Dear Linda,

You've been a dear friend for 13 [?]. I honestly can't imagine school without you. I know changes are inevitable, however I really don't like this one. I will miss you dearly. I pray for God's hand on you in this new position. May your decisions, attitude and walk glorify Him. Best Wishes.

Cathy Davis

Numbers 6:24-26

July 15, 1991

STANDING FIRM IN
JESUS

STANDING FIRM IN JESUS

SARAH HORNSBY

Published by

✓ chosen books

FLEMING H. REVELL COMPANY
OLD TAPPAN, NEW JERSEY

All Scripture quotations in this book are from the Holy Bible, New International Version, copyright © 1973, 1978, 1984 International Bible Society. Used by permission of Zondervan Bible Publishers.

Library of Congress Cataloging-in-Publication Data

Hornsby, Sarah.
    Standing firm in Jesus / Sarah Hornsby.
        p. cm.
    ISBN 0-8007-9167-3
    1. Devotional calendars.   I. Title.
BV4811.H646   1990
242′.2—dc20   90-38109
                                            CIP

A Chosen Book
Copyright © 1990 by Sarah Hornsby

Chosen Books are published by
Fleming H. Revell Company
Old Tappan, New Jersey
Printed in the United States of America

To
Doña Julia Lopez de Cardoza
in gratitude that Jesus has enabled me to share her life
and learn more of His healing ways by living across the
street from her this past year in Matagalpa, Nicaragua.

Special thanks to: Jane Campbell and Ann McMath, faithful, encouraging editors at Chosen Books.

Also thanks to: Andy Hornsby, Lorraine Stuart, Delores Winder, Tish Anderson, Jo Hornsby, Nancy and Wallace Braud, and the many who have told us that they not only read my books, but pray for us every day!

And appreciation for ideas for some of the borders from:
The Scriptorium—All Saints Convent, Cantonville, Maryland
Nicaraguan Primitive Art Calendars
Alex and Marta Benavidis
Matthew Hornsby
Jesus People USA / *Cornerstone* magazine

Contents

Introduction

Yesterday the finished manuscript and artwork rested in a neat package on my table, awaiting someone to hand-carry it to the States.

This book speaks of spiritual warfare in a daily, practical way, looking at Scripture, interpreting it in the ordinary events of a housewife's day, yet with the added spice of a different setting—Nicaragua. Here in the mountains of Matagalpa I have been blessed to see events from the perspective of Nicaraguan brothers and sisters in Christ—events in the family, neighborhood and between nations.

I write meditationally, for my own information and yours. Sometimes I reminisce about past experiences in the Young Life camping ministry in the mountains of North Carolina or of the inner city in Jacksonville, Florida, where we had youth ministry for fourteen years during the '60s and '70s.

People are important in my life and book. Jim, my rugged, bearded husband, who almost died of malaria this year, gives me space to write. He brings into my life those who have a vision for working with youth who no longer have hope or purpose, to show them the Jesus who walks their streets and cares about making a better community with them.

James, our 26-year-old son, is on the ministry team and anoints our rough places with soothing oil of wisdom, fresh perspective and sweet songs.

Matthew, in the tender/terrible year of thirteen, is our North American son, and the same size as Daniel Matamoros (seventeen) who lived with us the year this book was written. Daniel called me "Mama"; his own mother had gone with the contras to the mountains of Honduras years before. Daniel and Matthew had become good friends when we lived next door to his grandmother in rural Northwest Chinandega, where we worked with Habitat for Humanity from 1984 to 1986.

Evangelical pastor Amansio Sanchez and his daughter, Elda (nine), live just around the corner in our neighborhood—El Progreso. We first met the Sanchez family in 1986 after a mine exploded, leaving them both amputees.

Doña Julia Cardoza, a Catholic charismatic prayer group leader, lives across the street. To Doña Julia I take the Catholics who come to us North American missionaries for help and medicine, not realizing that within their own tradition and community is the source for healing of body, soul and spirit.

My first year at the University of Tennessee Presbyterian Student Center in 1956, Sandy Roddy gave a talk on the armor of God and the visual pictures made an impression. Another speaker years later described how ridiculous it is for Christians to go naked into the daily spiritual battles we face in the world. I discovered there are many qualities that don't just grow from within, as fruit of the Spirit. We are to make a conscious decision to *put on* many aspects of the Christian life in order to *stand firm.*

I discovered that Jesus is my spiritual armor. He is Salvation, Truth, Righteousness, Peace, the Word of God. We are given faith, but must take hold of it, use it for protection and in the offensive against satanic powers, which hold us, our loved ones and nations hostage.

I cannot be a passive bystander, but must choose to listen for God's direction as to *how* and *when* to be involved. *What* is my part in this cosmic battle called life?

This book is really a companion to *At the Name of Jesus*, because in the prayers after each meditation on the armor of God, I pray in a specific name or attribute of Jesus.

I also sought out names and attributes of God, the heavenly Father to whom Jesus prayed, and searched *Thompson's Chain Reference NIV* and the Psalms for more ways of addressing God.

Though the Greek word for *Father* in the Lord's Prayer includes the concept of parent—mother and father, I am not personally comfortable with using both male-female as I pray and write, so I leave you to add that to enrich the meaning.

Finally, please pray for me to keep growing in the fruit of God's Spirit, being filled more and more with all God is, and daily to make the choice, the decision, to put on the spiritual armor God provides . . . and I pray for you. . . .

> With love,
> Sarah Hornsby

To the Reader

It would add greatly to your overall understanding of
and meditation on the Scripture to look up the verse
and read it within its context, asking: To whom was
it written, when and why?

STANDING
FIRM IN
JESUS

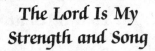

The Lord Is My Strength and Song

"The Lord is my strength and my song; he has become my salvation. . . . In your unfailing love you will lead the people you have redeemed. In your strength you will guide them to your holy dwelling."

Exodus 15:2, 13

Moses' song was a spontaneous expression of joy and triumph over the evil forces that seemed to win for so long. The wall of water, which meant freedom for the slaves, crashed down destroying those who sought their slavery again.
Justice of God's own choosing had been done by Him in His own timing. He performed it by His strength. He is worthy to be praised!

Father God, beginning a new year I look at those victories You have accomplished in my life. Written down they are a praise, a song! You lead Your people on a new journey . . . in the name of Jesus, the Alpha.

Love God
with All Your Strength

Hear, O Israel: The Lord our God, the Lord is one. Love
the Lord your God with all your heart and with all your
soul and with all your strength.
Deuteronomy 6:4–5

Love is the essence of all God showed
Moses on the mountain. Love is the
unsurpassed treasure to be taught
children before bed, at the start of the
day and in the midst of the day's
experiences.
Rabbi Jesus said that all the Law and
prophets hinge on loving our heavenly
Father with all our emotions, memories,
mental abilities, spirit, energies; and our
neighbors with the same enthusiasm as
we love ourselves
(Matthew 22:37–40).

Loving Father God, whether my strength is
great or small, I want to love You, and in
Your love, to love neighbor and self with
all of it!. . . in the name of Jesus, the
Rabbi who is Love.

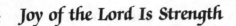

Joy of the Lord Is Strength

Nehemiah said, "Go and enjoy choice food and sweet drinks, and send some to those who have nothing prepared. This day is sacred to our Lord. Do not grieve, for the joy of the Lord is your strength."
Nehemiah 8:10

The people of Israel in family groups had worked hard to rebuild the walls of Jerusalem despite serious opposition. The cries of the poor were heard, Jerusalem's gates were rebuilt, and praisers were appointed. The people assembled to hear God's Word and wept.

When confronted by the living Word, I see that my best is not enough. The leap of faith is necessary, knowing that His love will bring me safely to that place where He wants me to be.

Father of joy, Your joy is my strength. You complete what You have begun . . . in the name of Jesus, the Fullness of joy!

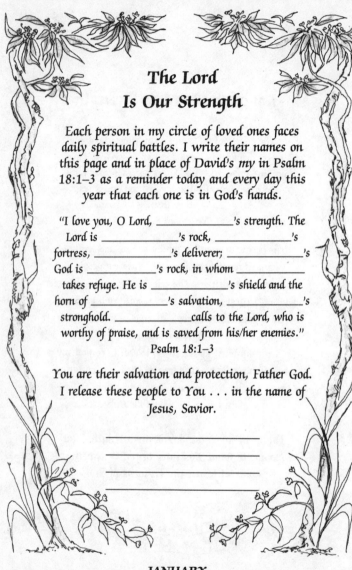

The Lord
Is Our Strength

Each person in my circle of loved ones faces daily spiritual battles. I write their names on this page and in place of David's *my* in Psalm 18:1–3 as a reminder today and every day this year that each one is in God's hands.

"I love you, O Lord, _____'s strength. The Lord is _____'s rock, _____'s fortress, _____'s deliverer; _____'s God is _____'s rock, in whom _____ takes refuge. He is _____'s shield and the horn of _____'s salvation, _____'s stronghold. _____ calls to the Lord, who is worthy of praise, and is saved from his/her enemies."
Psalm 18:1–3

You are their salvation and protection, Father God. I release these people to You . . . in the name of Jesus, Savior.

_____

_____

_____

_____

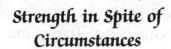

Strength in Spite of Circumstances

The Lord sits enthroned over the flood. . . . The Lord
gives strength to his people; the Lord blesses his
people with peace.
Psalm 29:10–11

My husband, Jim, our youngest son, Matthew, and I had
lived in our eighty-year-old adobe tile-roofed house in
Matagalpa, Nicaragua, only two days when Hurricane
Joan struck. After a long night we praised God for
safety! Others on the Atlantic Coast were praying, too,
but floodwaters destroyed thousands of dwellings. One
Moravian mother with three small children sought
shelter in a high school. In complete darkness, they had
to move to a safer place.
"I never lost faith through those hours of horror," she
said. "And to have been spared is like an experience of a
new birth, a chance to start life all over again."

Thank You, victorious Father God, for
strength in spite of circumstances . . . in
the name of Jesus, the Overcomer.

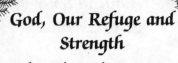

God, Our Refuge and Strength

God is our refuge and strength, an ever present help in trouble. Therefore we will not fear, though the earth give way and the mountains fall into the heart of the sea. . . . He makes wars cease to the ends of the earth. . . . "Be still, and know that I am God; I will be exalted among the nations."
Psalm 46:1–3, 9–10

Be still and know God, the psalmist says, and you will find out who He is, a place of refuge in a world shaken with natural disasters and the violence of wars.

Father of the nations, I pray for our nation's leaders to be still today and know You, to listen for Your direction in governing our land and its relations with other nations. Show me the leaders I can call or write to express the concerns You point out to me. Show me a troubled nation for which to pray, and teach me how to pray . . . in the name of Jesus, King of kings.

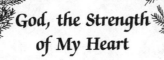

God, the Strength of My Heart

My flesh and my heart may fail, but God is the strength of my heart and my portion forever.
Psalm 73:26

Envy, grief and bitterness at seeing the rich grow richer despite their godless ways threatened to destroy the psalmist Asaph. He needed to remind himself of God's greatness, for God will bring about ultimate justice. Asaph decided to look at what God was doing in his life and keep a list that could be shared with others as a warning to some and an encouragement to others—a two-edged sword!

Compassionate Father, where I have allowed a seed of bitterness to take root, in the strength of Your Holy Spirit, I yank it out right now. Please fill that place with Your hope, Your encouragement, Your strength. Enable me to be part of the solution to those problems that cause envy, grief and bitterness . . . in the name of Jesus, Sower of good seed.

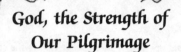

God, the Strength of
Our Pilgrimage

Blessed are those whose strength is in you, who have set their hearts on pilgrimage. As they pass through the Valley of Baca, they make it a place of springs. . . . They go from strength to strength till each appears before God in Zion.
Psalm 84:5–7

Through the dry valleys, I keep referring to His Guidebook, the Bible. The journey is difficult. The path is easy to lose because diversions are so logical and tempting. My companions can help or hinder me and I them, but I am responsible for my choices.

Father God, Lord of the journey, thank You for surprising me with fresh, clear springs of living water that quench my thirst and enable me to keep going in the right direction. Thank You for the inner knowing that You walk with me . . in the name of Jesus, my Companion.

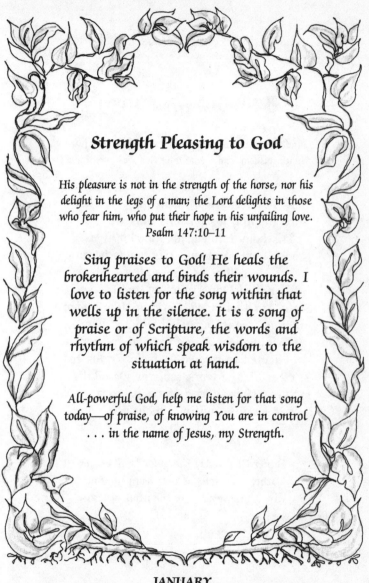

Strength Pleasing to God

His pleasure is not in the strength of the horse, nor his delight in the legs of a man; the Lord delights in those who fear him, who put their hope in his unfailing love.
Psalm 147:10–11

Sing praises to God! He heals the brokenhearted and binds their wounds. I love to listen for the song within that wells up in the silence. It is a song of praise or of Scripture, the words and rhythm of which speak wisdom to the situation at hand.

All-powerful God, help me listen for that song today—of praise, of knowing You are in control . . . in the name of Jesus, my Strength.

Jesus Grew . . . Strong

*And the child grew and became strong; he was filled
with wisdom, and the grace of God was upon him.*
Luke 2:40

The boy Jesus worked in the carpenter
shop helping Joseph. His muscles grew,
His body tanned, for the shop was
probably out-of-doors. His hands became
calloused and agile.
I watched Don Francisco and his son,
Carlos, in their woodworking shop under a
mango tree in our neighborhood here in
Matagalpa. A nod from his father
indicated to twelve-year-old Carlos to
clear off the work table as we adults
talked. There was a place for every tool,
and Carlos, smiling, knew just what
to do.

Father God, today I pray for families, for
fathers and sons as they learn to grow
strong together . . . in the name of Jesus,
Son of God.

With All Our Strength . . .

" 'Love the Lord your God with all your heart and with all your soul and with all your mind and with all your strength.' . . . 'Love your neighbor as yourself.' There is no commandment greater than these."

Mark 12:30–31

"You are not far from the Kingdom," Jesus told the Jewish teacher of the Law, who understood that at the very heart of God's commandments is the wisdom of loving relationships. My basic need is to seek God, hungering and thirsting for time alone with Him, sensing, craving His presence, His voice, His direction. I want to search out His will so that what I delight in is the very thing for which I was created and my relationships are soon filled up and covered with His love.

Loving Father, let me see in myself and in others today the possibility of change . . . in the name of Jesus, who gave His life for His friends.

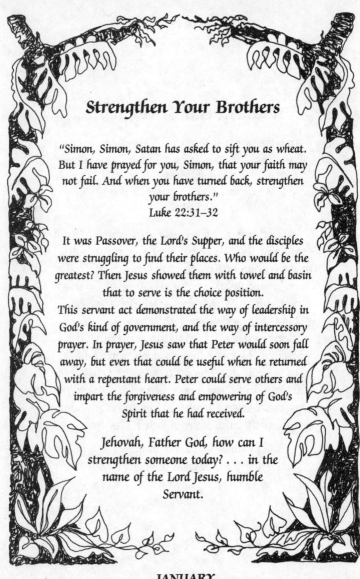

Strengthen Your Brothers

"Simon, Simon, Satan has asked to sift you as wheat.
But I have prayed for you, Simon, that your faith may
not fail. And when you have turned back, strengthen
your brothers."
Luke 22:31–32

It was Passover, the Lord's Supper, and the disciples
were struggling to find their places. Who would be the
greatest? Then Jesus showed them with towel and basin
that to serve is the choice position.

This servant act demonstrated the way of leadership in
God's kind of government, and the way of intercessory
prayer. In prayer, Jesus saw that Peter would soon fall
away, but even that could be useful when he returned
with a repentant heart. Peter could serve others and
impart the forgiveness and empowering of God's
Spirit that he had received.

Jehovah, Father God, how can I
strengthen someone today? . . . in the
name of the Lord Jesus, humble
Servant.

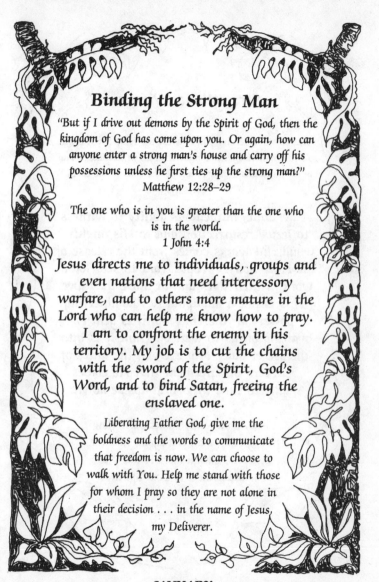

Binding the Strong Man

"But if I drive out demons by the Spirit of God, then the kingdom of God has come upon you. Or again, how can anyone enter a strong man's house and carry off his possessions unless he first ties up the strong man?"
Matthew 12:28–29

The one who is in you is greater than the one who is in the world.
1 John 4:4

Jesus directs me to individuals, groups and even nations that need intercessory warfare, and to others more mature in the Lord who can help me know how to pray. I am to confront the enemy in his territory. My job is to cut the chains with the sword of the Spirit, God's Word, and to bind Satan, freeing the enslaved one.

Liberating Father God, give me the boldness and the words to communicate that freedom is now. We can choose to walk with You. Help me stand with those for whom I pray so they are not alone in their decision . . . in the name of Jesus, my Deliverer.

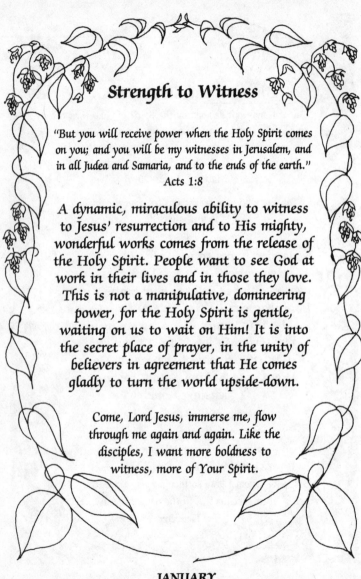

Strength to Witness

"But you will receive power when the Holy Spirit comes on you; and you will be my witnesses in Jerusalem, and in all Judea and Samaria, and to the ends of the earth."
Acts 1:8

A dynamic, miraculous ability to witness to Jesus' resurrection and to His mighty, wonderful works comes from the release of the Holy Spirit. People want to see God at work in their lives and in those they love. This is not a manipulative, domineering power, for the Holy Spirit is gentle, waiting on us to wait on Him! It is into the secret place of prayer, in the unity of believers in agreement that He comes gladly to turn the world upside-down.

Come, Lord Jesus, immerse me, flow through me again and again. Like the disciples, I want more boldness to witness, more of Your Spirit.

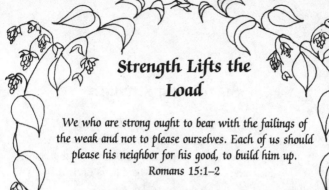

Strength Lifts the Load

We who are strong ought to bear with the failings of the weak and not to please ourselves. Each of us should please his neighbor for his good, to build him up.
Romans 15:1–2

Let the able use their ability to carry the load of those unable. Let the powerful person, the capable, use his/her strength to lift the weak, the impotent. Jesus, the all-powerful, prayed for His tormentors, the "strong" Roman imperialists and religious rulers who could not recognize God.
True strength is being yielded to God's will, His people in one accord.

Almighty Father God, may I see with new eyes those who appear strong in weaponry or religious zeal who torment and control others. Seeing apparent strength as weakness, I pray that those burdens be lifted from them. May my strength be as Jesus' on the cross . . . in His name, the obedient Lord.

Sustaining Strength

Therefore you do not lack any spiritual gift as you
eagerly wait for our Lord Jesus Christ to be revealed. He
will keep you strong to the end, so that you will be
blameless on the day of our Lord Jesus Christ.
1 Corinthians 1:7–8

God equips us with words and wisdom, and gives us
spiritual gifts that confirm the power of those words.
God continues to forgive, nurture and sustain us until
we are presented before Him, guiltless. The Corinthians
needed to know that God was at work among them and
would enable them to pull through the problems,
disagreements, confusions and persecutions.
Forgiven, loved by God, they were enabled to
be with Him forever. Jim, my husband, says Christians
are a society of forgiven failures; because of this we
learn to forgive and encourage others.

Forgiving Father God, thank You for strength
to forgive today, and gifts to share . . . in the
name of Jesus, our Intercessor.

In Our Weakness, His Strength

God chose the weak things of the world to shame the strong. . . . It is because of him that you are in Christ Jesus, who has become for us wisdom from God—that is, our righteousness, holiness and redemption. . . . "Let him who boasts boast in the Lord."
1 Corinthians 1:27, 30–31

Within every person are strengths and weaknesses. Within strength is the temptation to overpower others. If I am weak, then others can help me! God picked weak people to work with so others could see He was doing great things through them. When we do well, we often puff up with pride, but as Sam Shoemaker, founder of Alcoholics Anonymous, said, "The antidote to pride is a grateful heart."

Thank You, Creator of the universe, my Pride and Glory, for my strengths. I need wisdom and gentleness in using them. Thank You, Lord, for my weaknesses. Be strong and shine in them . . . in the name of Jesus, my Strength.

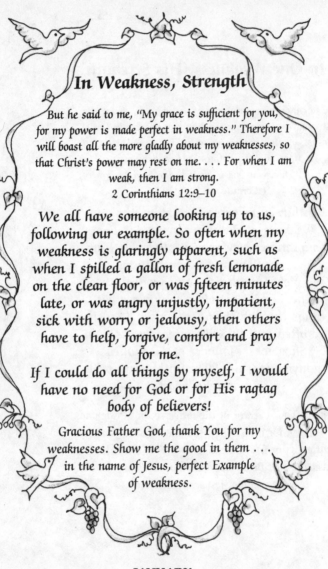

In Weakness, Strength

But he said to me, "My grace is sufficient for you, for my power is made perfect in weakness." Therefore I will boast all the more gladly about my weaknesses, so that Christ's power may rest on me. . . . For when I am weak, then I am strong.

2 Corinthians 12:9–10

We all have someone looking up to us, following our example. So often when my weakness is glaringly apparent, such as when I spilled a gallon of fresh lemonade on the clean floor, or was fifteen minutes late, or was angry unjustly, impatient, sick with worry or jealousy, then others have to help, forgive, comfort and pray for me.

If I could do all things by myself, I would have no need for God or for His ragtag body of believers!

Gracious Father God, thank You for my weaknesses. Show me the good in them . . . in the name of Jesus, perfect Example of weakness.

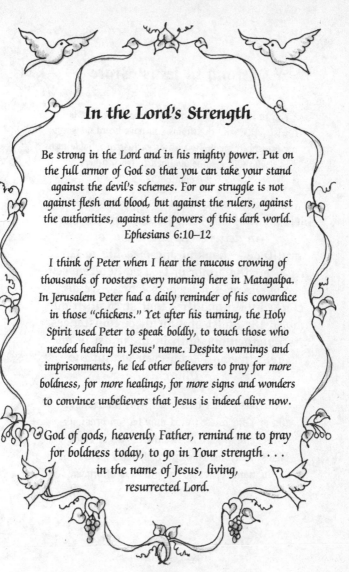

In the Lord's Strength

Be strong in the Lord and in his mighty power. Put on
the full armor of God so that you can take your stand
against the devil's schemes. For our struggle is not
against flesh and blood, but against the rulers, against
the authorities, against the powers of this dark world.
Ephesians 6:10–12

I think of Peter when I hear the raucous crowing of
thousands of roosters every morning here in Matagalpa.
In Jerusalem Peter had a daily reminder of his cowardice
in those "chickens." Yet after his turning, the Holy
Spirit used Peter to speak boldly, to touch those who
needed healing in Jesus' name. Despite warnings and
imprisonments, he led other believers to pray for *more*
boldness, for *more* healings, for *more* signs and wonders
to convince unbelievers that Jesus is indeed alive now.

God of gods, heavenly Father, remind me to pray
for boldness today, to go in Your strength . . .
in the name of Jesus, living,
resurrected Lord.

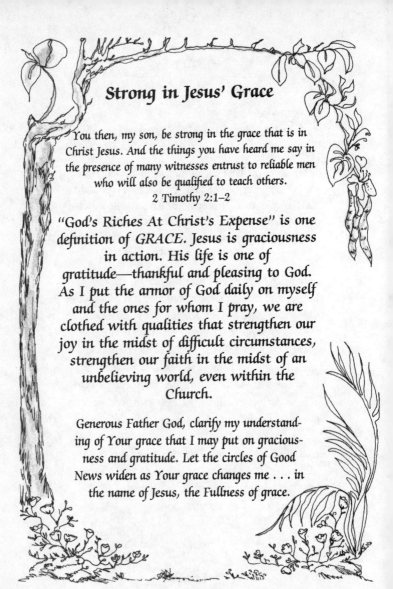

Strong in Jesus' Grace

You then, my son, be strong in the grace that is in Christ Jesus. And the things you have heard me say in the presence of many witnesses entrust to reliable men who will also be qualified to teach others.

2 Timothy 2:1–2

"God's Riches At Christ's Expense" is one definition of *GRACE*. Jesus is graciousness in action. His life is one of gratitude—thankful and pleasing to God. As I put the armor of God daily on myself and the ones for whom I pray, we are clothed with qualities that strengthen our joy in the midst of difficult circumstances, strengthen our faith in the midst of an unbelieving world, even within the Church.

Generous Father God, clarify my understanding of Your grace that I may put on graciousness and gratitude. Let the circles of Good News widen as Your grace changes me . . . in the name of Jesus, the Fullness of grace.

God Will Strengthen

And the God of all grace . . . after you have suffered a little while, will himself restore you and make you strong, firm and steadfast. To him be the power for ever and ever.

1 Peter 5:10–11

Peter taught a way of life for believers in the midst of situations when the devil prowls like a hungry lion. Some Christians of Peter's day were literally torn by lions in Roman arenas, so this was vivid imagery. We must: 1. Humble ourselves before God. 2. Give Him all anxieties. 3. Be sober, watchful. 4. Resist the devil, firm in faith. Then in the midst of suffering God will restore, establish and strengthen us. This strength is bodily vigor, spiritual power and knowledge that comes when we walk in obedience to God's will.

Father God, Lord of all power, thank You for the example of faithful Christians. I want to follow in their steps today . . . in the name of Jesus, Faithful in suffering, Triumphant in glory.

Faith Makes Strong

"By faith in the name of Jesus, this man whom you see and know was made strong. It is Jesus' name and the faith that comes through him that has given this complete healing to him, as you can all see."

Acts 3:16

The Author of life, Jesus, was killed by ignorance, but God raised Him from the dead. "We are witnesses," Peter declared boldly as the crippled man walked, leaped and praised God in the Temple. To those staring in curiosity or annoyance or in awe of the disciples, Peter declared, "Jesus is the one who heals, yesterday, today and forever!" He uses us as channels of His immense compassion.

Great Father God, I want to be an instrument of peace and healing in the midst of suffering . . . in the name of Jesus, divine Physician.

El Salvador

Resurrection Power!

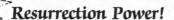

I pray also that the eyes of your heart may be enlightened in order that you may know . . . his incomparably great power for us who believe. That power is like the working of his mighty strength, which he exerted in Christ when he raised him from the dead.
Ephesians 1:18–20

What strength placed Jesus "above all rule and authority" and put "all things under His feet"? The same strength that walks with me in difficult places. This is the authority I have over evil, which is under my feet when I am in my proper place in the Body of Jesus. Nothing against God has any ultimate power, though at times when I see the immensity of evil I am discouraged, tempted to give up.

Victorious Father God, help me hold onto the victory in Jesus, live in it, walk in it persistently and be a light that draws others to Your resurrection hope . . . in the name of Jesus, the Victor.

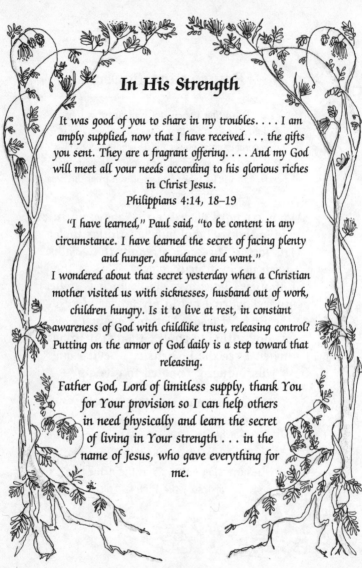

In His Strength

It was good of you to share in my troubles. . . . I am amply supplied, now that I have received . . . the gifts you sent. They are a fragrant offering. . . . And my God will meet all your needs according to his glorious riches in Christ Jesus.

Philippians 4:14, 18–19

"I have learned," Paul said, "to be content in any circumstance. I have learned the secret of facing plenty and hunger, abundance and want."

I wondered about that secret yesterday when a Christian mother visited us with sicknesses, husband out of work, children hungry. Is it to live at rest, in constant awareness of God with childlike trust, releasing control? Putting on the armor of God daily is a step toward that releasing.

Father God, Lord of limitless supply, thank You for Your provision so I can help others in need physically and learn the secret of living in Your strength . . . in the name of Jesus, who gave everything for me.

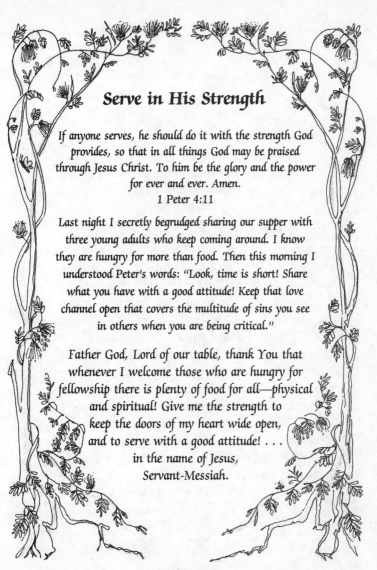

Serve in His Strength

If anyone serves, he should do it with the strength God
provides, so that in all things God may be praised
through Jesus Christ. To him be the glory and the power
for ever and ever. Amen.
1 Peter 4:11

Last night I secretly begrudged sharing our supper with
three young adults who keep coming around. I know
they are hungry for more than food. Then this morning I
understood Peter's words: "Look, time is short! Share
what you have with a good attitude! Keep that love
channel open that covers the multitude of sins you see
in others when you are being critical."

Father God, Lord of our table, thank You that
whenever I welcome those who are hungry for
fellowship there is plenty of food for all—physical
and spiritual! Give me the strength to
keep the doors of my heart wide open,
and to serve with a good attitude! . . .
in the name of Jesus,
Servant-Messiah.

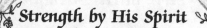

Strength by His Spirit

So he said to me, "This is the word of the Lord to
Zerubbabel: 'Not by might nor by power, but by my
Spirit,' says the Lord Almighty."
Zechariah 4:6

The foundation was laid for the Temple in
Jerusalem, but Zerubbabel needed
encouragement to continue rebuilding. In
his vision Zechariah saw the work
completed, the mountain become a plain,
and he heard the Lord's word, ". . . by My
Spirit." Small things accomplish His
purpose. My foundation is Jesus Himself
and the temple is my physical body as
well as our lives together as families,
churches—the whole family of God.

Heavenly Father, who fills Your Temple with the
sweet fragrance of Your Spirit, what steps do I
need to take today to be building? . . . in the name
of Jesus, Master Builder.

Jesus' Strength

Jesus returned to Galilee in the power of
the Spirit. . . . "The Spirit of the Lord is
on me, because he has anointed me to preach good news
to the poor. He has sent me to proclaim freedom for the
prisoners and recovery of sight for the blind, to release
the oppressed. . . ."
Luke 4:14, 18

Jesus began His ministry full of the Holy
Spirit and was led by the Spirit
immediately into the wilderness where the
devil waited to tempt Him. I am also
tempted to use my own spiritual strength
in ways that will meet physical,
recognition and control needs. The power
Satan offered to give Jesus belonged to
Him legitimately after He resisted the
temptations and clearly chose God's path.

Father God, fill me with Your Holy Spirit, with
Your living Word, that I may choose Your way
today . . . in the name of Jesus, Baptizer with
the Holy Spirit and with fire.

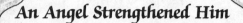

An Angel Strengthened Him

An angel from heaven appeared to him and strengthened him. And being in anguish, he prayed more earnestly, and his sweat was like drops of blood falling to the ground.
Luke 22:43–44

After facing Satan's temptations, Jesus received strength from ministering angels. When He was agonizing in prayer in the Garden an angel ministered to Him. The writer of Hebrews says we sometimes entertain angels when we are hospitable to strangers. I have read of angels who appear as ordinary people but do extraordinary things to help many who have reached their own limits.

Thank You, Father God, Lord of the supernatural, that I am not limited by my own strength when You are in my life! . . . in the name of Jesus, unimaginable Surprise!

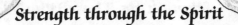

Strength through the Spirit

I pray that . . . he may strengthen you with power
through his Spirit in your inner being, so that Christ
may dwell in your hearts through faith . . . [and that
you] may have power . . . to grasp how wide and long
and high and deep is the love of Christ.
Ephesians 3:16–18

Paul prayed that I may have, through God's Holy Spirit
at work in me, the strengthening of His dynamic,
miracle-working power. After seeing a movie with bad
language recently, curse words kept coming into my
thoughts whenever things went wrong. What I put into
my mind and spirit breeds and reproduces—for good or
for evil. What comes from within reveals whether I am
polluted or a pure, fresh spring of living water.

Thank You, dynamic Father God, for Your
powerful cleansing that washes through me,
scrubbing away those effects of the
world—more than I can ask or think! . . .
in the name of the indwelling Lord Jesus.

Strength for Those Who Wait

He gives strength to the weary and increases the power
of the weak. . . . Those who hope in the Lord will renew
their strength. They will soar on wings like eagles; they
will run and not grow weary, they will walk and not be
faint.

Isaiah 40:29, 31

*To wait in Hebrew means "to bind together by twisting,
to expect patiently." Like the disciples bound together in
prayer waiting for the promised Holy Spirit, we can
receive a new boldness and strength to communicate the
Good News. The saints who have gone before are pulling
for us. Battalions of angels are camped around us. There
are people who need me and I them so that together we
can receive His power.*

All-powerful Father God, help me to confess my
faults honestly to my brothers and sisters and pray
for healing so that we can "run and not be weary,
walk and not faint" . . . in the name of Jesus,
Number One in the race!

Through Pressure . . . Strength

We also rejoice in our sufferings, because we know that suffering produces perseverance; perseverance, character; and character, hope. And hope does not disappoint us, because God has poured out his love into our hearts.

Romans 5:3–5

Every believer is under necessary pressure, like lumps of coal being formed into diamonds. My emotions resist those afflictions, burdens, anguish, troubles and persecutions. "Why me?" I cry out. Or, "Why does my friend or country seem to suffer too much?" Paul had a long list of hardships, but used each one as a valuable teaching tool. He learned the secret of joy: in the midst of pain to transform suffering.

Father God, Lord of hope, right now I yield my sufferings to You to transform them into the ingredients of eternal life: faith, hope and love . . . in the name of Jesus, my blessed Hope.

Stand Firm . . . See Deliverance

Moses answered the people, "Do not be afraid. Stand firm and you will see the deliverance the Lord will bring you today. The Egyptians you see today you will never see again. The Lord will fight for you; you need only to be still."

Exodus 14:13–14

"Stand, stay, remain in that place that denies fear," Moses exhorted the trembling Israelites. "You will see God at work to save you from very real danger." Then God brought His people out in His time and in a way that drew attention, not to the efforts of His children, but to His way of working. Moses stayed in that listening place to hear God's calm instructions in spite of the crisis.

Father God, Lord of liberation, I want to hear You today in the presence of my enemies, in the midst of fear or destructive power greater than my own in the name of Jesus, the Liberator.

Stand Every Morning

The duty of the Levites was to . . . be in charge of the
courtyards, the side rooms. . . . They were in charge of
the bread set out on the table . . . the baking and the
mixing. . . . They were also to stand every morning to
thank and praise the Lord.
1 Chronicles 23:28–30

Each person in our household has
responsibilities. Mine, like the Levites in
the first Temple, most often include
cooking and cleaning. The Levites were
also to thank and praise God continually.
An attitude of thanking and praising God
is the constant that makes my home or
church a holy place. *To stand* in Hebrew
includes abiding, enduring, remaining firm.

Father God, Lord of my everyday duties, I stand
still before You. Thank You for this morning, and
this evening, every day. . . . Fill our
household with Your Presence as You did
the Temple! . . . in the name of Jesus, the
sweet Fragrance of God's Spirit.

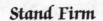

Stand Firm

"You will not have to fight this battle. Take up your positions; stand firm and see the deliverance the Lord will give you, O Judah and Jerusalem."
2 Chronicles 20:17

Enemy armies were marching against King Jehoshaphat; he called the people to fast and pray. "We do not know what to do, but our eyes are upon Thee." The answer came: "Take your positions, stand still and see the victory of the Lord. . . ." When I come to God with my fear and need, He speaks. I must listen and act on that wisdom. When our family goes our own way, refusing to do what we know is a clear word from God, He patiently draws us back from trying to do battle with spiritual forces on our own.

All-wise God, I want to take time to listen, to act on Your quiet wisdom and praise You for the deliverance! . . . in the name of Jesus, the Deliverer.

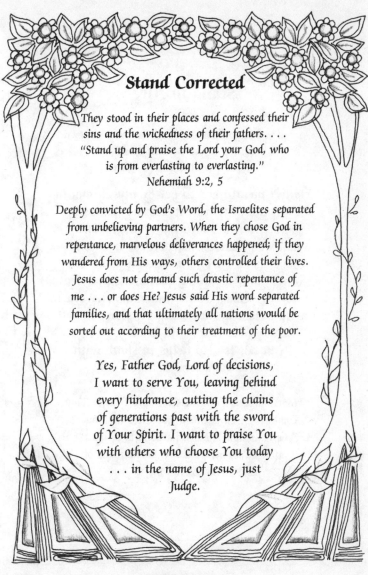

Stand Corrected

They stood in their places and confessed their
sins and the wickedness of their fathers. . . .
"Stand up and praise the Lord your God, who
is from everlasting to everlasting."
Nehemiah 9:2, 5

Deeply convicted by God's Word, the Israelites separated
from unbelieving partners. When they chose God in
repentance, marvelous deliverances happened; if they
wandered from His ways, others controlled their lives.
Jesus does not demand such drastic repentance of
me . . . or does He? Jesus said His word separated
families, and that ultimately all nations would be
sorted out according to their treatment of the poor.

Yes, Father God, Lord of decisions,
I want to serve You, leaving behind
every hindrance, cutting the chains
of generations past with the sword
of Your Spirit. I want to praise You
with others who choose You today
. . . in the name of Jesus, just
Judge.

Stand in Awe

Stand in awe, and sin not: commune with your own heart upon your bed, and be still.
Psalm 4:4, King James Version

Many times I need to get by myself and in a variety of ways express my angers or fears (from the Hebrew word for *awe*), rage at injustice, my deepest emotions. Sometimes I write a letter to God, but other times I have a gut-wrenching cry that only God's Spirit understands. When in the midst of much suffering and unable to help, this is all I can do. It also helps to share with others who believe.

Understanding Father God, thank You for Your comfort, encouragement, for the Holy Spirit's groans, and the brilliant shafts of light that direct my path . . . in the name of Jesus, who teaches me to pray.

Stand Upright

Some trust in chariots and some in horses, but we trust
in the name of the Lord our God. They are brought to
their knees and fall, but we rise up and stand firm.
Psalm 20:7–8

Around the corner from our house lives Amansio
Sanchez, a pastor with only one leg. In October 1986 he
was riding a civilian truck crowded with 52 people on
his way to a prayer meeting for peace. A mine exploded
causing six deaths and leaving eleven as amputees,
including his seven-year-old daughter, Elda. Now,
Amansio and Elda stand in church singing praises to
God. They have shown me how to stand upright in the
presence of enemies. I am learning from them about
forgiveness and faith.

Trustworthy Father God, I pray for my own
nation to fear You more than other nations, to
learn to use spiritual weapons instead of
those that can destroy the innocent . . .
in the name of Jesus, Prince of Peace.

Standing in the Holy Place

Who may stand in his holy place? He who has clean hands and a pure heart, who does not lift up his soul to an idol or swear by what is false.

Psalm 24:3–4

My hands are clean from washing clothes and dishes today. Pilate washed his hands, too. Jesus ate with unwashed hands!

How can I know my own heart? The publican knew his heart was unclean so cried, "Lord be merciful to me a sinner." His prayer was heard.

How can I discern my own soul, the ways I have been polluted by the world's values? I stand not on my own goodness, but on the One who said no one is good but God alone. He paid the price.

Holy heavenly Father, trembling I stand before You, forgiven with grateful heart . . . in the name of the perfect Lord Jesus.

Stand Up for God

Judgment will again be founded on righteousness, and all
the upright in heart will follow it. Who will rise up for
me against the wicked? Who will take a stand for me
against evildoers?
Psalm 94:15–16

The psalmist saw injustice made legal and
felt helpless. God sees what is going on,
the hurt of widows, orphans, refugees;
after all, He made eyes! The Lord Himself
will stand with the one who resists the
arrogant evil of leaders. Eliot Ness in seeking to cleanse Chicago of Al Capone's gang
found himself doing the very things he
hated, becoming like his enemy. Within
each human is the capacity for evil as well
as the ability to change.

Almighty Father God, I pray for my nation's
leaders to have the courage to see the poor from
Your perspective, to act as Your ambassadors today
. . . in the name of Jesus, King of kings.

Who Shall Stand?

Out of the depths I cry to you, O Lord. . . . Let your
ears be attentive to my cry for mercy. If you, O Lord,
kept a record of sins, O Lord, who could stand? But
with you there is forgiveness; therefore you are feared.

Psalm 130:1–4

Out of the depths the psalmist cries to the
Lord, "If You, Lord, keep account of
wrongs done, who can stand?" The
implied answer is nobody! I can stand
only in His forgiveness. When we had a
camping ministry in North Carolina and
took our baths in an icy mountain stream,
Jim often described our forgiveness in Jesus
as a delicious, warm, full-headed shower
of super-saturated, holy, tender loving
care!

Merciful heavenly Father, I imagine myself
standing in a continuous cleansing stream
of Jesus' poured-out blood (1 John 1:7–9).
Help me to be honest with myself and
others as I stand before You today . . . in
the name of Jesus, the Sanctifier.

Stand By Night

Praise the Lord, all you servants of the Lord who
minister by night in the house of the Lord. Lift up your
hands in the sanctuary and praise the Lord.

Psalm 134:1

In the Temple at Jerusalem some priests
had the night shift, to stand and bless the
Lord. I never could force myself to stay
awake to pray, having an inner clock that
clicks off about 9:30 P.M. Often I waken,
alert in the silent spaces of night. I have
learned to nestle quietly beside my
husband's warmth and let my thoughts be
instructed by the familiar, still voice of
the Lord. Then He corrects a wrong
attitude, illumines a dream or a troubling
situation, shares His joy.

Father God, who never sleeps, some have
complained of insomnia. Be with them in those
long stretches and help them join those
who stand in the night watches in Your
loving Presence . . . in the name of Jesus,
the Upholder.

Stand Watch

I will stand at my watch and station myself on the ramparts; I will look to see what he will say to me, and what answer I am to give to this complaint.
Habakkuk 2:1

The prophet Habakkuk, on seeing the rich take advantage of the poor, cried to God that justice was not being done. God answered that He punishes the wicked with the more wicked. God wants us to ask hard questions about our society, about those who use Jesus' name but continue to increase their comfort while the poor get poorer. Where is justice? In the courts? In prisons? Where and how and with whom can I stand against the overpowering forces of evil that pretend to be good?

Father God, Lord of all insight, give me the vision and ability to run and to wait at Your direction . . . in the name of Jesus, who overturned the tables in Your name.

Stand Praying and Forgive

"Therefore I tell you, whatever you ask for in prayer,
believe that you have received it, and it will be yours.
And when you stand praying, if you hold anything
against anyone, forgive him, so that your Father in
heaven may forgive you your sins."
Mark 11:24–25

Whenever I stand praying, I must forgive. To
stand—to persevere, be stationary. When I take hold
of what seems to be a mountain that can be moved
only by prayer, my heart must be clear of all
resentment, anger, bitterness, hatred. "Our words are
powerful," our son James said, reminding me that once
at our house during the Jesus People
days a young believer cursed our fig trees, and
they never again bore fruit. "We must be careful
how we pray."

Illuminating Father God, show me today any
unforgiveness that I have hidden from myself.
Wash me so I can stand fast in the prayers You
put on my heart . . . in the name of the cleansing
Lord Jesus.

Stand Beside Jesus

But Jesus knew what they were thinking and said to the man with the shriveled hand, "Get up and stand in front of everyone." So he got up and stood there. . . . He looked around at them all, and then said to the man, "Stretch out your hand." He did so, and his hand was completely restored.
Luke 6:8–10

"Come stand beside Me," Jesus said to the man with the withered hand, whose mind must have been full of questions: *I don't want to stand out, to be subject to the criticism of our church leaders.*
I don't want to interrupt the order of the service by doing something different, even ridiculous, like going to the front and standing with Jesus. But there was something strong, attractive, a compelling warmth, hope and compassion that drew him. His hand was restored!

Close Companion, Lord Jesus, today I want to stand with You, be healed and be Your instrument of healing.

Stand Before Them

". . . Then know this, you and everyone else in Israel: It is by the name of Jesus Christ of Nazareth, whom you crucified but whom God raised from the dead, that this man stands before you completely healed."
Acts 4:10

Through the Holy Spirit at work in the disciples, a crippled beggar, more than forty years old and one of Jerusalem's homeless, was healed. In the initial excitement of being able to walk, the man jumped, skipped, leaped and danced in praise to God. The day after, however, he had to decide: "Will I stand with these through whom I have experienced God's power, even though it may mean prison or death?" He decided to stand, to place himself on exhibit as proof of Jesus' resurrection.

Jesus Christ of Nazareth, I want to stand up with the beggar, jump and dance. I want to stand boldly, filled with Your Spirit today.

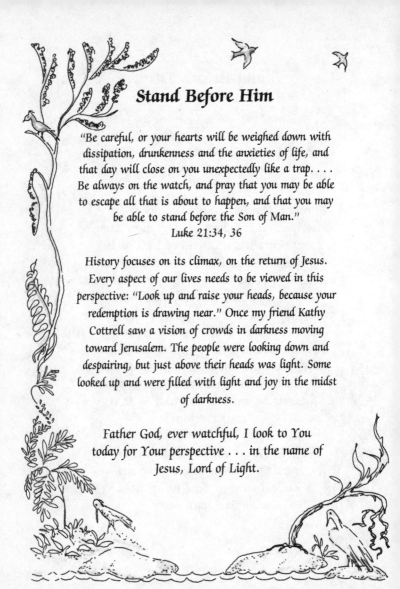

Stand Before Him

"Be careful, or your hearts will be weighed down with
dissipation, drunkenness and the anxieties of life, and
that day will close on you unexpectedly like a trap. . . .
Be always on the watch, and pray that you may be able
to escape all that is about to happen, and that you may
be able to stand before the Son of Man."

Luke 21:34, 36

History focuses on its climax, on the return of Jesus.
Every aspect of our lives needs to be viewed in this
perspective: "Look up and raise your heads, because your
redemption is drawing near." Once my friend Kathy
Cottrell saw a vision of crowds in darkness moving
toward Jerusalem. The people were looking down and
despairing, but just above their heads was light. Some
looked up and were filled with light and joy in the midst
of darkness.

Father God, ever watchful, I look to You
today for Your perspective . . . in the name of
Jesus, Lord of Light.

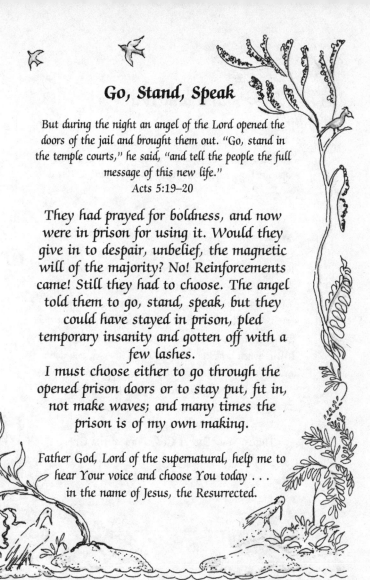

Go, Stand, Speak

But during the night an angel of the Lord opened the doors of the jail and brought them out. "Go, stand in the temple courts," he said, "and tell the people the full message of this new life."

Acts 5:19–20

They had prayed for boldness, and now were in prison for using it. Would they give in to despair, unbelief, the magnetic will of the majority? No! Reinforcements came! Still they had to choose. The angel told them to go, stand, speak, but they could have stayed in prison, pled temporary insanity and gotten off with a few lashes.

I must choose either to go through the opened prison doors or to stay put, fit in, not make waves; and many times the prison is of my own making.

Father God, Lord of the supernatural, help me to hear Your voice and choose You today . . . in the name of Jesus, the Resurrected.

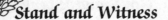

Stand and Witness

" 'I am Jesus, whom you are persecuting,' the Lord
replied. 'Now get up and stand on your feet. I have
appeared to you to appoint you as a servant and as a
witness.' "
Acts 26:15–16

Saul, a self-righteous murderer, was made physically
blind in an encounter with Jesus, but received his
healing touch from a courageous Christian who prayed
for Saul's eyes to be opened. To stand, Saul needed to
fall in the presence of Jesus. To serve, he was first
served. To witness, he first experienced the reality of the
living Lord, the forgiveness and faith that make whole.
It was when a pastor said, "Don't witness if you don't
have anything to witness to," that I stopped trying to be
"religious" and began searching for the real,
living Jesus who found me!

Thank You, Father God, Lord of the Good
News, for making me a witness . . . in
the name of Jesus, the Persecuted.

Stand in Grace

Therefore, since we have been justified through faith, we have peace with God through our Lord Jesus Christ, through whom we have gained access by faith into this grace in which we now stand.
Romans 5:1–2

We are made right with God by faith. This nutshell description of the Christian life in Romans came as a revelation to Martin Luther. I stand, continue, abide. I am established in the goodness of God poured out as peace through Jesus, love through the Holy Spirit. In this security I am able to rejoice in sufferings and because of them to be strengthened with endurance. This endurance will form character, which, based in the reality of God's love, produces hope.

Thank You, Father God, Lord of grace, that I need not focus on the spiritual enemy or on the problems, but I stand energized by Your faithful love today . . . in the name of Jesus, the Justifier.

God Makes the Servant Stand

Who are you to judge someone else's servant? To his own master he stands or falls. And he will stand, for the Lord is able to make him stand.

Romans 14:4

As I read Romans 14:4, my friend who supervises a Christian hostel in Nicaragua's capital city, Managua, is screaming at the teenage maid. The tile floor looks polished to me, but my friend finds fault in a torrent of Spanish. *How can the girl stand this abuse?* I wonder, praying for her and for my friend, whom I see embittered from repeatedly giving vent to her anger. I can share this Scripture with the maid, but my friend feels she is so right. . . .

Father God, Lord of patience, thank You for taking the part of the weak; heal us in our strengths where they injure others . . . in the name of Jesus, the Suffering Servant.

Stand Firm

Stand firm. Let nothing move you. Always give
yourselves fully to the work of the Lord, because you
know that your labor in the Lord is not in vain. . . . Be
on your guard; stand firm in the faith.
1 Corinthians 15:58, 16:13

"Persevere, stand fast, be stationary in the
faith," Paul admonishes the Corinthian
church. "Be on your guard, courageous,
strong, loving."
This kind of command only makes me
discouraged. How can I stand firm just
because someone tells me to? I need to get
my eyes off my feelings and what I can
do, and look to Jesus. Maybe I should seek
out a spiritual parent for prayer. The Lord
did not create me to be Superwoman,
but to share with others the gifts and
fruits of His Spirit.

Father God, Lord of our labor, thank You
for brothers and sisters who help me
stand firm!. . . in the name of Jesus,
forever the Same.

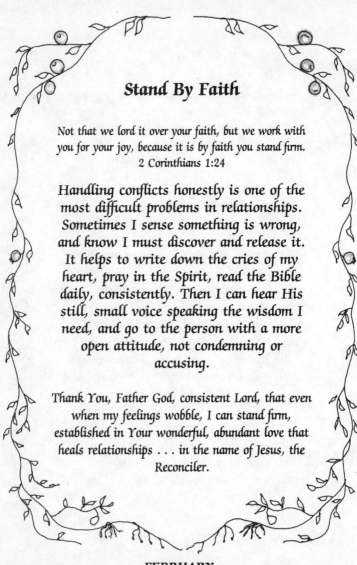

Stand By Faith

Not that we lord it over your faith, but we work with
you for your joy, because it is by faith you stand firm.
2 Corinthians 1:24

Handling conflicts honestly is one of the
most difficult problems in relationships.
Sometimes I sense something is wrong,
and know I must discover and release it.
It helps to write down the cries of my
heart, pray in the Spirit, read the Bible
daily, consistently. Then I can hear His
still, small voice speaking the wisdom I
need, and go to the person with a more
open attitude, not condemning or
accusing.

Thank You, Father God, consistent Lord, that even
when my feelings wobble, I can stand firm,
established in Your wonderful, abundant love that
heals relationships . . . in the name of Jesus, the
Reconciler.

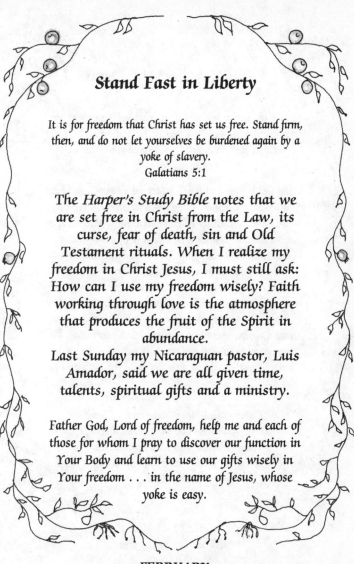

Stand Fast in Liberty

It is for freedom that Christ has set us free. Stand firm,
then, and do not let yourselves be burdened again by a
yoke of slavery.
Galatians 5:1

The *Harper's Study Bible* notes that we
are set free in Christ from the Law, its
curse, fear of death, sin and Old
Testament rituals. When I realize my
freedom in Christ Jesus, I must still ask:
How can I use my freedom wisely? Faith
working through love is the atmosphere
that produces the fruit of the Spirit in
abundance.
Last Sunday my Nicaraguan pastor, Luis
Amador, said we are all given time,
talents, spiritual gifts and a ministry.

Father God, Lord of freedom, help me and each of
those for whom I pray to discover our function in
Your Body and learn to use our gifts wisely in
Your freedom . . . in the name of Jesus, whose
yoke is easy.

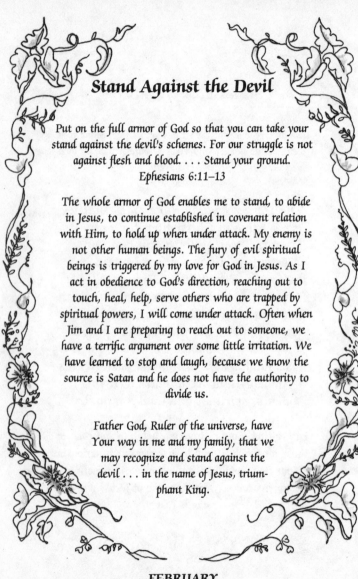

Stand Against the Devil

Put on the full armor of God so that you can take your
stand against the devil's schemes. For our struggle is not
against flesh and blood. . . . Stand your ground.
Ephesians 6:11–13

The whole armor of God enables me to stand, to abide
in Jesus, to continue established in covenant relation
with Him, to hold up when under attack. My enemy is
not other human beings. The fury of evil spiritual
beings is triggered by my love for God in Jesus. As I
act in obedience to God's direction, reaching out to
touch, heal, help, serve others who are trapped by
spiritual powers, I will come under attack. Often when
Jim and I are preparing to reach out to someone, we
have a terrific argument over some little irritation. We
have learned to stop and laugh, because we know the
source is Satan and he does not have the authority to
divide us.

Father God, Ruler of the universe, have
Your way in me and my family, that we
may recognize and stand against the
devil . . . in the name of Jesus, triumphant King.

Stand in One Spirit

Whatever happens, conduct yourselves in a manner
worthy of the gospel of Christ. Then . . . I will know
that you stand firm in one spirit, contending as one man
for the faith of the gospel without being frightened in
any way by those who oppose you.
Philippians 1:27–28

I need to get my eyes off things that divide and keep in
focus the goal of sharing the life of Jesus with those
who do not know Him. It is not easy when close
relationships rub and grate, making raw wounds. Last
night, instead of giving in to jealous feelings for the
beautiful Nicaraguan woman half my age who is helping
us here, I chose to participate with her. It was a
decision. Her giftedness shone and I was able to
encourage her. Eighty young people filled our living room
with laughter and praise songs, and I saw my part more
clearly.

Father God, Lord of oneness, I decide
today to stand in Your one Spirit with
those you have placed in my circle . . .
in the name of Jesus, Repairer of the
breach.

Stand Fast in the Lord

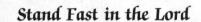

Therefore, my brothers, you whom I love and long for,
my joy and crown, that is how you should stand firm in
the Lord, dear friends!
Philippians 4:1

"Stand fast, persevere," Paul wrote from
prison, "in living like those whom you
admire and look up to in Jesus." The
Philippians were Paul's joy and crown. He
wanted so much for them to be firm,
growing in the faith, strong in courage
. . . to resist pressures to be like the
crowd, to overindulge, to believe Satan's
lies. . . . And those who are watching me?

Faithful Lord, without seeming to nag, be critical
or self-righteous, help me encourage those special
few who are my joy and crown to stand fast in
You today. Show me, Lord, Your way of
encouraging . . . in the name of Jesus,
dearest Friend.

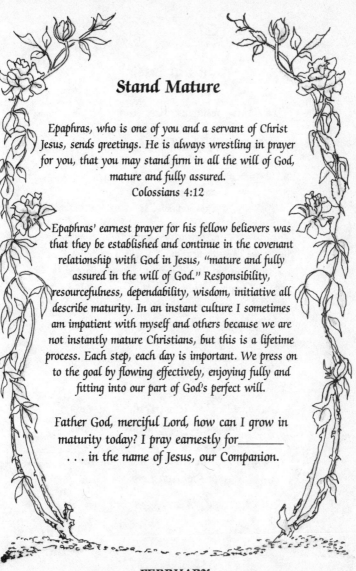

Stand Mature

Epaphras, who is one of you and a servant of Christ Jesus, sends greetings. He is always wrestling in prayer for you, that you may stand firm in all the will of God, mature and fully assured.

Colossians 4:12

Epaphras' earnest prayer for his fellow believers was that they be established and continue in the covenant relationship with God in Jesus, "mature and fully assured in the will of God." Responsibility, resourcefulness, dependability, wisdom, initiative all describe maturity. In an instant culture I sometimes am impatient with myself and others because we are not instantly mature Christians, but this is a lifetime process. Each step, each day is important. We press on to the goal by flowing effectively, enjoying fully and fitting into our part of God's perfect will.

Father God, merciful Lord, how can I grow in maturity today? I pray earnestly for_____
. . . in the name of Jesus, our Companion.

Stand Fast

For now we really live, since you are standing
firm in the Lord. How can we thank God enough
for you in return for all the joy we have in the
presence of our God because of you? Night and
day we pray most earnestly that we
may see you again.
1 Thessalonians 3:8–10

Paul was encouraged when he learned that the young
believers in Thessalonica had not drifted away from the
truth of the Gospel, but remained firm, steadfast in the
Lord, like deeply rooted plants. How wonderful to see
the abundance that comes from carefully prepared soil,
which lives mixed with manure and composted garbage
aerated by worms! Ugh! In the soil of my life today,
what is God transforming into necessary nutrients that
produce the fruit of God's Spirit?

Thank You, steadfast Father God, for
those things that help me grow and for
the young believers who stand fast in
You . . . in the name of Jesus, the Sun
of Righteousness.

Stand Firm

So then, brothers, stand firm and hold to the
teachings we passed on to you, whether by word
of mouth or by letter.
2 Thessalonians 2:15

"Eat the meat and throw away the bones"
is a helpful saying when traditions are
being taught. So many manmade doctrines
are called divine, yet become legal
bondages and divisive. Are my traditions
God's kind of love, His kind of service to
those in need, making narrower the gap
between rich and poor, building bridges,
healing? I want to examine and let them
go if they do not serve me well.

Father God, Lord of history, help me
to see clearly my church's traditions,
and others', too, standing firm in what
is true and letting the rest go . . . in
the name of Jesus, called blasphemer
and Sabbath-breaker!

Stand Fast

Be self-controlled and alert. Your enemy the devil prowls around like a roaring lion looking for someone to devour. Resist him, standing firm in the faith, because you know that your brothers throughout the world are undergoing the same kind of sufferings.
1 Peter 5:8–9

Paul describes our enemy as the devil with principalities, powers, rulers of the darkness of this world, spiritual wickedness in high places (Ephesians 6:12). Yet greater is He who is in us than he who is in the world (1 John 4:4). To pray against, take authority over evil and say no to it is part of my inheritance as a Christian. If I see evil in another, I can bind that evil, but ultimately the responsibility for saying yes to God and no to evil rests with that person. My prayer opens doors.

All-powerful Father God, I praise You that before You no evil can stand, but You lift up the humble and bruised . . . in the name of Jesus, the Despised, Rejected, Crushed and Pierced.

In My Mouth, Truth

Then the woman said to Elijah, "Now I know that you
are a man of God and that the word of the Lord from
your mouth is the truth."
1 Kings 17:24

There was no rain for years in Israel; Elijah had told
King Ahab the truth. Elijah's own food was a daily
miracle as the widow and her son shared bread from the
jar of meal and jar of oil that were amazingly
replenished. When the widow's son died, however, her
reason for living died, too, and she blamed Elijah.
To feel the intense emotions of this true story, I imagine
I am there, taking the part of each person, without
knowing the happy ending!
Elijah told the woman, "Your son lives," after he was
resurrected. Those words were convincing because they
were true.

Father, God of Truth, may I
grow so close to You that my
words also speak what is true in
Your creative plan . . . in the
name of Jesus, Truth
personified.

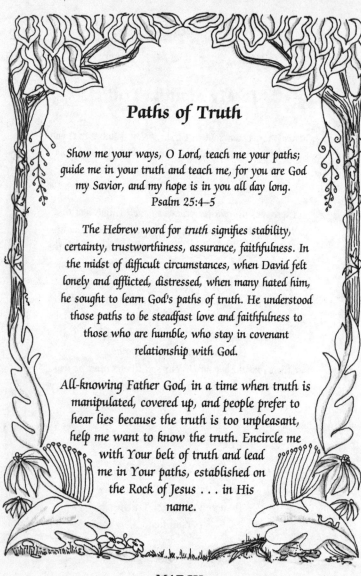

Paths of Truth

*Show me your ways, O Lord, teach me your paths;
guide me in your truth and teach me, for you are God
my Savior, and my hope is in you all day long.*
Psalm 25:4–5

The Hebrew word for *truth* signifies stability,
certainty, trustworthiness, assurance, faithfulness. In
the midst of difficult circumstances, when David felt
lonely and afflicted, distressed, when many hated him,
he sought to learn God's paths of truth. He understood
those paths to be steadfast love and faithfulness to
those who are humble, who stay in covenant
relationship with God.

All-knowing Father God, in a time when truth is
manipulated, covered up, and people prefer to
hear lies because the truth is too unpleasant,
help me want to know the truth. Encircle me
with Your belt of truth and lead
me in Your paths, established on
the Rock of Jesus . . . in His
name.

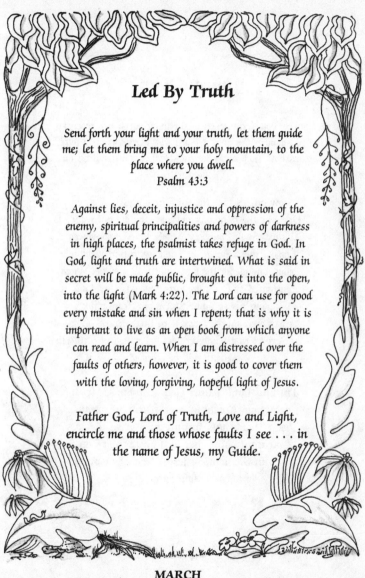

Led By Truth

*Send forth your light and your truth, let them guide
me; let them bring me to your holy mountain, to the
place where you dwell.*
Psalm 43:3

Against lies, deceit, injustice and oppression of the
enemy, spiritual principalities and powers of darkness
in high places, the psalmist takes refuge in God. In
God, light and truth are intertwined. What is said in
secret will be made public, brought out into the open,
into the light (Mark 4:22). The Lord can use for good
every mistake and sin when I repent; that is why it is
important to live as an open book from which anyone
can read and learn. When I am distressed over the
faults of others, however, it is good to cover them
with the loving, forgiving, hopeful light of Jesus.

Father God, Lord of Truth, Love and Light,
encircle me and those whose faults I see . . . in
the name of Jesus, my Guide.

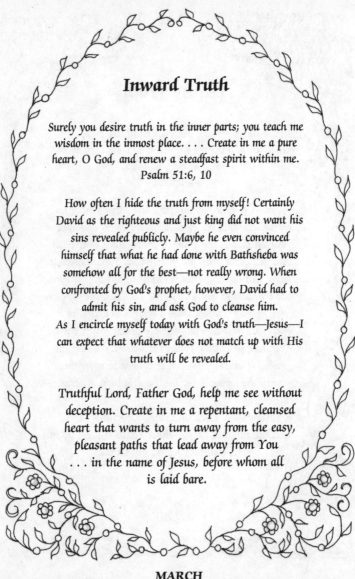

Inward Truth

Surely you desire truth in the inner parts; you teach me
wisdom in the inmost place. . . . Create in me a pure
heart, O God, and renew a steadfast spirit within me.
Psalm 51:6, 10

How often I hide the truth from myself! Certainly
David as the righteous and just king did not want his
sins revealed publicly. Maybe he even convinced
himself that what he had done with Bathsheba was
somehow all for the best—not really wrong. When
confronted by God's prophet, however, David had to
admit his sin, and ask God to cleanse him.
As I encircle myself today with God's truth—Jesus—I
can expect that whatever does not match up with His
truth will be revealed.

Truthful Lord, Father God, help me see without
deception. Create in me a repentant, cleansed
heart that wants to turn away from the easy,
pleasant paths that lead away from You
. . . in the name of Jesus, before whom all
is laid bare.

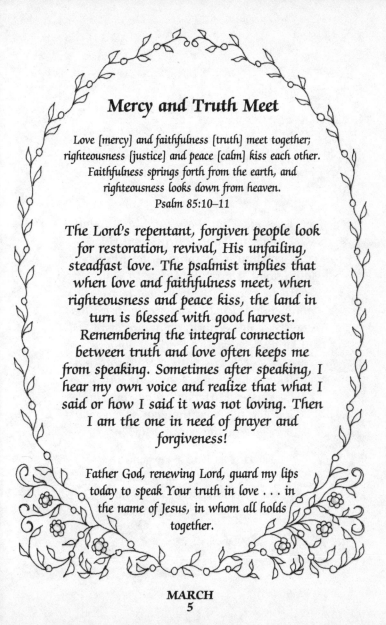

Mercy and Truth Meet

Love [mercy] and faithfulness [truth] meet together;
righteousness [justice] and peace [calm] kiss each other.
Faithfulness springs forth from the earth, and
righteousness looks down from heaven.

Psalm 85:10–11

The Lord's repentant, forgiven people look
for restoration, revival, His unfailing,
steadfast love. The psalmist implies that
when love and faithfulness meet, when
righteousness and peace kiss, the land in
turn is blessed with good harvest.
Remembering the integral connection
between truth and love often keeps me
from speaking. Sometimes after speaking, I
hear my own voice and realize that what I
said or how I said it was not loving. Then
I am the one in need of prayer and
forgiveness!

Father God, renewing Lord, guard my lips
today to speak Your truth in love . . . in
the name of Jesus, in whom all holds
together.

Walk in Truth

Teach me your way, O Lord, and I will walk in your truth; give me an undivided heart, that I may fear your name. I will praise you, O Lord my God, with all my heart; I will glorify your name forever.

Psalm 86:11–12

"Teach me Your way, Lord, and I will walk in Your truth, stability, trustworthiness, assurance, faithfulness," said David. He realized that to walk this path he needed an undivided heart. "A doubleminded man is unstable in all his ways," James echoed, "blown and tossed like a wave on the sea." As long as I earnestly seek His path, keep on asking, seeking, knocking, I know it will be clear. Sister Patterson, a pastor, said, "God doesn't open the door when you are in the parking lot!"

Father God, Lord of my path, I want to walk with You in paths of truth and peace today . . . in the name of Jesus, the Open Door.

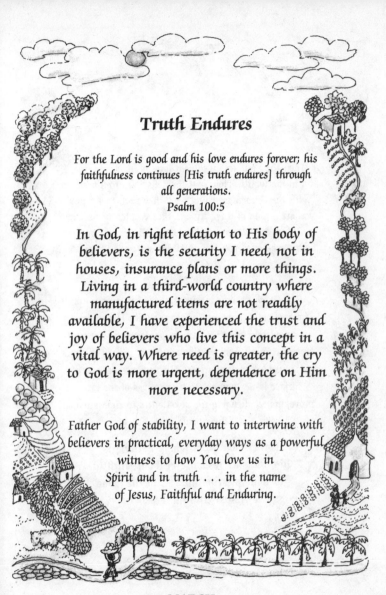

Truth Endures

For the Lord is good and his love endures forever; his
faithfulness continues [His truth endures] through
all generations.
Psalm 100:5

In God, in right relation to His body of
believers, is the security I need, not in
houses, insurance plans or more things.
Living in a third-world country where
manufactured items are not readily
available, I have experienced the trust and
joy of believers who live this concept in a
vital way. Where need is greater, the cry
to God is more urgent, dependence on Him
more necessary.

Father God of stability, I want to intertwine with
believers in practical, everyday ways as a powerful
witness to how You love us in
Spirit and in truth . . . in the name
of Jesus, Faithful and Enduring.

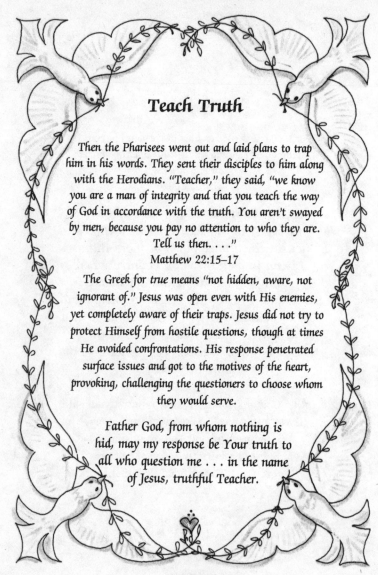

Teach Truth

Then the Pharisees went out and laid plans to trap
him in his words. They sent their disciples to him along
with the Herodians. "Teacher," they said, "we know
you are a man of integrity and that you teach the way
of God in accordance with the truth. You aren't swayed
by men, because you pay no attention to who they are.
Tell us then. . . ."
Matthew 22:15–17

The Greek for *true* means "not hidden, aware, not
ignorant of." Jesus was open even with His enemies,
yet completely aware of their traps. Jesus did not try to
protect Himself from hostile questions, though at times
He avoided confrontations. His response penetrated
surface issues and got to the motives of the heart,
provoking, challenging the questioners to choose whom
they would serve.

Father God, from whom nothing is
hid, may my response be Your truth to
all who question me . . . in the name
of Jesus, truthful Teacher.

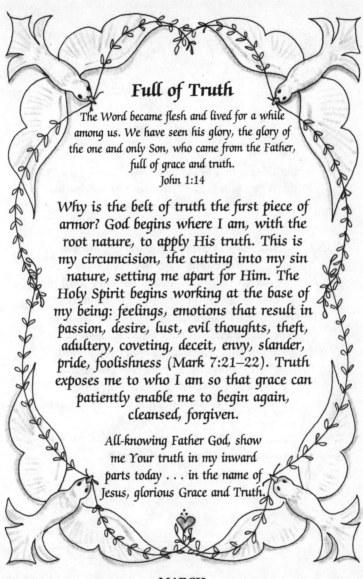

Full of Truth

The Word became flesh and lived for a while among us. We have seen his glory, the glory of the one and only Son, who came from the Father, full of grace and truth.
John 1:14

Why is the belt of truth the first piece of armor? God begins where I am, with the root nature, to apply His truth. This is my circumcision, the cutting into my sin nature, setting me apart for Him. The Holy Spirit begins working at the base of my being: feelings, emotions that result in passion, desire, lust, evil thoughts, theft, adultery, coveting, deceit, envy, slander, pride, foolishness (Mark 7:21–22). Truth exposes me to who I am so that grace can patiently enable me to begin again, cleansed, forgiven.

All-knowing Father God, show me Your truth in my inward parts today . . . in the name of Jesus, glorious Grace and Truth.

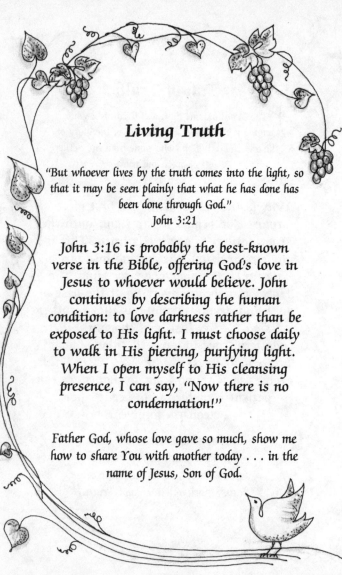

Living Truth

*"But whoever lives by the truth comes into the light, so
that it may be seen plainly that what he has done has
been done through God."*
John 3:21

John 3:16 is probably the best-known
verse in the Bible, offering God's love in
Jesus to whoever would believe. John
continues by describing the human
condition: to love darkness rather than be
exposed to His light. I must choose daily
to walk in His piercing, purifying light.
When I open myself to His cleansing
presence, I can say, "Now there is no
condemnation!"

Father God, whose love gave so much, show me
how to share You with another today . . . in the
name of Jesus, Son of God.

Worship in Truth

"True worshipers will worship the Father in spirit and
truth, for they are the kind of worshipers the Father
seeks. God is spirit, and his worshipers must worship
in spirit and in truth."
John 4:23–24

Jesus spoke to the woman at the well as to an equal.
To her He revealed that He is the One for whom both
Jews and Samaritans wait, God's truth in a Person.
"This drink, this spring of water that never grows dry,
is for you," He told her, and she received it eagerly.
She could not help but run and call those who had
judged, condemned, ridiculed her, "Come and see!"
They saw the difference in her, were curious and
came because she had worshiped in spirit and in
truth that day.

Father God, gracious Judge, I want to worship in
spirit and in truth; I want to drink today from
Your living waters and share them with all who
will come . . . in the name of Jesus,
the true Source.

Truth Makes Free

To the Jews who had believed him, Jesus said, "If you
hold to my teaching, you are really my disciples. Then
you will know the truth, and the truth will set you
free."

John 8:31–32

God is true, Jesus said, steadfast, loyal,
honest, just. He is real and essential,
consistent. Jesus revealed God in human
form by doing and speaking only what
pleased His Father. What an intimate
relationship! What love and gratitude are
necessary to hear His voice consistently!
To act on those inner urgings, I must
decrease so that He can increase in me.
All my good efforts are trash (Isaiah
64:6). What counts are those things done
with God's joy filling them.

Honest Father God, speak to me in this
quiet moment specific truth You have for
me today. Wrap it around me as a
pleasing garment of praise . . . in the
name of Jesus, Revealer of Truth.

Jesus Is Truth

Jesus answered, "I am the way and the truth and the
life. No one comes to the Father except through me. . . .
I tell you the truth, anyone who has faith in me will do
what I have been doing. He will do even greater things
than these, because I am going to the Father."
John 14:6, 12

"There must be more to the Christian life than this!" I
cried out in 1969 when we were working with inner-
city teenagers in Jacksonville, Florida, and that began
my search. Soon I found others who knew that
everything Jesus said was true, right now, in the
midst of real crises and pressing needs.
The way, the truth, the life: This is who Jesus is.
As I seek to walk in His footsteps, God promises to
lead me into all the fullness He has prepared for me,
to do those "greater things" through me.

Great God who is in control, lead me in Jesus'
way today, doing what He would do in those
situations beyond my control . . .
in His name.

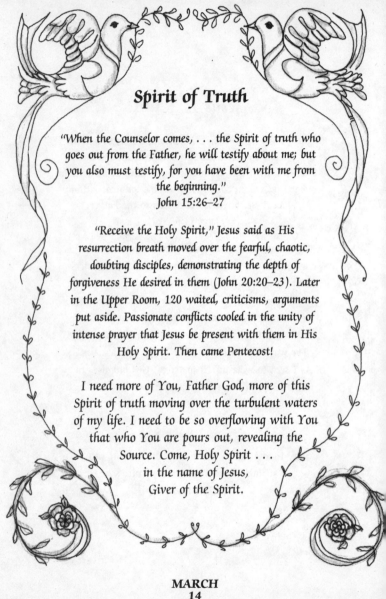

Spirit of Truth

"When the Counselor comes, . . . the Spirit of truth who
goes out from the Father, he will testify about me; but
you also must testify, for you have been with me from
the beginning."
John 15:26–27

"Receive the Holy Spirit," Jesus said as His
resurrection breath moved over the fearful, chaotic,
doubting disciples, demonstrating the depth of
forgiveness He desired in them (John 20:20–23). Later
in the Upper Room, 120 waited, criticisms, arguments
put aside. Passionate conflicts cooled in the unity of
intense prayer that Jesus be present with them in His
Holy Spirit. Then came Pentecost!

I need more of You, Father God, more of this
Spirit of truth moving over the turbulent waters
of my life. I need to be so overflowing with You
that who You are pours out, revealing the
Source. Come, Holy Spirit . . .
in the name of Jesus,
Giver of the Spirit.

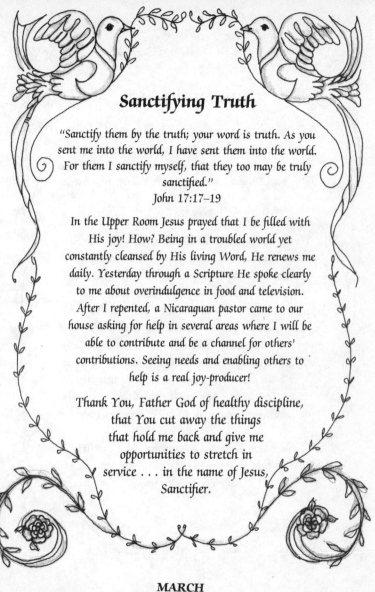

Sanctifying Truth

"Sanctify them by the truth; your word is truth. As you sent me into the world, I have sent them into the world. For them I sanctify myself, that they too may be truly sanctified."
John 17:17–19

In the Upper Room Jesus prayed that I be filled with His joy! How? Being in a troubled world yet constantly cleansed by His living Word, He renews me daily. Yesterday through a Scripture He spoke clearly to me about overindulgence in food and television. After I repented, a Nicaraguan pastor came to our house asking for help in several areas where I will be able to contribute and be a channel for others' contributions. Seeing needs and enabling others to help is a real joy-producer!

Thank You, Father God of healthy discipline, that You cut away the things that hold me back and give me opportunities to stretch in service . . . in the name of Jesus, Sanctifier.

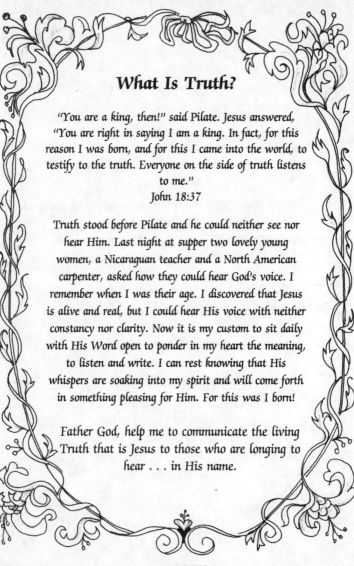

What Is Truth?

"You are a king, then!" said Pilate. Jesus answered,
"You are right in saying I am a king. In fact, for this
reason I was born, and for this I came into the world, to
testify to the truth. Everyone on the side of truth listens
to me."
John 18:37

Truth stood before Pilate and he could neither see nor
hear Him. Last night at supper two lovely young
women, a Nicaraguan teacher and a North American
carpenter, asked how they could hear God's voice. I
remember when I was their age. I discovered that Jesus
is alive and real, but I could hear His voice with neither
constancy nor clarity. Now it is my custom to sit daily
with His Word open to ponder in my heart the meaning,
to listen and write. I can rest knowing that His
whispers are soaking into my spirit and will come forth
in something pleasing for Him. For this was I born!

Father God, help me to communicate the living
Truth that is Jesus to those who are longing to
hear . . . in His name.

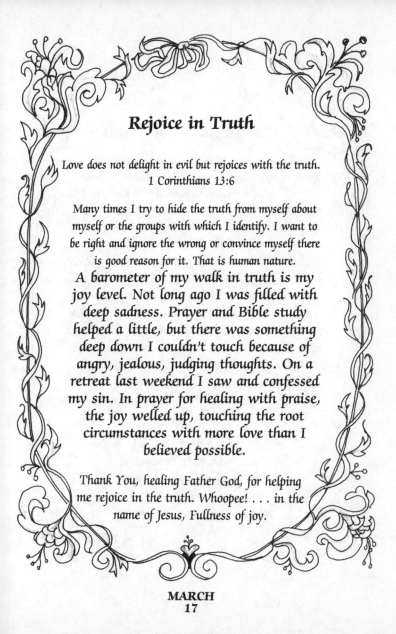

Rejoice in Truth

Love does not delight in evil but rejoices with the truth.
1 Corinthians 13:6

Many times I try to hide the truth from myself about
myself or the groups with which I identify. I want to
be right and ignore the wrong or convince myself there
is good reason for it. That is human nature.

A barometer of my walk in truth is my
joy level. Not long ago I was filled with
deep sadness. Prayer and Bible study
helped a little, but there was something
deep down I couldn't touch because of
angry, jealous, judging thoughts. On a
retreat last weekend I saw and confessed
my sin. In prayer for healing with praise,
the joy welled up, touching the root
circumstances with more love than I
believed possible.

Thank You, healing Father God, for helping
me rejoice in the truth. Whoopee! . . . in the
name of Jesus, Fullness of joy.

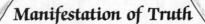

Manifestation of Truth

We have renounced secret and shameful ways; we
do not use deception, nor do we distort the word
of God. On the contrary, by setting forth the
truth plainly we commend ourselves to every
man's conscience in the sight of God.
2 Corinthians 4:2

Moses wore a veil over his face because God's splendor
was too great for ordinary people to bear. The veil in the
Temple was torn when Jesus died on the cross, for in
Him the Holiest is open, available for those who seek.
Now I, with unveiled face, come into His light, exposed,
open, available, vulnerable. My life is to be like a moon,
dead to my own warts and wishes, but gloriously
attractive in reflecting His great love in the darkness,
dancing my part in the rhythm of His immense,
universal plan.

Splendid, Holy Father God, help me be
open and honest, transparent
in the way I communicate
Your joyful good news . . . in
the name of Jesus, Lord of the
dance.

Speaking Truth in Love

Instead, speaking the truth in love, we will in all
things grow up into him who is the Head, that
is, Christ.
Ephesians 4:15

The goal is maturity, growing up in harmony, in unity
with other believers, not influenced by those who would
deceive. Speaking the truth in love, Paul says, is the
way to grow, fitting into the place designed for me in
the Body of Christ. Judge as I would be judged, Jesus
said. Speak the truth as I would have others speak. Take
the log out. . . . Easier said than done. Often I notice
and am antagonized by something in others that is my
own tendency or failing.

All-knowing and accepting Father God, turn the
spotlight away from the glaring faults of others
and show what is in me that needs
Your truth spoken in love! . . .
in the name of Jesus, the
true Light.

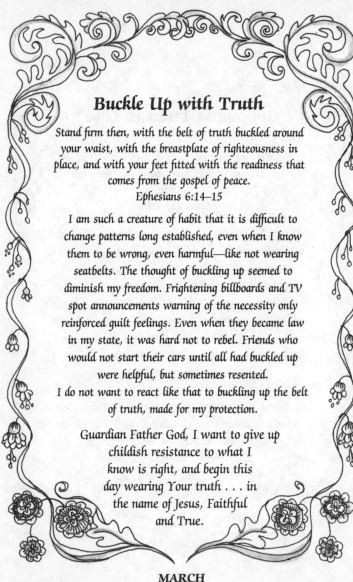

Buckle Up with Truth

Stand firm then, with the belt of truth buckled around your waist, with the breastplate of righteousness in place, and with your feet fitted with the readiness that comes from the gospel of peace.

Ephesians 6:14–15

I am such a creature of habit that it is difficult to change patterns long established, even when I know them to be wrong, even harmful—like not wearing seatbelts. The thought of buckling up seemed to diminish my freedom. Frightening billboards and TV spot announcements warning of the necessity only reinforced guilt feelings. Even when they became law in my state, it was hard not to rebel. Friends who would not start their cars until all had buckled up were helpful, but sometimes resented.
I do not want to react like that to buckling up the belt of truth, made for my protection.

Guardian Father God, I want to give up
childish resistance to what I
know is right, and begin this
day wearing Your truth . . . in
the name of Jesus, Faithful
and True.

Dividing the Word of Truth

*Do your best to present yourself to God as one approved,
a workman who does not need to be ashamed and who
correctly handles the word of truth.*
2 Timothy 2:15

What works? What is effective in communicating to
others the Good News of Jesus' resurrection?
Arguments over doctrines do not help. Avoid them,
Paul says, in order to focus on what is positive.
Last night in our living room gathered six Nicaraguan
Christian leaders, each with strong doctrines,
traditions, opinions, beliefs that cause them to exclude
the others. Having been with each in his own setting,
I knew the prejudices that would keep them from
considering a joint project. Yet Jesus Christ is central
to each; His presence enabled them to see something
good in the others.

One and only Father God, help me today
to absorb and share Your true
Word in ways that build up
. . . in the name of Jesus,
Lion of Judah and Passover
Lamb.

Truth and Godliness

Paul, a servant of God and an apostle of Jesus Christ for the faith of God's elect and the knowledge of the truth that leads to godliness—a faith and knowledge resting on the hope of eternal life, which God, who does not lie, promised before the beginning of time. . . .
Titus 1:1–2

God never lies! When I grow in Him, I grow more like Him, more truthful, honest, transparent. To understand what a Christian is like, I read between the lines of those I respect and admire in the Lord. For years I wore a mask of religiosity until I was confronted, penetrated by the warmth and real presence of a living Jesus. Now I do not admire those who "seem" holy, but I try to look beyond the appearances to the honest inner core, the vulnerable part standing openly in need of forgiving prayer.

All-seeing Father God, thank You for revealing the truth to me . . . in the name of Jesus, Chosen of God, Firstborn, First and Last.

Straying from Truth

My brothers, if one of you should wander from the truth
and someone should bring him back, remember this:
Whoever turns a sinner from the error of his way will
save him from death and cover over a multitude of sins.
James 5:19–20

James described a healthy Christian fellowship like
this: Believers gather around to pray for those
suffering. With the cheerful, they rejoice, praising God
together. The sick are anointed with oil and forgiven
in a healing prayer that includes confession of sins.
Joyfully those believers see God at work answering
prayer! If I really care about the one who once
shared with me but is now going away from the light
of truth, I will persistently go after him or her, never
giving up, not giving in to gossip.

Pursuing Father God, show me for whom You
would have me pray fervently today, not giving
up, covering a multitude of sins with Your
forgiving love . . . in the name of Jesus,
Shepherd and Overseer of souls.

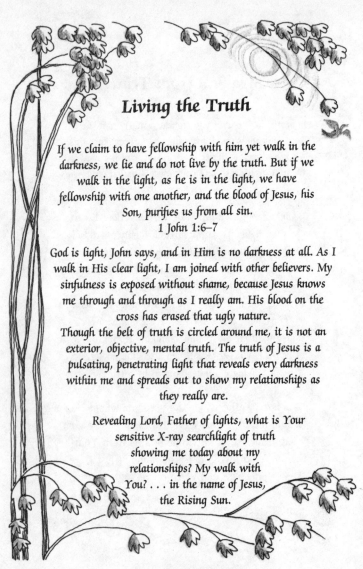

Living the Truth

If we claim to have fellowship with him yet walk in the
darkness, we lie and do not live by the truth. But if we
walk in the light, as he is in the light, we have
fellowship with one another, and the blood of Jesus, his
Son, purifies us from all sin.
1 John 1:6–7

God is light, John says, and in Him is no darkness at all. As I
walk in His clear light, I am joined with other believers. My
sinfulness is exposed without shame, because Jesus knows
me through and through as I really am. His blood on the
cross has erased that ugly nature.
Though the belt of truth is circled around me, it is not an
exterior, objective, mental truth. The truth of Jesus is a
pulsating, penetrating light that reveals every darkness
within me and spreads out to show my relationships as
they really are.

Revealing Lord, Father of lights, what is Your
sensitive X-ray searchlight of truth
showing me today about my
relationships? My walk with
You? . . . in the name of Jesus,
the Rising Sun.

In Deed and Truth

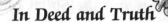

Dear children, let us not love with words or
tongue but with actions and in truth.
1 John 3:18

If anyone has the world's goods and sees his brother in
need, yet closes his heart against him, how does God's
love abide in him (1 John 3:17)? How can I love in
deed and in truth? A product of North American
culture, I can view tragedies all around the world
instantly, my senses bombarded with huge needs
impossible for me to meet. I, in despair, become callous
in soul. How to keep an open heart?

Millard Fuller, founder of Habitat for Humanity, says
each of us can do something; he has the goal of
eliminating poverty housing. It is exciting to see what
can happen when people, rich and poor, black, white,
brown, with different abilities and interests, join
together to share resources.

Thank You, Father God of impossible dreams, for
opening my heart and showing me ways I can be
a part . . . in the name of Jesus, the Cornerstone.

Knowing the Spirit of Truth

We are from God, and whoever knows God listens to us;
but whoever is not from God does not listen to us.
This is how we recognize the Spirit of truth and the
spirit of falsehood.
1 John 4:6

For years I questioned, wondering, "How could one
man's death mean so much? So many have died cruel
deaths." I could not believe in the resurrection, though I
was very religious and critical of others. One day in our
apartment Jim's last year in seminary the Scriptures
came alive. I am the living Bread, the living Water, He
seemed to be saying to me, and there was a warm
Presence in the room I could not deny. He is alive! And
it makes all the difference!

Thank You, Father God, for Your Presence
in Jesus who comes to me personally, in
ways that lift my expectations to include
Your Spirit and resurrection living . . . in the
name of Jesus, Source of eternal salvation.

Knowing the Spirit of Truth

Who is it that overcomes the world? Only he who
believes that Jesus is the Son of God. This is the one
who came by water and blood—Jesus Christ. . . . And it
is the Spirit who testifies, because the Spirit is the
truth.
1 John 5:5–6

There are three witnesses to the fact that Jesus is who
He claims to be: 1. The *water* of His baptism when
God said, "This is My beloved Son"; 2. The *blood*
poured out at the cross crying out from the ground
with the Roman soldier, "Surely this is the Son of
God"; 3. The *Holy Spirit* whom Jesus, in His
resurrection body, breathed into His disciples, who
came at Pentecost with wind and fire and gave ability
to communicate, without fear, languages of praise and
witness. "More, I want more of that Spirit, more
boldness," they cried out, and so do I.

Father God, my heart longs for Your Spirit
of truth to plunge through me in rivers of
living water; this is Your will!. . . in the
name of Jesus, Baptizer with the Spirit and
with fire.

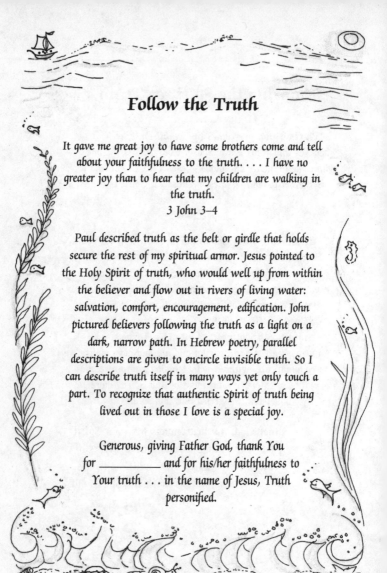

Follow the Truth

It gave me great joy to have some brothers come and tell
about your faithfulness to the truth. . . . I have no
greater joy than to hear that my children are walking in
the truth.
3 John 3–4

Paul described truth as the belt or girdle that holds
secure the rest of my spiritual armor. Jesus pointed to
the Holy Spirit of truth, who would well up from within
the believer and flow out in rivers of living water:
salvation, comfort, encouragement, edification. John
pictured believers following the truth as a light on a
dark, narrow path. In Hebrew poetry, parallel
descriptions are given to encircle invisible truth. So I
can describe truth itself in many ways yet only touch a
part. To recognize that authentic Spirit of truth being
lived out in those I love is a special joy.

Generous, giving Father God, thank You
for _____ and for his/her faithfulness to
Your truth . . . in the name of Jesus, Truth
personified.

Fellow Workers in the Truth

You are faithful in what you are doing for the brothers,
even though they are strangers to you. . . . It was for
the sake of the Name that they went out, receiving no
help from the pagans. We ought therefore to show
hospitality to such men so that we may work together
for the truth.
3 John 5, 7–8

The truth is the Gospel itself, the Good News that Jesus
is alive, working in mighty ways here and now. It
includes supporting others whose mission is to share the
Gospel. When visitors come unexpectedly at mealtime,
it seems the Lord takes joy in my serving them. At
other times, when I am reluctant and say there is
not enough, inevitably their portion is left over. When
I am gracious and share, the food stretches and I
am blessed as well.

Father God of abundant provision, I want to
be a channel of Your Good News . . . in the
name of Jesus, whose life was one with His
message.

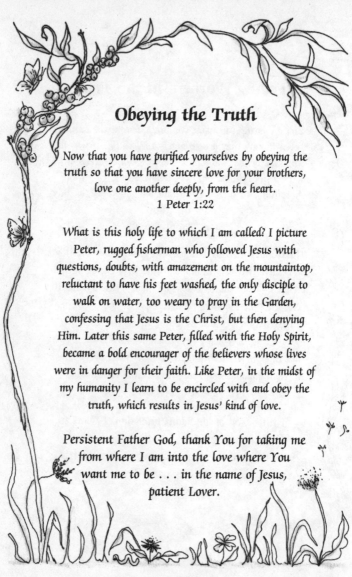

Obeying the Truth

Now that you have purified yourselves by obeying the truth so that you have sincere love for your brothers, love one another deeply, from the heart.
1 Peter 1:22

What is this holy life to which I am called? I picture Peter, rugged fisherman who followed Jesus with questions, doubts, with amazement on the mountaintop, reluctant to have his feet washed, the only discile to walk on water, too weary to pray in the Garden, confessing that Jesus is the Christ, but then denying Him. Later this same Peter, filled with the Holy Spirit, became a bold encourager of the believers whose lives were in danger for their faith. Like Peter, in the midst of my humanity I learn to be encircled with and obey the truth, which results in Jesus' kind of love.

Persistent Father God, thank You for taking me from where I am into the love where You want me to be . . . in the name of Jesus, patient Lover.

Receiving the Truth

Let us draw near to God with a sincere heart in full
assurance of faith, having our hearts sprinkled to cleanse
us from a guilty conscience. . . . Let us . . . spur one
another on toward love and good deeds . . . after we
have received the knowledge of the truth.

Hebrews 10:22, 24, 26

It is easy to read only pleasant Scriptures that encourage
and make me feel warm, loved, accepted. The writer of
Hebrews is true to the heritage of awesome seriousness
that Moses revealed as he shattered the Ten
Commandments at the foot of the mountain. Our
freedom was bought at great cost and in the spirit of
gratitude I hold on, keep going even when it is tough. I
need others to keep those supply lines open, to keep me
encouraged and determined never to turn back.

Father God, Consuming Fire, show me my
support system. Thank You for each one who
comes to mind and knit me even more closely
with these brothers and sisters . . . in the name
of Jesus, our older Brother.

Counted As Righteousness

He took him outside and said, "Look up at the heavens
and count the stars—if indeed you can count them."
Then he said to him, "So shall your offspring be."
Abram believed the Lord, and he credited it to him as
righteousness.
Genesis 15:5–6

Old Abram standing under the stars could not point to
his child, but trusted God's promise that from him
would come uncounted millions of children! What is
God's promise to *me*? What is that dream that rises
from deep within my spirit, the part connected to God's
Spirit? Though it may seem impossible, He does what
He says if I yield to His working.
With Abram I stand under the stars and am thankful for
such a magnificent God who does far more than I can
ask or think.

Father God of dreamers, give me
strength to put my dreams on
Your altar, relinquishing them
totally into Your plan, Your
timing . . . in the name of Jesus,
who is the "Yes!"

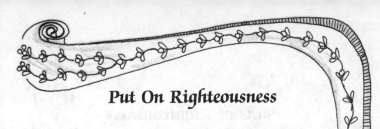

Put On Righteousness

I put on righteousness as my clothing; justice was my
robe and my turban. I was eyes to the blind and feet to
the lame. I was a father to the needy; I took up the case
of the stranger. I broke the fangs of the wicked and
snatched the victims from their teeth.

Job 29:14–17

Righteousness and justice—hand-in-hand,
defining each other—are the ways pleasing
to God. Job put on righteousness and
justice like clothing. This meant action on
behalf of the poor, widows, orphans,
blind, lame, and action against those who
created injustice. Good deeds did not
prevent his being severely tested by Satan.

Father God of all that is truly right,
how can I put on righteousness today?
Not self-righteously. Whom can I
serve today? Who needs my resources
in order to sing for joy? . . . in the
name of Jesus, the I AM.

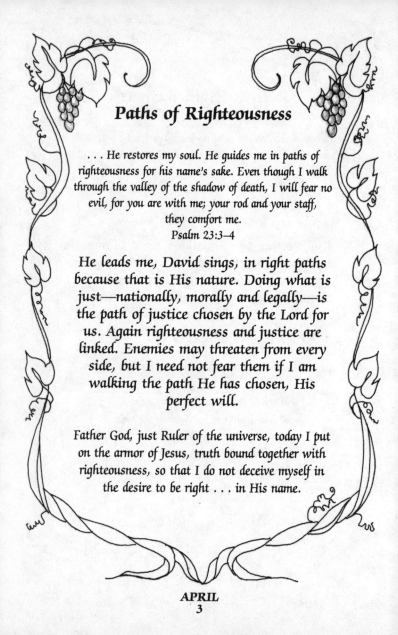

Paths of Righteousness

... He restores my soul. He guides me in paths of
righteousness for his name's sake. Even though I walk
through the valley of the shadow of death, I will fear no
evil, for you are with me; your rod and your staff,
they comfort me.
Psalm 23:3–4

He leads me, David sings, in right paths
because that is His nature. Doing what is
just—nationally, morally and legally—is
the path of justice chosen by the Lord for
us. Again righteousness and justice are
linked. Enemies may threaten from every
side, but I need not fear them if I am
walking the path He has chosen, His
perfect will.

Father God, just Ruler of the universe, today I put
on the armor of Jesus, truth bound together with
righteousness, so that I do not deceive myself in
the desire to be right ... in His name.

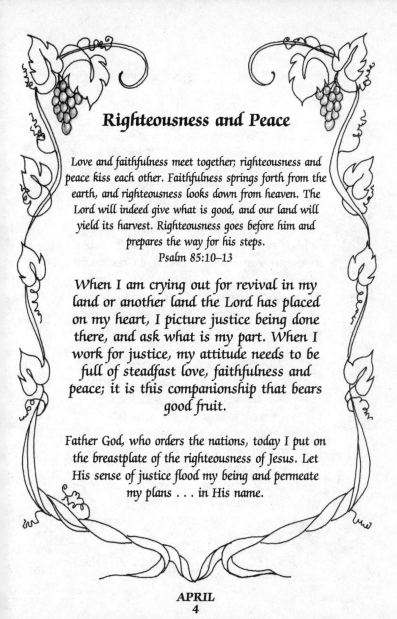

Righteousness and Peace

Love and faithfulness meet together; righteousness and peace kiss each other. Faithfulness springs forth from the earth, and righteousness looks down from heaven. The Lord will indeed give what is good, and our land will yield its harvest. Righteousness goes before him and prepares the way for his steps.

Psalm 85:10–13

When I am crying out for revival in my land or another land the Lord has placed on my heart, I picture justice being done there, and ask what is my part. When I work for justice, my attitude needs to be full of steadfast love, faithfulness and peace; it is this companionship that bears good fruit.

Father God, who orders the nations, today I put on the breastplate of the righteousness of Jesus. Let His sense of justice flood my being and permeate my plans . . . in His name.

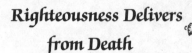

Righteousness Delivers from Death

He is a shield to those whose walk is blameless, for he guards the course of the just. . . . Then you will understand what is right and just and fair—every good path. For wisdom will enter your heart.

Proverbs 2:7–10

Seekers for wisdom and understanding, which are gifts of the Holy Spirit, learn awesome respect for God. From reverence comes wisdom; in this path the Lord Himself is a shield. He is my protection as I step out, act on His directions to do what is right, pursue justice, love mercy.

All-wise Father God, as I think of
_____who needs guidance and wisdom
today, and of_____
who is following a path that is
obviously wrong, whether deliberately
or from ignorance of the true path, I
need Your wisdom to help relate to
them in ways they can receive . . . in
the name of Jesus, the Way and
the Life.

Showing Righteousness

The wicked man earns deceptive wages, but he who sows righteousness reaps a sure reward. . . . The fruit of the righteous is a tree of life, and he who wins souls is wise.

Proverbs 11:18, 30

I love it when meditating on one verse in the Bible brings forth a whole parade of thoughts, companion verses, greater understanding, embellishing, harmonizing, expanding the imagination. The proverb about sowing righteousness and kindness brought to mind the Parable of the Sower, the tree of life, the pruned and fruitful vine, the healing leaves.

Thank You, Father God of the Harvest, for Your planting in me. Remove from me whatever prevents the fruitfulness You desire . . . in the name of Jesus, the Vine.

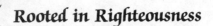

Rooted in Righteousness

A man cannot be established through wickedness, but the righteous cannot be uprooted. . . . In the way of righteousness there is life; along that path is immortality.

Proverbs 12:3, 28

As I seek to understand more about this righteousness that I put on as a breastplate, protecting my heart, vital organs and physical life, many proverbs expand my understanding. Righteousness, justice, doing what pleases God, is something that goes down deep into my being with durable roots. Righteousness unifies my body, soul and spirit. My thoughts focused on what is right in God's eyes result in kind actions and truthful, healing words.

All-righteous Father God, unite my heart today. Cleanse me of those things that keep me from being fully pleasing to You. Help my thoughts, words and actions this day to reflect Your life in me . . . in the name of Jesus, One with the Father.

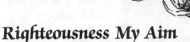

Righteousness My Aim

But you, man of God, flee from all this, and pursue
righteousness, godliness, faith, love, endurance and
gentleness. Fight the good fight of the faith.
1 Timothy 6:11–12

"The Lord . . . loves those who pursue
righteousness" (Proverbs 15:9). Daniel,
the teenager living with us, wants a tape
recorder, a motorcycle, dark mirror
glasses—none of which is wrong in itself,
but what is the goal? I remember poring
over the Sears Christmas catalog and
Seventeen magazine making my wish list
far beyond my parents' post-Depression
means. How do we change from things
possessing us to holding all things lightly
as a trust of which we are stewards?

Father God, my ultimate Goal, today I take the
sword of the Spirit to cut me free from the love of
things that hold me, and those I love . . . in the
name of Jesus, my Righteousness.

Way of Righteousness

In a large house there are articles not only of gold and silver, but also of wood and clay; some are for noble purposes and some for ignoble. If a man cleanses himself from the latter, he will be an instrument for noble purposes, made holy, useful to the Master and prepared to do any good work.

2 Timothy 2:20–21

In order to wear a breastplate of righteousness, the righteousness of Jesus who alone knows and is what is perfectly just and right, I must seek it out. Whatever my sphere of influence—friends, family, neighbors, church, school, work, government leaders—I am responsible to seek after God's righteous path and His strength to walk in it.

Father God, who is living Spirit and Fire, I submit my will, passions, ambitions, desires and delights to the heat of Your tempering, purifying flame, to melt and shape me into a useful vessel . . . in the name of Jesus, the Righteous One.

Reward of Righteousness

The kingdom of God is . . . righteousness, peace and joy
in the Holy Spirit, because anyone who serves Christ in
this way is pleasing to God and approved by men. Let us
therefore make every effort to do what leads to peace.
Romans 14:17–19

Solomon said that the person who pursues what is right
will find life and honor (Proverbs 21:21). Jim, my
husband, was not looking for life and honor when he
heard God call him to Nicaragua six years ago. On his
heart were the staggering conditions from years of
injustice and greed that could be seen in the eyes of the
hungry children, houses made of junk covered with
plastic, Christian friends with limbs blown off by mines.
His decision was unpopular with many. But Jim was
looking for peace, and he has found it here, in obedience
to God's call.

Longsuffering Father God, thank You that You
are present wherever there is suffering. Enable us
to learn Your way of peace . . . in the name of
Jesus, Prince of Peace.

Judge in Righteousness

He will not judge by what he sees with his eyes, . . .
but with righteousness he will judge the needy, with
justice he will give decisions for the poor of the
earth. . . . Righteousness will be his belt and
faithfulness the sash around his waist.

Isaiah 11:3–5

The prophet Isaiah described Jesus, the
One God would send, as having right
judgment as His clothing. I take Jesus as
my spiritual armor today. His right
judgment in favor of the needy, weak and
depressed will be part of who I am.
Today I repent of any ways I hold others
in contempt, accusing or blaming them for
their condition.

Show me, Father God, how to strengthen the
weak, enable the poor to have meaningful
employment, give the depressed hope and
reason to live. Show my nation any ways we
are wicked and cleanse us in these specific
areas: _____ . . . in the name of
Jesus, our righteous Judge.

Result of Righteousness

[When] the Spirit is poured upon us from on high . . .
Justice will dwell in the desert and righteousness
live in the fertile field. The fruit of righteousness
will be peace; the effect of righteousness will be
quietness and confidence forever.
Isaiah 32:15–17

The Spirit of God filling me, covering my land, guiding
my occupation, results in righteousness and justice. One
pastor from a squatters' settlement in Costa Rica said
that peace is not just absence of the military but work,
dignity and a place to live. Jim often says that one of
the first results of the Holy Spirit's coming at Pentecost
was that the believers sold their excess and shared so all
had enough.

Generous Father God, show me today my
excess and what to share and with whom.
Come, Holy Spirit, Convicter, Comforter,
Counselor, and bring healing in our land. Let
Your way of peace begin in me . . . in the
name of Jesus, the Sun of Righteousness.

Righteousness and Strength

"I am God, and there is no other. . . . Before me every knee will bow; by me every tongue will swear. They will say of me, 'In the Lord alone are righteousness and strength.'"
Isaiah 45:22–24

In Isaiah is another clue about my armor of righteousness. God's creative word, the word that formed the earth, the word that took human shape in Jesus the Messiah, was sent forth in an atmosphere, a living breath, of righteousness. That word said, "To Me every knee shall bow and every tongue confess. . . ."
Only God is perfectly right. People on their own do what is "right" in their own eyes (Judges 21:25) and justify their actions.

Merciful Father God, when I live in Your holy breath as my necessary air, the enemies who attack me really come against You and will have to answer to You. I release them into Your compassionate hands; I want You to be the judge instead of me . . . in the name of Jesus, who threw no stones.

Righteousness As Breastplate

He was appalled that there was no one to intercede; so his own arm worked salvation for him, and his own righteousness sustained him. He put on righteousness as his breastplate, and the helmet of salvation on his head.
Isaiah 59:16–17

Though Paul wrote of the armor of God as if for the individual's daily spiritual battles, the prophet Isaiah clearly saw the need for a nation under God to be responsible for its use as well. Israel received God's protection and blessing only after sincere repentance and turning from lies, violence and injustice. The Lord Himself puts on the armor of justice and the helmet of salvation. He also puts on vengeance to punish those who destroy the innocent.

As a Christian, I am responsible to participate with You, holy Father God, by interceding in the cleansing process. Those principalities and powers of darkness seem so great, but You are greater! Show me my part today . . . in the name of Jesus, our Redemption.

Trees of Righteousness

I delight greatly in the Lord; my soul rejoices in my God. For he has clothed me with garments of salvation and arrayed me in a robe of righteousness. . . . For as the soil makes the sprout come up and a garden causes seeds to grow, so the Sovereign Lord will make righteousness and praise spring up before all nations.
Isaiah 61:10–11

Ends do not justify the means. Every person and nation will be judged by how we relate to the poor. What are the poor saying of me? What are the captives, the refugees saying of me? Am I opening the prisons? healing wounds? Am I enabling them to rejoice in the Lord like a strong oak tree lifting its leafy arms in praise?

Father God, who searches my heart, if the answer to the above questions is yes, then I am thankful. If the answer is no, then there is something to be done today. Please show me . . . in the name of Jesus, "the least of these," my Brother.

Stream of Righteousness

Hate evil, love good; maintain justice in the courts.
Perhaps the Lord God Almighty will have mercy. . . .
"Let justice roll on like a river, righteousness like
a never-failing stream!"
Amos 5:15, 24

Amos says the evidence of true spirituality
is presented by the quality of justice in
our land, not by towering steeples or
padded sanctuaries. In fairness and in
legal rights for every citizen is found the
fresh, pure, flowing waters of justice and
righteousness.

Sovereign Father God, today I pray for our legal
system, for judges and lawyers not to be influenced
by the rich and powerful. I pray for the refugee,
the elderly, the homeless, for racial minorities to
have justice in my land. Here I put names and
faces to these groupings so that my prayer is not
anonymous but personal: _____ . . . in
the name of Jesus, the Lawyer who took our place.

Sun of Righteousness

"For you who revere my name, the sun of righteousness
will rise with healing in [His] wings. And you will go
out and leap like calves."
Malachi 4:2

One time when I felt I could not face the next day, Jim
placed his hand on my head and prayed quietly. I felt
something soft, like a breath of air from angel wings,
and the thought came, *There is healing in His wings.* In
that moment came the tender presence of Jesus and a
healing of my mind.

To read Malachi 3–4 is to understand that there is a
price for entering into a relationship with a holy and
just God. To those in need He is kind, responsive, a
tender lover. To those in rebellion, whose hearts are
hardened by gaining at the expense of others, He is
stern, direct, pointing out His commandments. There is
cause and effect for going my own way.

Today, impartial Father God, I put on Jesus'
righteousness, which has healing woven into it
. . . in His precious name.

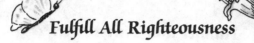

Fulfill All Righteousness

Then Jesus came from Galilee to the Jordan to be
baptized by John. . . . Jesus [said], "Let it be so now; it
is proper for us to do this to fulfill all righteousness."
Matthew 3:13–15

By being baptized Jesus showed His
humility, His willingness to fit into God's
plan for His life, to "fulfill all
righteousness."
Webster's dictionary says that to be
justified by God is to prove to be just,
right or reasonable. Baptism is a public,
outward sign that my life is sealed with
the stamp of approval of God's Holy
Spirit. I am no longer my own to do with
as I please. I belong to the loving Father,
who gave His only Son for me.

Today I will share this Scripture with someone
who has not been baptized, but You, tender Father
God, are the One who can touch
his/her heart and draw him/her into
the joy of fitting into Your plan . . .
in the name of Jesus, the
submissive One.

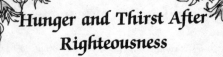

Hunger and Thirst After Righteousness

"Blessed are those who hunger and thirst for righteousness, for they will be filled. . . . For I tell you that unless your righteousness surpasses that of the Pharisees and the teachers of the law, you will certainly not enter the kingdom of heaven."
Matthew 5:6, 20

When I am "religious" I take on a haughty, self-righteous, better-than-thou attitude, so that I see anyone against me as persecuting me! Perhaps that is one of the enemy's tactics to get me diverted from true righteousness. Instead I am to crave Jesus and His kind of righteousness as essential.

Nurturing Father God, right now I repent of ways I have thought and acted superior to others as well as ways I have looked at myself as inferior. Lord, show me the balance and cover me today with Your righteousness . . . in the name of Jesus, the living Bread and living Water who fills my hunger and thirst.

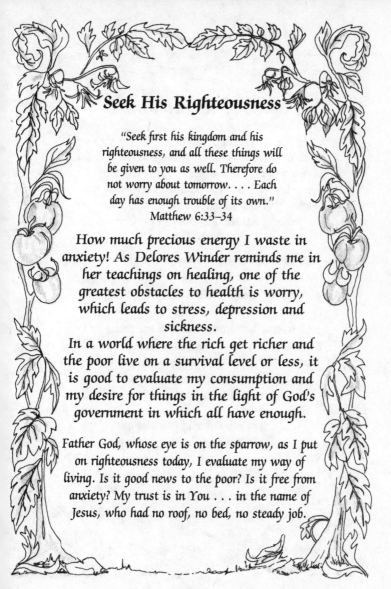

Seek His Righteousness

"Seek first his kingdom and his
righteousness, and all these things will
be given to you as well. Therefore do
not worry about tomorrow. . . . Each
day has enough trouble of its own."
Matthew 6:33–34

How much precious energy I waste in
anxiety! As Delores Winder reminds me in
her teachings on healing, one of the
greatest obstacles to health is worry,
which leads to stress, depression and
sickness.
In a world where the rich get richer and
the poor live on a survival level or less, it
is good to evaluate my consumption and
my desire for things in the light of God's
government in which all have enough.

Father God, whose eye is on the sparrow, as I put
on righteousness today, I evaluate my way of
living. Is it good news to the poor? Is it free from
anxiety? My trust is in You . . . in the name of
Jesus, who had no roof, no bed, no steady job.

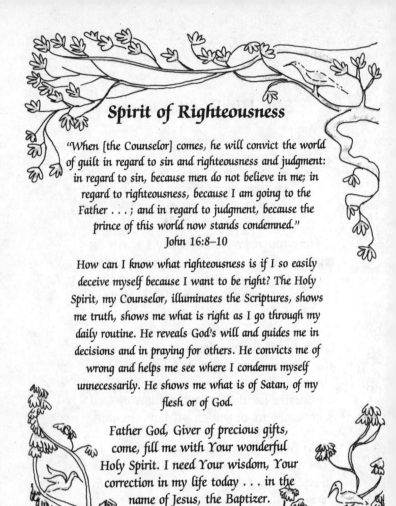

Spirit of Righteousness

"When [the Counselor] comes, he will convict the world of guilt in regard to sin and righteousness and judgment: in regard to sin, because men do not believe in me; in regard to righteousness, because I am going to the Father . . . ; and in regard to judgment, because the prince of this world now stands condemned."
John 16:8–10

How can I know what righteousness is if I so easily deceive myself because I want to be right? The Holy Spirit, my Counselor, illuminates the Scriptures, shows me truth, shows me what is right as I go through my daily routine. He reveals God's will and guides me in decisions and in praying for others. He convicts me of wrong and helps me see where I condemn myself unnecessarily. He shows me what is of Satan, of my flesh or of God.

Father God, Giver of precious gifts, come, fill me with Your wonderful Holy Spirit. I need Your wisdom, Your correction in my life today . . . in the name of Jesus, the Baptizer.

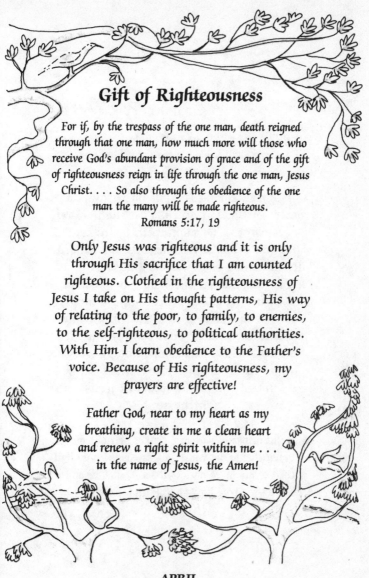

Gift of Righteousness

For if, by the trespass of the one man, death reigned
through that one man, how much more will those who
receive God's abundant provision of grace and of the gift
of righteousness reign in life through the one man, Jesus
Christ. . . . So also through the obedience of the one
man the many will be made righteous.

Romans 5:17, 19

Only Jesus was righteous and it is only
through His sacrifice that I am counted
righteous. Clothed in the righteousness of
Jesus I take on His thought patterns, His way
of relating to the poor, to family, to enemies,
to the self-righteous, to political authorities.
With Him I learn obedience to the Father's
voice. Because of His righteousness, my
prayers are effective!

Father God, near to my heart as my
breathing, create in me a clean heart
and renew a right spirit within me . . .
in the name of Jesus, the Amen!

Alive Because of Righteousness

But if Christ is in you, your body is dead because of sin,
yet your spirit is alive because of righteousness.
Romans 8:10

The righteousness I put on today is a matter of life and death! Last night Karen celebrated her eighteenth birthday, giggling in embarrassment as she tugged her miniskirt over shapely thighs. We all knew after dinner she would be drinking, not caring what happened. "She's happy," her friend Martina said. But to me she seemed like a little boat on a stormy sea with no anchor, rudder or pilot. A worldly life is really death, Paul warned, as he shared the joy he found in Jesus' righteousness.

Merciful heavenly Father, I cannot be righteous on my own energy nor can I save anyone. I pray that each of my loved ones will see Your love and accept their true Lover and Friend, Jesus . . . in His name.

Righteousness, Peace and Joy

The kingdom of God is not a matter of eating and drinking, but of righteousness, peace and joy in the Holy Spirit.
Romans 14:17

Some are vegetarians and others eat meat both are in God's will if what they do is in faith. Some worship God from a rich liturgical style, observing the Christian calendar with traditions, vestments, colors and fasts. Others prefer unadorned simplicity, counting every day as holy. Some like classical music and others hand-clapping choruses with electric guitars; both can please God. The question is: Does what I do build others up and contribute to a joyful, peaceful, positive way of life?

Father, God of peace, am I condemning someone today for being different from me in ways that do not matter to You? Do I have a critical attitude? a spectator spirit? Lord, cleanse me today of anything that unnecessarily separates me from those who please You in their own way . . . in the name of Jesus, our Acceptance.

Jesus Our Righteousness

It is because of him that you are in Christ Jesus, who
has become for us wisdom from God—that is, our
righteousness, holiness and redemption. . . . "Let him
who boasts boast in the Lord."
1 Corinthians 1:30–31

"No man is good," said Cesar Gonzalez,
the Managua dentist who bubbles with
joy in Jesus. Even Jesus asked, "Why do
you call Me good, for only My heavenly
Father is good?" Jesus did only what God
told Him to do and became our wisdom,
righteousness, holiness. This was so my
pride, my joy can be in what He is doing
through me.

Excellent Father God, I give you all my energies
and desires today . . . in the name of Jesus, my
Righteousness and Reward.

Righteousness and the Poor

Each man should give what he has decided in his
heart to give, not reluctantly or under compulsion, for
God loves a cheerful giver. . . . As it is written: "He
has scattered abroad his gifts to the poor; his
righteousness endures forever."
2 Corinthians 9:7, 9

The connection between righteousness and cheerful
sharing is crucial. So much depends on attitude!
Sometimes I am fearful that someone will steal what I
have; sometimes I focus too much on desire for more
things. Doña Julia, my neighbor, has a house full of
family and her husband has been out of work for a year,
but they are helping two poor families build homes. "We
are poor," said Doña Julia, "but there are always people
poorer than we are whom we can help in Jesus' name."

Blessed Father God, today I count my blessings and offer
them to You, with a desire to share cheerfully . . . in
the name of Jesus, the Arm
of the Lord.

Fruit of Righteousness

No discipline seems pleasant at the time, but painful.
Later on, however, it produces a harvest of righteousness
and peace for those who have been trained by it.
Hebrews 12:11

Peacemakers who sow in peace raise a
harvest of righteousness.
James 3:18

It is not an easy thing to put on righteousness daily if it
must come by shaking free of the things in my life that
hold me back from God's perfect way for me. *The Little
Prince,* as told by Antoine de Saint-Exupery, described
the importance of pulling up sprouts of baobab trees
daily. Once the sole inhabitant of a small planet allowed
three baobabs to grow; their roots spread out and
destroyed the entire planet.

Father God, consuming Fire, root out the
"baobabs" of my angers, jealousies, fears,
bitternesses, etc., so that righteousness and
peace have room to grow . . . in the name of
Jesus, the Refining Fire.

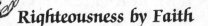

Righteousness by Faith

When they hurled their insults at him, he did not
retaliate; when he suffered, he made no threats. Instead,
he entrusted himself to him who judges justly. He
himself bore our sins in his body on the tree, so that we
might die to sins and live for righteousness; by his
wounds you have been healed.

1 Peter 2:23–24

Noah listened to God's voice calling him to build an ark.
Though it seemed crazy to everyone in the world, Noah
and his family climbed inside and waited for rain.
Everyone turned against Jesus, too. Even His closest
followers and family stood by helplessly and God's way
was ridiculed and rejected. Jesus obeyed God's voice,
which called Him to die; He went through the fires of
hell in order to rescue me. To put on righteousness
today is to be willing to be considered foolish by the
world. It is also to accept the healing provided by Jesus'
wounds.

Father God, my Refuge, I put on healing today
as a penetrating light for myself and for . . . in
the name of Jesus, the Rejected.

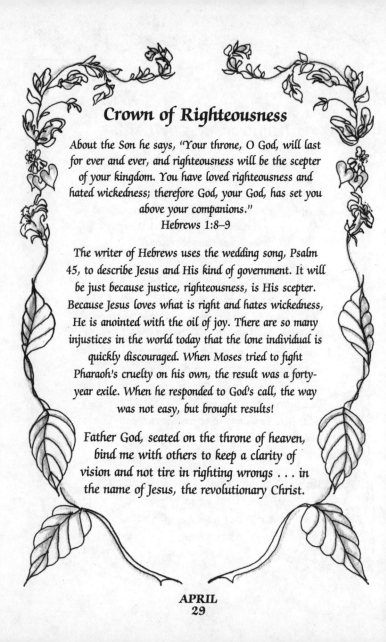

Crown of Righteousness

About the Son he says, "Your throne, O God, will last
for ever and ever, and righteousness will be the scepter
of your kingdom. You have loved righteousness and
hated wickedness; therefore God, your God, has set you
above your companions."
Hebrews 1:8–9

The writer of Hebrews uses the wedding song, Psalm
45, to describe Jesus and His kind of government. It will
be just because justice, righteousness, is His scepter.
Because Jesus loves what is right and hates wickedness,
He is anointed with the oil of joy. There are so many
injustices in the world today that the lone individual is
quickly discouraged. When Moses tried to fight
Pharaoh's cruelty on his own, the result was a forty-
year exile. When he responded to God's call, the way
was not easy, but brought results!

Father God, seated on the throne of heaven,
bind me with others to keep a clarity of
vision and not tire in righting wrongs . . . in
the name of Jesus, the revolutionary Christ.

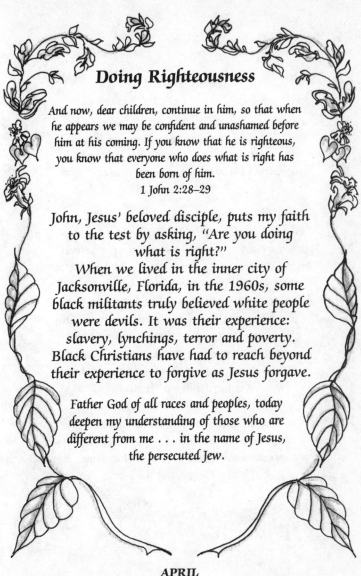

Doing Righteousness

And now, dear children, continue in him, so that when he appears we may be confident and unashamed before him at his coming. If you know that he is righteous, you know that everyone who does what is right has been born of him.

1 John 2:28–29

John, Jesus' beloved disciple, puts my faith to the test by asking, "Are you doing what is right?"

When we lived in the inner city of Jacksonville, Florida, in the 1960s, some black militants truly believed white people were devils. It was their experience: slavery, lynchings, terror and poverty. Black Christians have had to reach beyond their experience to forgive as Jesus forgave.

Father God of all races and peoples, today deepen my understanding of those who are different from me . . . in the name of Jesus, the persecuted Jew.

Seek Peace

Come, my children, listen to me; I will teach you the fear of the Lord. . . . Turn from evil and do good; seek peace and pursue it. . . . The Lord is close to the brokenhearted and saves those who are crushed in spirit.
Psalm 34:11, 14, 18

When landowners hold huge unused tracts of land and a mass of landless, hungry, poorly paid workers has nothing, there is injustice and need for change. In Jesus the rich share what they have so all have enough. The poor trust God to show them how to provide for their families, believing and working for positive change. If the changes do not come soon enough, violent revolution occurs with wounds that take generations to heal.

Father God, whose wrath is against injustice, use me today in Your plan that makes meaningful peace . . . in the name of Jesus, Defender of the poor.

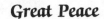

Great Peace

Great peace have they who love your law, and nothing can make them stumble.
Psalm 119:165

The psalmist was persecuted without cause in a land where lies reigned. How could he find peace? By understanding that great peace is found by those who love God's Word; nothing can make them stumble. Daniel found peace in the luxurious court of a pagan king. Shadrach, Meshach and Abednego found peace even in a fiery furnace. Jesus had peace in the midst of Satan's temptations. Paul and Silas used God's Word to praise Him from their prison cells.

Father God, my Refuge, today as I humbly seek Your specific Word for my life, illumined by the Son of Your great Love, Jesus, I will find great peace. Help me to share it . . . in His name.

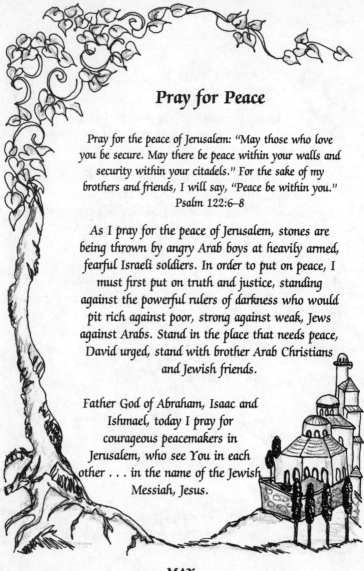

Pray for Peace

Pray for the peace of Jerusalem: "May those who love you be secure. May there be peace within your walls and security within your citadels." For the sake of my brothers and friends, I will say, "Peace be within you." Psalm 122:6–8

As I pray for the peace of Jerusalem, stones are being thrown by angry Arab boys at heavily armed, fearful Israeli soldiers. In order to put on peace, I must first put on truth and justice, standing against the powerful rulers of darkness who would pit rich against poor, strong against weak, Jews against Arabs. Stand in the place that needs peace, David urged, stand with brother Arab Christians and Jewish friends.

Father God of Abraham, Isaac and Ishmael, today I pray for courageous peacemakers in Jerusalem, who see You in each other . . . in the name of the Jewish Messiah, Jesus.

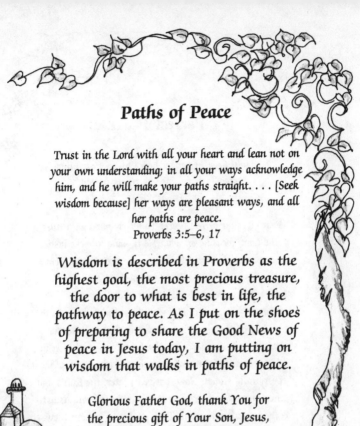

Paths of Peace

Trust in the Lord with all your heart and lean not on
your own understanding; in all your ways acknowledge
him, and he will make your paths straight. . . . [Seek
wisdom because] her ways are pleasant ways, and all
her paths are peace.
Proverbs 3:5–6, 17

Wisdom is described in Proverbs as the
highest goal, the most precious treasure,
the door to what is best in life, the
pathway to peace. As I put on the shoes
of preparing to share the Good News of
peace in Jesus today, I am putting on
wisdom that walks in paths of peace.

Glorious Father God, thank You for
the precious gift of Your Son, Jesus,
who is wisdom, righteousness and
peace. I want to walk in His steps
today . . . in His name.

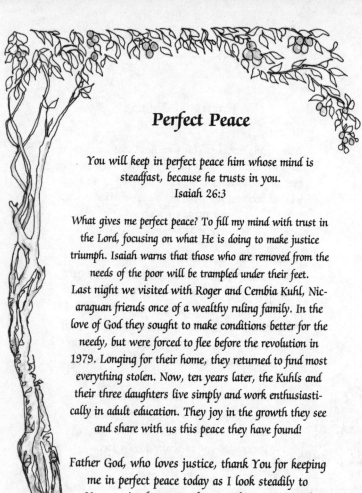

Perfect Peace

You will keep in perfect peace him whose mind is
steadfast, because he trusts in you.
Isaiah 26:3

What gives me perfect peace? To fill my mind with trust in
the Lord, focusing on what He is doing to make justice
triumph. Isaiah warns that those who are removed from the
needs of the poor will be trampled under their feet.
Last night we visited with Roger and Cembia Kuhl, Nicaraguan friends once of a wealthy ruling family. In the
love of God they sought to make conditions better for the
needy, but were forced to flee before the revolution in
1979. Longing for their home, they returned to find most
everything stolen. Now, ten years later, the Kuhls and
their three daughters live simply and work enthusiasti-
cally in adult education. They joy in the growth they see
and share with us this peace they have found!

Father God, who loves justice, thank You for keeping
me in perfect peace today as I look steadily to
You . . . in the name of Jesus, the Carpenter of
Nazareth.

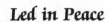

Led in Peace

"You will go out in joy and be led forth in peace; the
mountains and hills will burst into song before you, and
all the trees of the field will clap their hands."
Isaiah 55:12

Yesterday in the breathtaking mountains
above Matagalpa, with a troop of children,
we rejoiced with coffee-pickers who four
years before had formed a fish cooperative.
We came to celebrate the first harvest of
fish. We remembered those who lost their
lives in war, but God's presence abounded
in our midst. He had led them in peace!
The children danced around a small girl
holding high a Bible. The mountains,
hills, trees in all their strength and beauty
did indeed seem to rejoice with us.

Father God, Lord of the harvest, thank You for
peace, the simple goodness of living, for Your
provision . . . in the name of Jesus, the Captain
who makes us fishers for men!

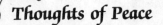

Thoughts of Peace

"Seek the peace and prosperity of the city to which I
have carried you into exile . . . because if it prospers,
you too will prosper. . . . You will seek me and find me
when you seek me with all your heart. I will be found
by you," declares the Lord, "and will bring you back
from captivity."
Jeremiah 29:7, 13–14

I prayed with a mother, a pastor's wife, whose 25-year-old
son has been in Honduras avoiding the draft for five years.
She has not heard from him in all that time. Weeping with
her, I remembered God's assurance that He would work to
bring the exiles back with joy.

Within a week she received word that her son was in
Guatemala with relatives and wanted to come home! Praise
the Lord!

Overshadowing Father God, I am so grateful for the
experiences of the people of Israel, who learned that
You are in control, even of nations and peoples, of refugees, of their returning. You
care, You enable us to beat our swords into
plowshares . . . in the name of
Jesus, the Deliverer.

Walk in Peace

"My covenant was with [Levi], a covenant of life and
peace, and I gave them to him; this called for reverence
and he revered me and stood in awe of my name. True
instruction was in his mouth and nothing false was
found on his lips. He walked with me in peace and
uprightness, and turned many from sin."
Malachi 2:5–6

The whole thrust of Malachi's prophecy is
that the people of God were blind to their
need for repentance. Their religiosity was
an offense to God. He could not hear their
prayers, because they did not arise from
compassionate hearts.

Father God who reproves, today as I put
on the shoes of the Good News of peace, I
examine my style of worship and my
attitude toward those in need . . . in the
name of Jesus, Wonderful Counselor.

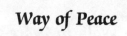

Way of Peace

"... Because of the tender mercy of our God, by which
the rising sun [Jesus] will come to us from heaven to
shine on those living in darkness and in the shadow of
death, to guide our feet into the path of peace."
Luke 1:78–79

God's covenant with His people includes rescue from
enemies, freedom from fear and forgiveness of sins. As
Zechariah spoke, his people were slaves under imperial
Rome, but Jesus came in God's timing to show His way
of peace. This same Word comes to me as light, whether
I live in a country under oppressive rule, or in a country
in authority over others. He shows me how to be light
in the place and time where He has me.

Father God, today I pray for my enemies to be
filled with Your love ... for my fears to be
dissolved in Your light ... for my sins to be
cleansed with Jesus' blood, so that I may see Your
paths of peace ... in the name of Jesus, Light of
the world.

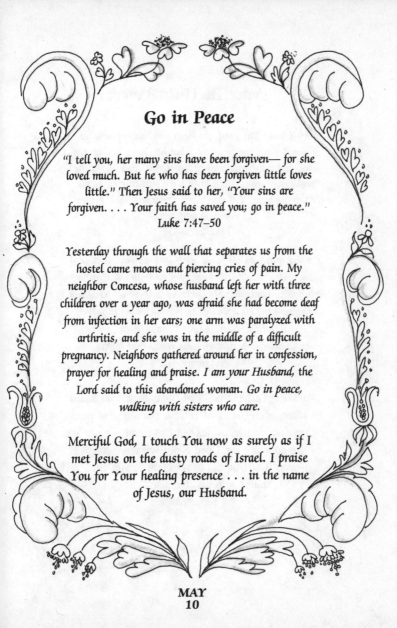

Go in Peace

"I tell you, her many sins have been forgiven— for she loved much. But he who has been forgiven little loves little." Then Jesus said to her, "Your sins are forgiven. . . . Your faith has saved you; go in peace."
Luke 7:47–50

Yesterday through the wall that separates us from the hostel came moans and piercing cries of pain. My neighbor Concesa, whose husband left her with three children over a year ago, was afraid she had become deaf from infection in her ears; one arm was paralyzed with arthritis, and she was in the middle of a difficult pregnancy. Neighbors gathered around her in confession, prayer for healing and praise. *I am your Husband,* the Lord said to this abandoned woman. *Go in peace, walking with sisters who care.*

Merciful God, I touch You now as surely as if I met Jesus on the dusty roads of Israel. I praise You for Your healing presence . . . in the name of Jesus, our Husband.

Peace Be Unto You

"It is true! The Lord has risen and has appeared to
Simon." Then the two told what had happened on the
way, and how Jesus was recognized by them when he
broke the bread. While they were still talking about
this, Jesus himself stood among them and said to them,
"Peace be with you."
Luke 24:34–36

The disciples had all failed Jesus in the hour He needed
them most. Would the risen Lord come to them in fiery
wrath with punishment? "Peace be unto you," Jesus said
the moment He appeared to them, coming into the
locked room. It took them a while
to believe it, that He was really that loving
and forgiving.

Searching Father God, You come again and again
to accept me in spite of myself. Put shoes of peace
on my feet that Jesus has washed clean. Enable me
to go share the Good News with someone
who is still afraid of rejection . . . in the
name of Jesus, Despised and
Rejected.

Jesus' Peace

"But the Counselor, the Holy Spirit, whom the Father will send in my name, will teach you all things and will remind you of everything I have said to you. Peace I leave with you."
John 14:26–27

The Holy Spirit Himself is peace; He is the Counselor Jesus sends. As I write, it is Pentecost Sunday and I have been angry with everyone in the house! All my anger did not achieve the results I wanted—a God-filled family and ministry! Instead my eyes were riveted on their faults. How to get from my anger to my goal? 1. Offer honest confession; 2. Look for good and be thankful; 3. Reject the rejection of others; 4. Release them and my own failures to the Lord; 5. Expect Him to work.

Father God, who is angry for a little while, thank You for Your Holy Spirit, Your peace like a dove that enables me to be more than the sum of my abilities, emotions and energies. You enable us to overcome and be one . . . in the name of Jesus, the Uniter.

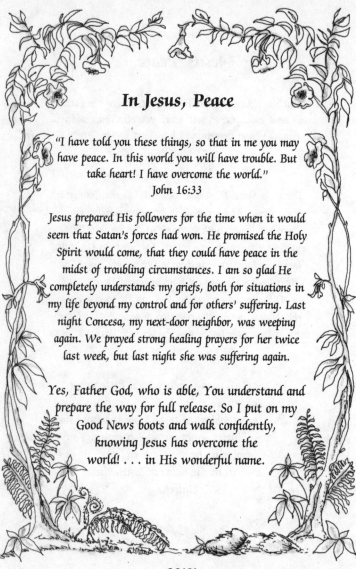

In Jesus, Peace

"I have told you these things, so that in me you may
have peace. In this world you will have trouble. But
take heart! I have overcome the world."
John 16:33

Jesus prepared His followers for the time when it would
seem that Satan's forces had won. He promised the Holy
Spirit would come, that they could have peace in the
midst of troubling circumstances. I am so glad He
completely understands my griefs, both for situations in
my life beyond my control and for others' suffering. Last
night Concesa, my next-door neighbor, was weeping
again. We prayed strong healing prayers for her twice
last week, but last night she was suffering again.

Yes, Father God, who is able, You understand and
prepare the way for full release. So I put on my
Good News boots and walk confidently,
knowing Jesus has overcome the
world! . . . in His wonderful name.

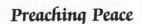

Preaching Peace

"This is the message God sent to the people of
Israel, telling the good news of peace through
Jesus Christ, who is Lord of all . . . how God
anointed Jesus of Nazareth with the Holy Spirit
and power, and how he went around doing good
and healing all who were under the power of the
devil."

Acts 10:36, 38

As I put on shoes of peace today, Peter tells me three
ways Jesus demonstrated peace: 1. Telling about it; 2.
Doing good; 3. Healing all under the power of the devil.
Peace in Greek means "quietness, rest, set at one again,
joined," all elements of healing. I need God's healing
power flowing through me.

Thank You, saving Father God, that You do not
leave me alone to stumble blindly through this
world, but You illumine my path and
empower me to do those things Jesus
demonstrated on earth. He lives in
me! . . . in the name of Jesus, mighty
Mediator.

Way of Peace

As it is written: "There is no one righteous, not even one; there is no one who understands, no one who seeks God. . . . and the way of peace they do not know."
Romans 3:10–11, 17

I want to be thought O.K. I want to be admired, respected, appreciated in my own self, but am learning the value of confession. My neighbor, Doña Julia, has a steady flame of hope and joy in the midst of trying circumstances, and regular confession to a priest is important to her. "I believe in the priesthood of all believers," I told her yesterday. She just laughed and said there are things you don't want to tell anyone because they might create a scandal, so it is better to go to a priest!

Omniscient, all-knowing Father God, I want to go deeper, be cleaner, more certain in this path of peace so that Your Holy Spirit has room to flow freely through me to do Your will . . . in the name of Jesus, our Guide.

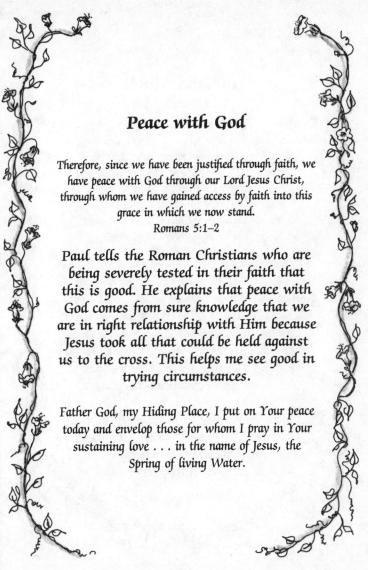

Peace with God

Therefore, since we have been justified through faith, we
have peace with God through our Lord Jesus Christ,
through whom we have gained access by faith into this
grace in which we now stand.

Romans 5:1–2

Paul tells the Roman Christians who are
being severely tested in their faith that
this is good. He explains that peace with
God comes from sure knowledge that we
are in right relationship with Him because
Jesus took all that could be held against
us to the cross. This helps me see good in
trying circumstances.

Father God, my Hiding Place, I put on Your peace
today and envelop those for whom I pray in Your
sustaining love . . . in the name of Jesus, the
Spring of living Water.

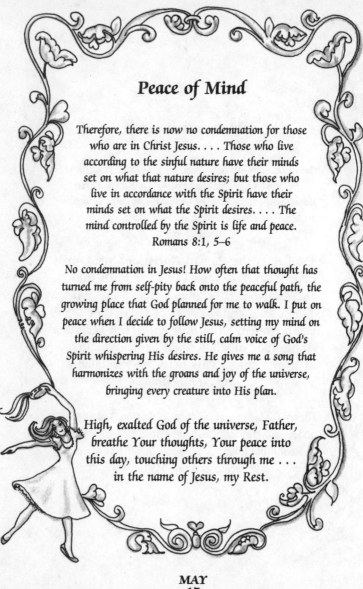

Peace of Mind

Therefore, there is now no condemnation for those
who are in Christ Jesus. . . . Those who live
according to the sinful nature have their minds
set on what that nature desires; but those who
live in accordance with the Spirit have their
minds set on what the Spirit desires. . . . The
mind controlled by the Spirit is life and peace.
Romans 8:1, 5–6

No condemnation in Jesus! How often that thought has
turned me from self-pity back onto the peaceful path, the
growing place that God planned for me to walk. I put on
peace when I decide to follow Jesus, setting my mind on
the direction given by the still, calm voice of God's
Spirit whispering His desires. He gives me a song that
harmonizes with the groans and joy of the universe,
bringing every creature into His plan.

High, exalted God of the universe, Father,
breathe Your thoughts, Your peace into
this day, touching others through me . . .
in the name of Jesus, my Rest.

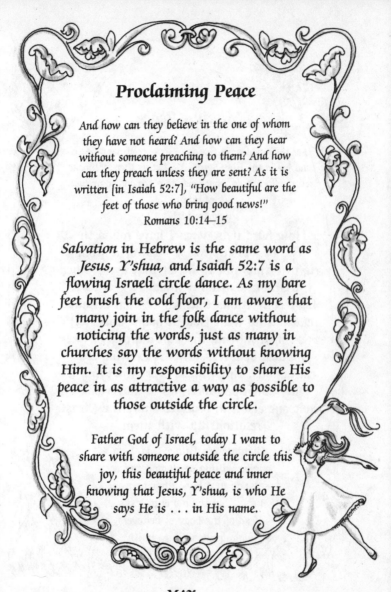

Proclaiming Peace

*And how can they believe in the one of whom
they have not heard? And how can they hear
without someone preaching to them? And how
can they preach unless they are sent? As it is
written [in Isaiah 52:7], "How beautiful are the
feet of those who bring good news!"*
Romans 10:14–15

Salvation in Hebrew is the same word as
Jesus, *Y'shua,* and Isaiah 52:7 is a
flowing Israeli circle dance. As my bare
feet brush the cold floor, I am aware that
many join in the folk dance without
noticing the words, just as many in
churches say the words without knowing
Him. It is my responsibility to share His
peace in as attractive a way as possible to
those outside the circle.

Father God of Israel, today I want to
share with someone outside the circle this
joy, this beautiful peace and inner
knowing that Jesus, Y'shua, is who He
says He is . . . in His name.

Making Peace

For the kingdom of God is . . . righteousness, peace
and joy in the Holy Spirit. . . . Let us therefore make
every effort to do what leads to peace and to mutual
edification.

Romans 14:17, 19

How hard it is when I have found the
way of worship, or service, or a group
right for me, not to insist that every other
Christian fit into my mold. It is good to
have convictions that result from genuine
relationship with God through Jesus, with
His Spirit moving through a group of like-
minded believers. This is exciting and
contagious. But I must ever be willing to
lay down pet doctrines and overlook
someone else's in order to share the Christ
relationship with them.

Omnipresent Father God, help
me be willing to change and to
see You in others different from
me . . . in the name of Jesus,
Head of the body of believers,
who draws us into unity

God of Peace

Everyone has heard about your obedience, so I am full of joy over you; but I want you to be wise about what is good, and innocent about what is evil. The God of peace will soon crush Satan under your feet.

Romans 16:19–20

Wherever I go, directed by the God of peace, Satan will be crushed under my feet! Even though some have gone forth following God's directions and been crushed by evil forces (Hebrews 11), I can still go out confidently, trusting that He will bring good out of evil that touches me. Joseph's slavery and two-year imprisonment were used by God for good, as were Moses' forty years in the desert, and Shadrach, Meshach and Abednego's punishment in the fiery furnace.

Father God, my Fortress, with Peter I pray for boldness and more of Your Spirit to keep me steady and obedient in spite of evil . . . in the name of Jesus, the Wounded One.

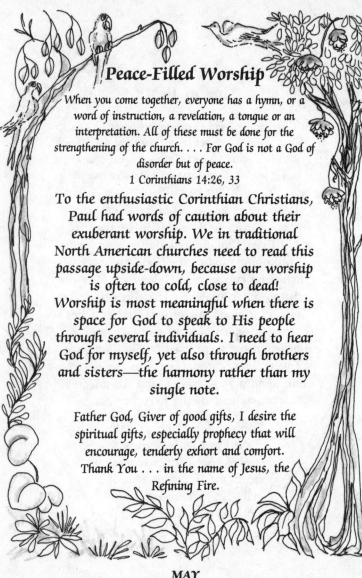

Peace-Filled Worship

When you come together, everyone has a hymn, or a
word of instruction, a revelation, a tongue or an
interpretation. All of these must be done for the
strengthening of the church. . . . For God is not a God of
disorder but of peace.

1 Corinthians 14:26, 33

To the enthusiastic Corinthian Christians,
Paul had words of caution about their
exuberant worship. We in traditional
North American churches need to read this
passage upside-down, because our worship
is often too cold, close to dead!
Worship is most meaningful when there is
space for God to speak to His people
through several individuals. I need to hear
God for myself, yet also through brothers
and sisters—the harmony rather than my
single note.

Father God, Giver of good gifts, I desire the
spiritual gifts, especially prophecy that will
encourage, tenderly exhort and comfort.
Thank You . . . in the name of Jesus, the
Refining Fire.

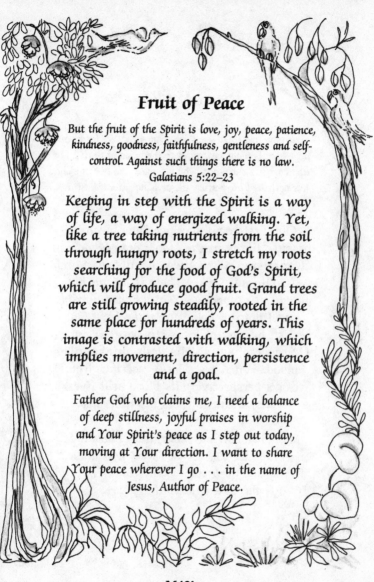

Fruit of Peace

But the fruit of the Spirit is love, joy, peace, patience, kindness, goodness, faithfulness, gentleness and self-control. Against such things there is no law.
Galatians 5:22–23

Keeping in step with the Spirit is a way of life, a way of energized walking. Yet, like a tree taking nutrients from the soil through hungry roots, I stretch my roots searching for the food of God's Spirit, which will produce good fruit. Grand trees are still growing steadily, rooted in the same place for hundreds of years. This image is contrasted with walking, which implies movement, direction, persistence and a goal.

Father God who claims me, I need a balance of deep stillness, joyful praises in worship and Your Spirit's peace as I step out today, moving at Your direction. I want to share Your peace wherever I go . . . in the name of Jesus, Author of Peace.

Jesus, My Peace

*But now in Christ Jesus you who once were far away
have been brought near through the blood of Christ. For
he himself is our peace, who has made the two one and
has destroyed the barrier, the dividing wall of hostility.*
Ephesians 2:13–14

Old Testament sacrifices had meaning
because life is in the blood; only blood can
cleanse sin. When I was a child in church
I could not sing, "There is a fountain
filled with blood. . . ." It sounded horrible
and I did not believe it to be true. The
Jewish hearers of Jesus cringed, too, when
He spoke of eating His flesh, drinking His
blood. When I see Jesus' sacrifice from
God's perspective, His blood still lives,
heals, liberates; it is my necessity.

Most High heavenly Father, today I need to be
washed in the blood of the Savior, who died and
lives again, in order to walk in Your peace . . . in
the name of Jesus, the Purifier.

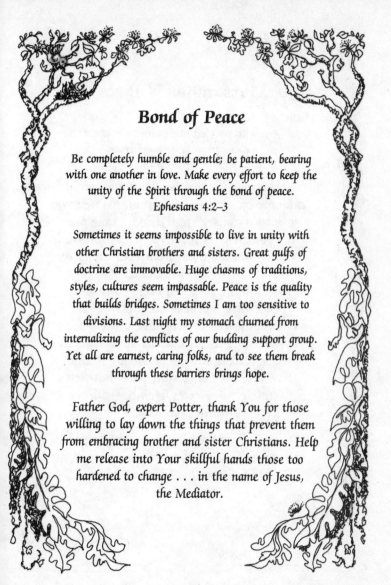

Bond of Peace

Be completely humble and gentle; be patient, bearing
with one another in love. Make every effort to keep the
unity of the Spirit through the bond of peace.
Ephesians 4:2–3

Sometimes it seems impossible to live in unity with
other Christian brothers and sisters. Great gulfs of
doctrine are immovable. Huge chasms of traditions,
styles, cultures seem impassable. Peace is the quality
that builds bridges. Sometimes I am too sensitive to
divisions. Last night my stomach churned from
internalizing the conflicts of our budding support group.
Yet all are earnest, caring folks, and to see them break
through these barriers brings hope.

Father God, expert Potter, thank You for those
willing to lay down the things that prevent them
from embracing brother and sister Christians. Help
me release into Your skillful hands those too
hardened to change . . . in the name of Jesus,
the Mediator.

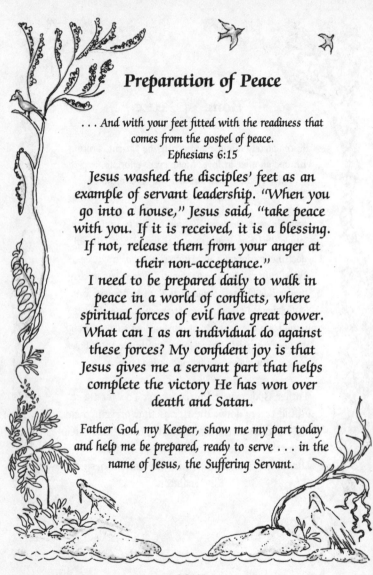

Preparation of Peace

... And with your feet fitted with the readiness that
comes from the gospel of peace.

Ephesians 6:15

Jesus washed the disciples' feet as an
example of servant leadership. "When you
go into a house," Jesus said, "take peace
with you. If it is received, it is a blessing.
If not, release them from your anger at
their non-acceptance."
I need to be prepared daily to walk in
peace in a world of conflicts, where
spiritual forces of evil have great power.
What can I as an individual do against
these forces? My confident joy is that
Jesus gives me a servant part that helps
complete the victory He has won over
death and Satan.

Father God, my Keeper, show me my part today
and help me be prepared, ready to serve ... in the
name of Jesus, the Suffering Servant.

Peace Passes Understanding

Rejoice in the Lord always. . . . Do not be anxious about
anything, but in everything, by prayer and petition, with
thanksgiving, present your requests to God. And the
peace of God, which transcends all understanding, will
guard your hearts and your minds in Christ Jesus.
Philippians 4:4, 6–7

Paul promises that I will find profound levels of
understanding in God's peace as I rejoice and take every
stress over circumstances to Him in prayer. Some of my
Nicaraguan Christian friends seem to be in impossible
circumstances: Three in my Sunday school class have
had husbands or family members kidnapped for over a
year! I find myself weeping out the grief in the healing
prayer group. God does act in amazing ways when we
release our cares to Him.

Omnipresent Father God, thank You for being
close to all who cry out to You . . . in
the name of Jesus, the Way Home.

Fellowship of Peace

Strengthen your feeble arms and weak knees. "Make level paths for your feet," so that the lame may not be disabled, but rather healed. Make every effort to live in peace with all men and to be holy; without holiness no one will see the Lord.
Hebrews 12:12–14

If those near me are weak and lame, the writer of Hebrews suggests I can be with them in ways that heal. As I teach embroidery to Elda, a nine-year-old amputee, I see another lameness that needs healing. "I can't," she says at each new skill. There are some things she cannot do due to her handicap, but there is much she can do if she has confidence to try.

Father God, great Shepherd of the sheep, help me strengthen and discipline myself today, preparing a level path for those who need healing . . . in the name of Jesus, Wisdom from God.

Depart in Peace

Suppose a brother or sister is without clothes
and daily food. If one of you says to him, "Go,
I wish you well; keep warm and well fed," but
does nothing about his physical needs, what
good is it? In the same way, faith by itself, if
it is not accompanied by action, is dead.
James 2:15–17

James warns that faith must include physical action.
Beautiful words are empty to the hungry, ragged,
imprisoned, sick, hopeless. I need God's wisdom to reach
out and connect in meaningful ways. Sometimes pity
motivates me to do a bit of charity, but it only makes
the receiver more helpless, dependent. Jesus touched in a
healing way that fed and clothed those in need with
dignity.

Heavenly Father God, whose thoughts
toward us cannot be numbered, show me
today the infinite value You place on every
person, no matter how needy. Move through
me with Your compassionate touch . . . in
the name of Jesus, our Brother.

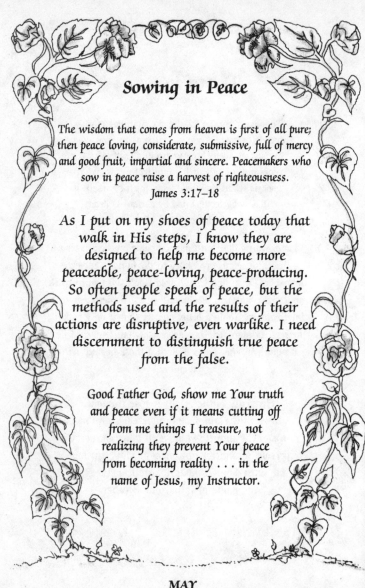

Sowing in Peace

The wisdom that comes from heaven is first of all pure;
then peace loving, considerate, submissive, full of mercy
and good fruit, impartial and sincere. Peacemakers who
sow in peace raise a harvest of righteousness.
James 3:17–18

As I put on my shoes of peace today that
walk in His steps, I know they are
designed to help me become more
peaceable, peace-loving, peace-producing.
So often people speak of peace, but the
methods used and the results of their
actions are disruptive, even warlike. I need
discernment to distinguish true peace
from the false.

Good Father God, show me Your truth
and peace even if it means cutting off
from me things I treasure, not
realizing they prevent Your peace
from becoming reality . . . in the
name of Jesus, my Instructor.

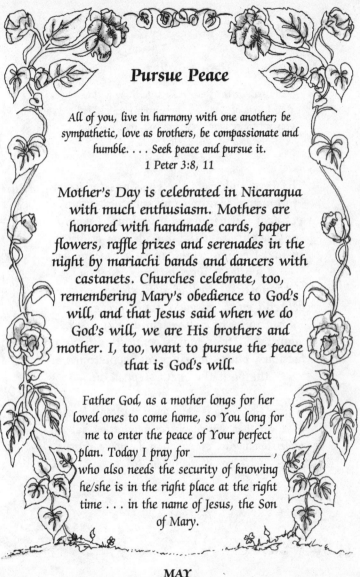

Pursue Peace

All of you, live in harmony with one another; be sympathetic, love as brothers, be compassionate and humble. . . . Seek peace and pursue it.
1 Peter 3:8, 11

Mother's Day is celebrated in Nicaragua with much enthusiasm. Mothers are honored with handmade cards, paper flowers, raffle prizes and serenades in the night by mariachi bands and dancers with castanets. Churches celebrate, too, remembering Mary's obedience to God's will, and that Jesus said when we do God's will, we are His brothers and mother. I, too, want to pursue the peace that is God's will.

Father God, as a mother longs for her loved ones to come home, so You long for me to enter the peace of Your perfect plan. Today I pray for _____ , who also needs the security of knowing he/she is in the right place at the right time . . . in the name of Jesus, the Son of Mary.

Peacemakers

*"Blessed are the peacemakers, for they will be
called sons of God . . . . Love your enemies and
pray for those who persecute you, that you may
be sons of your Father in heaven."*
Matthew 5:9, 44–45

The Beatitudes, as the blessings for Jesus'
followers, reinforce the spiritual armor,
yet deal with inner motivations. I cannot
be one thing on the outside and another
inside. I cannot claim to be a peacemaker
while at war within myself.
I cannot use warlike methods to achieve
peaceful ends, an advocate of peace in one
situation while threatening violence in
another. A peacemaker connects differing
factions, builds a bridge and sometimes is
the path that gets stepped on.

Father God, who is One, what gulf can I bridge
today that will enable communication and
understanding to grow? . . . in the name of Jesus,
Son of the living God.

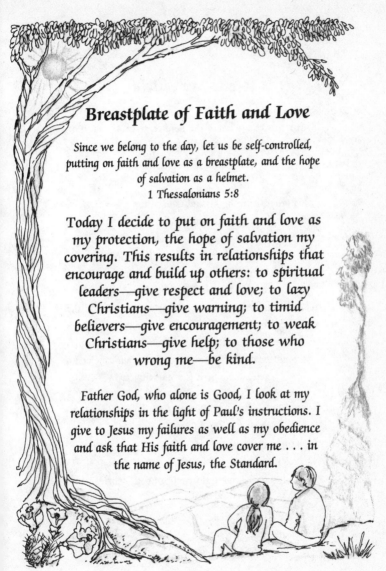

Breastplate of Faith and Love

Since we belong to the day, let us be self-controlled,
putting on faith and love as a breastplate, and the hope
of salvation as a helmet.
1 Thessalonians 5:8

Today I decide to put on faith and love as
my protection, the hope of salvation my
covering. This results in relationships that
encourage and build up others: to spiritual
leaders—give respect and love; to lazy
Christians—give warning; to timid
believers—give encouragement; to weak
Christians—give help; to those who
wrong me—be kind.

Father God, who alone is Good, I look at my
relationships in the light of Paul's instructions. I
give to Jesus my failures as well as my obedience
and ask that His faith and love cover me . . . in
the name of Jesus, the Standard.

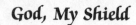

God, My Shield

After this, the word of the Lord came to Abram in a
vision: "Do not be afraid, Abram. I am your shield,
your very great reward."
Genesis 15:1

God promised to be Abram's shield, his reward. This
understanding came long after Abram left his homeland
to journey in faith, not knowing what or where the end
would be. Fear leads away from God.
"Do not be afraid," God told Abram in many ways.
Jesus, also, told His disciples not to fear, especially
when He did things they could not understand. On the
Mount of Transfiguration, at the Last Supper, when He
walked on water and after the Resurrection, Jesus said,
"Do not be afraid." He wants to walk with me and
release me from fear and anxiety.

Father God, my Hiding Place, right now I put
every fear in Your hands. I am so glad You are a
supernatural God who does things I cannot
understand . . . in the name of Jesus,
perfect Love who casts out all fear!

God of Israel

"Blessed are you, O Israel! Who is like you, a people saved by the Lord? He is your shield and helper and your glorious sword."
Deuteronomy 33:29

Moses knew God as protector, defender, shield of His people in dramatic, tangible, miraculous ways: the plagues, the Red Sea opening, the cloud by day, fire by night—which protected them from the harsh sun and desert cold. Jesus quoted from Deuteronomy more than any other book, and must have recalled the ways God protected His people as He observed the Passover and other feasts and fasts. Though Roman soldiers occupied the land of these historic events, Jesus could see God's hand at work and offered Himself as a channel for that work.

Father God, Lord of history, today I review my own history and give thanks for Your protection. I offer myself as an instrument of Your liberation . . . in the name of Jesus, the Jewish Messiah.

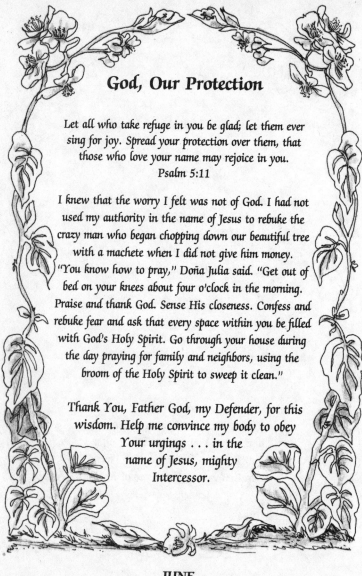

God, Our Protection

Let all who take refuge in you be glad; let them ever sing for joy. Spread your protection over them, that those who love your name may rejoice in you.
Psalm 5:11

I knew that the worry I felt was not of God. I had not used my authority in the name of Jesus to rebuke the crazy man who began chopping down our beautiful tree with a machete when I did not give him money. "You know how to pray," Doña Julia said. "Get out of bed on your knees about four o'clock in the morning. Praise and thank God. Sense His closeness. Confess and rebuke fear and ask that every space within you be filled with God's Holy Spirit. Go through your house during the day praying for family and neighbors, using the broom of the Holy Spirit to sweep it clean."

Thank You, Father God, my Defender, for this wisdom. Help me convince my body to obey Your urgings . . . in the name of Jesus, mighty Intercessor.

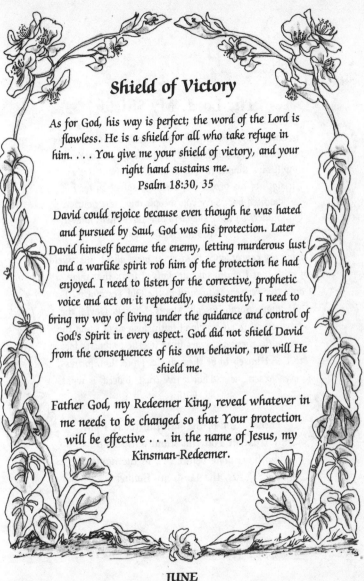

Shield of Victory

As for God, his way is perfect; the word of the Lord is
flawless. He is a shield for all who take refuge in
him. . . . You give me your shield of victory, and your
right hand sustains me.
Psalm 18:30, 35

David could rejoice because even though he was hated
and pursued by Saul, God was his protection. Later
David himself became the enemy, letting murderous lust
and a warlike spirit rob him of the protection he had
enjoyed. I need to listen for the corrective, prophetic
voice and act on it repeatedly, consistently. I need to
bring my way of living under the guidance and control of
God's Spirit in every aspect. God did not shield David
from the consequences of his own behavior, nor will He
shield me.

Father God, my Redeemer King, reveal whatever in
me needs to be changed so that Your protection
will be effective . . . in the name of Jesus, my
Kinsman-Redeemer.

The Lord, My Shield

The Lord is my strength and my shield; my heart trusts
in him, and I am helped. My heart leaps for joy and I
will give thanks to him in song. The Lord is the
strength of his people, a fortress of salvation for his
anointed one. Save your people and bless your
inheritance; be their shepherd and carry them forever.
Psalm 28:7–9

Using my concordance to discover more about this shield
of faith that I am to take up daily, I learn that there are
only two references to *faith* in the Old Testament. Yet
Abraham, Sarah, Joseph, Moses, Miriam, David, the
prophets were all people of faith. Instead of using the
word *faith*, these ancestors lived it. The psalmists looked
to God Himself to be their shield, protection, fortress,
ever-present help. That active trust, indeed, is what
faith is.

Father, God of the faithful, today I put
my trust in You and stand with all those
who have gone before . . . in the name of
Jesus, the Lord, my Banner.

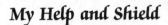

My Help and Shield

The eyes of the Lord are on those . . . whose hope is in
his unfailing love. . . . We wait in hope for the Lord; he
is our help and our shield. In him our hearts rejoice, for
we trust in his holy name.
Psalm 33:18, 20–21

The psalmist leads me into praise, into new songs and joyful
shouts. My imagination is stretched to picture God speaking the
heavens into existence, birthing galaxies with His breath. This
great God cares for everyone whose life is entrusted to Him. He
is my protection, the psalmist reminds us.

On June 7, 1960, Jim and I were married; we celebrated this
year by holding hands and eating pizza reminiscing about people
we have known through the years. What joy to remember those
who have grown in the Lord, kept the faith and kept in touch
with us!

Father God, there is none like You. Your
faithfulness is a shield, a covering invisible yet
tangible over me and those I bring to You in
prayer through the years . . . in the name of
Jesus, the Spoiler of Satan's territory.

God, Our Defender

Better is one day in your courts than a thousand
elsewhere; I would rather be a doorkeeper in the house
of my God than dwell in the tents of the wicked.
Psalm 84:10

Today I went to a meeting for youth leaders. The priest,
Padre Zenon, had proposed a way to help youths who
have drug problems; a psychologist from Wisconsin was
present to see how North Americans could help. "How
do you deal with serious drug problems?" he asked Doña
Julia. She explained that their healing group prays and
in the name of Jesus young people are set free from the
desire for drugs. Then they become involved in the life of
the Christian community. "I've never heard of anything
like that," said the psychologist, "bringing God into it."

Thank You, Father of all wisdom,
for stirring our hearts to desire You
above all else . . . in the name of
Jesus, the Answer.

His Faithfulness, My Shield

He who dwells in the shelter of the Most High will rest
in the shadow of the Almighty. . . . He will cover you
with his feathers, and under his wings you will find
refuge; his faithfulness will be your shield and rampart.

Psalm 91:1, 4

The shield of faith is that covering which
the Lord Himself is, as I find protection,
warmth, maternal nurturing, nestling
under His wings. Jesus, when He wept
over Jerusalem, desired to gather His
people like a hen with chicks under
His wings.

Thank You, divine Protector,
heavenly Father, that I can face
tomorrow because the Sun of
Righteousness lives, risen with
healing in His wings! . . . in His
name I pray.

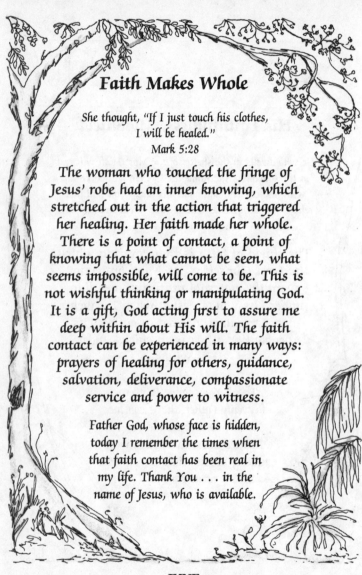

Faith Makes Whole

She thought, "If I just touch his clothes,
I will be healed."
Mark 5:28

The woman who touched the fringe of
Jesus' robe had an inner knowing, which
stretched out in the action that triggered
her healing. Her faith made her whole.
There is a point of contact, a point of
knowing that what cannot be seen, what
seems impossible, will come to be. This is
not wishful thinking or manipulating God.
It is a gift, God acting first to assure me
deep within about His will. The faith
contact can be experienced in many ways:
prayers of healing for others, guidance,
salvation, deliverance, compassionate
service and power to witness.

Father God, whose face is hidden,
today I remember the times when
that faith contact has been real in
my life. Thank You . . . in the
name of Jesus, who is available.

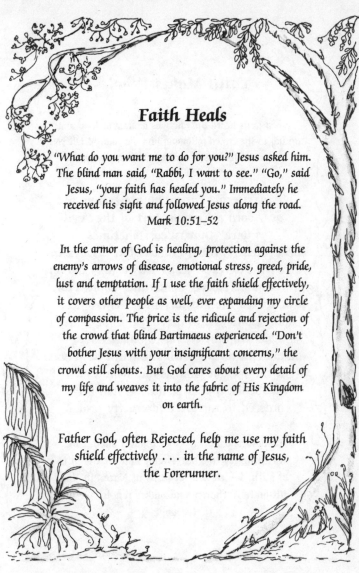

Faith Heals

"What do you want me to do for you?" Jesus asked him.
The blind man said, "Rabbi, I want to see." "Go," said
Jesus, "your faith has healed you." Immediately he
received his sight and followed Jesus along the road.
Mark 10:51–52

In the armor of God is healing, protection against the
enemy's arrows of disease, emotional stress, greed, pride,
lust and temptation. If I use the faith shield effectively,
it covers other people as well, ever expanding my circle
of compassion. The price is the ridicule and rejection of
the crowd that blind Bartimaeus experienced. "Don't
bother Jesus with your insignificant concerns," the
crowd still shouts. But God cares about every detail of
my life and weaves it into the fabric of His Kingdom
on earth.

Father God, often Rejected, help me use my faith
shield effectively . . . in the name of Jesus,
the Forerunner.

Faith Makes Whole

When Jesus heard this, he was amazed at him, and turning to the crowd following him, he said, "I tell you, I have not found such great faith even in Israel."
Luke 7:9

He was Jesus' enemy by profession and race, born a Roman, part of the "evil empire" that ruled sometimes benevolently, often cruelly, but always in its own interests. Jesus was a Jew, one of the conquered; yet something about Him attracted the military man. The officer was accustomed to getting the job done. I picture him trying to balance his distasteful duties with the truth he found in the Jewish God. What would have happened if this centurion had been ordered to torture and crucify Jesus?

All-powerful Father God, today I submit all my authority to You. Thank You for the gift of faith, which sees in Jesus of Nazareth the ultimate Authority and makes whole . . . in His name.

Mustard Seed Faith

He replied, "If you have faith as small as a mustard seed, you can say to this mulberry tree, 'Be uprooted and planted in the sea,' and it will obey you."
Luke 17:6

The disciples asked Jesus to increase their faith. His answer was that even a tiny, practically invisible faith can accomplish marvelous things. Use the little you have, and it will grow by itself. Whenever I pray, see and thank God for the answer, my faith increases. Did the nine lepers who were healed have faith as well as the one who returned and gave thanks (Luke 17:11–19)? Perhaps, but since it was not bathed in thanksgiving, they missed the intimate contact with Jesus Himself, the Source of healing and faith.

Gracious God of wholeness and harmony, today I look back to see how You have led me in faith, giving thanks for answers that make a journal of praise . . . in the name of Jesus, my Yoke.

Faith in His Name

"By faith in the name of Jesus, this man whom you see
and know was made strong. It is Jesus' name and the
faith that comes through him that has given this
complete healing to him, as you can all see."
Acts 3:16

*At the Name of Jesus was written for use
in my prayer group in Cullowhee, North
Carolina, that we might see more fully
His greatness as we pray "in His name."
Again and again I need to return to this
basic, living, moving, having my being in
Him, my first love. Through Him comes
faith and that is the source of healing!*

Heavenly Father of our Lord Jesus Christ, today I
look at Him, at who He is: His greatness and
humility; His love and sacrifice; His wounds and
blood; His invitation to me to come, be forgiven,
cleansed, set free. Lord, I want to be an
instrument of His healing and His peace in this
sick, war-weary world . . . in His name.

Justified by Faith

Therefore, since we have been justified through faith, we have peace with God through our Lord Jesus Christ.
Romans 5:1

As I come to know Jesus and allow who He is to touch all that I know of myself, I realize that His healing presence can make whole even the parts of myself I do not know. God gives me a gift to open, a present of faith, a childlike trust. I picture Jesus, risen and forgiving, appearing to me as He did to the disciples, smiling, accepting, loving me. He walks into my dark memories to shine His light there. He comes into my woundedness to touch me with His wounds, bathe my own wounds with His sparkling, pure, ever-effective poured-out blood.

Tender-loving Father God, thank You for the security of the relationship You made possible through Jesus. Today as I rest in Your love, help me receive those in need around me as I would receive You . . . in the name of Jesus, the Wounded Healer.

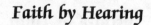

Faith by Hearing

Consequently, faith comes from hearing the message,
and the message is heard through the word of Christ.
Romans 10:17

The living Word, Jesus, is as near as my
breathing. Faith in Him comes through
my hearing, an open attitude of listening,
sorting out the many clanging, insistent
voices that demand attention. I will know
His voice, Jesus said. That certainty is the
faith that defuses the explosives thrown at
me by Satan. I can distinguish lies from
truth by using this filter of faith, the
living presence of Jesus, as I commune
daily reading, studying, meditating on His
Word.

Father God, whose face is hidden,
open my ears that I may hear, and
my mouth that I may speak Your
words that build faith . . . in the
name of Jesus, the great Shepherd of
my soul.

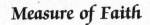

Measure of Faith

Do not think of yourself more highly than you ought,
but rather think of yourself with sober judgment, in
accordance with the measure of faith God has given you.
Romans 12:3

I am given a portion of faith to use in spiritual
battles. That faith is enough to do those greater
things Jesus said I would do. Yet it is not enough
to do everything I want all by myself! I need to fit
my faith with that of my brothers and sisters in
order to fulfill God's perfect plan for family,
church, community, nation. When I cut off any
group or individual from myself, I cut off the
possibility of their gifts and faith increasing mine.
Jesus' example of forgiveness on the cross made
it possible for Roman imperialists and rigid
religionists to come to Him, in spite of the
suffering and death they were causing!

Father God, just Judge, thank You
that in Jesus is all the faith I need
for today's battle, today's
opportunity . . . in His
wonderful name.

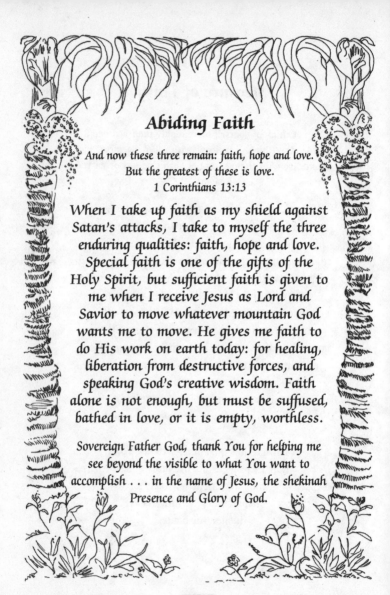

Abiding Faith

And now these three remain: faith, hope and love.
But the greatest of these is love.
1 Corinthians 13:13

When I take up faith as my shield against Satan's attacks, I take to myself the three enduring qualities: faith, hope and love. Special faith is one of the gifts of the Holy Spirit, but sufficient faith is given to me when I receive Jesus as Lord and Savior to move whatever mountain God wants me to move. He gives me faith to do His work on earth today: for healing, liberation from destructive forces, and speaking God's creative wisdom. Faith alone is not enough, but must be suffused, bathed in love, or it is empty, worthless.

Sovereign Father God, thank You for helping me see beyond the visible to what You want to accomplish . . . in the name of Jesus, the shekinah Presence and Glory of God.

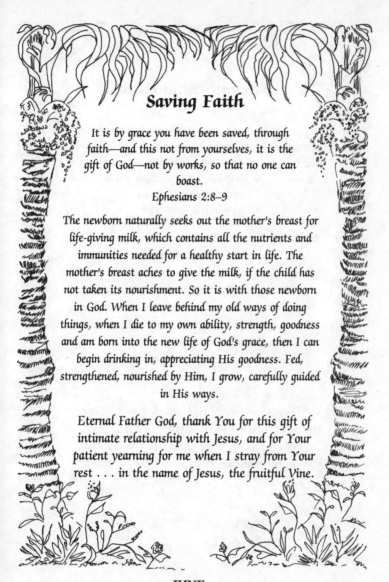

Saving Faith

It is by grace you have been saved, through faith—and this not from yourselves, it is the gift of God—not by works, so that no one can boast.
Ephesians 2:8–9

The newborn naturally seeks out the mother's breast for life-giving milk, which contains all the nutrients and immunities needed for a healthy start in life. The mother's breast aches to give the milk, if the child has not taken its nourishment. So it is with those newborn in God. When I leave behind my old ways of doing things, when I die to my own ability, strength, goodness and am born into the new life of God's grace, then I can begin drinking in, appreciating His goodness. Fed, strengthened, nourished by Him, I grow, carefully guided in His ways.

Eternal Father God, thank You for this gift of intimate relationship with Jesus, and for Your patient yearning for me when I stray from Your rest . . . in the name of Jesus, the fruitful Vine.

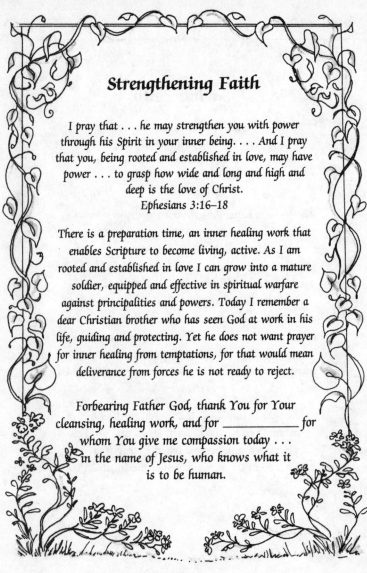

Strengthening Faith

*I pray that . . . he may strengthen you with power
through his Spirit in your inner being. . . . And I pray
that you, being rooted and established in love, may have
power . . . to grasp how wide and long and high and
deep is the love of Christ.*
Ephesians 3:16–18

There is a preparation time, an inner healing work that
enables Scripture to become living, active. As I am
rooted and established in love I can grow into a mature
soldier, equipped and effective in spiritual warfare
against principalities and powers. Today I remember a
dear Christian brother who has seen God at work in his
life, guiding and protecting. Yet he does not want prayer
for inner healing from temptations, for that would mean
deliverance from forces he is not ready to reject.

Forbearing Father God, thank You for Your
cleansing, healing work, and for _____ for
whom You give me compassion today . . .
in the name of Jesus, who knows what it
is to be human.

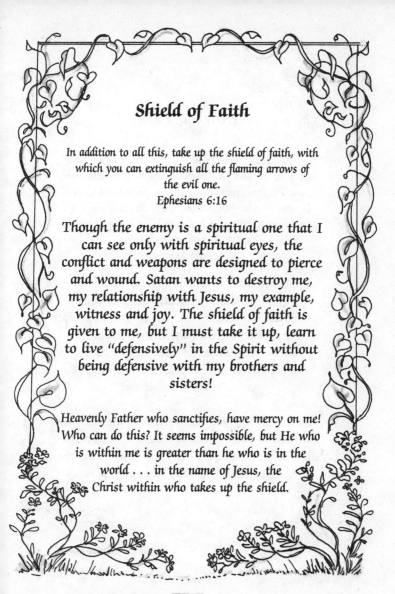

Shield of Faith

In addition to all this, take up the shield of faith, with
which you can extinguish all the flaming arrows of
the evil one.
Ephesians 6:16

Though the enemy is a spiritual one that I
can see only with spiritual eyes, the
conflict and weapons are designed to pierce
and wound. Satan wants to destroy me,
my relationship with Jesus, my example,
witness and joy. The shield of faith is
given to me, but I must take it up, learn
to live "defensively" in the Spirit without
being defensive with my brothers and
sisters!

Heavenly Father who sanctifies, have mercy on me!
Who can do this? It seems impossible, but He who
is within me is greater than he who is in the
world . . . in the name of Jesus, the
Christ within who takes up the shield.

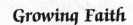

Growing Faith

We ought always to thank God for you, brothers, and
rightly so, because your faith is growing more and more,
and the love every one of you has for each other is
increasing. Therefore, among God's churches we boast
about your perseverance and faith in all the persecutions
and trials you are enduring.
2 Thessalonians 1:3–4

To see other believers come through
difficulties is an encouragement and
motivation. "How can you be so happy in
the Lord when things are so hard?" I
asked the mother of Matthew's tutor.
"Oh, He gives us surprises every day, like
you coming to visit us."

Father God, the only real Security, I want to put
my trust in You and not in things. Thank You for
the example of believers like this mother . . . in the
name of Jesus, who rewards and refreshes.

Fight of Faith

The love of money is a root of all kinds of evil. Some
people, eager for money, have wandered from the faith
and pierced themselves with many griefs.
1 Timothy 6:10

Wanting money or things exposes me to
never-ending desires for more. Growing up
at the end of the Depression, I felt
deprived in hand-me-down clothes. After I
learned to sew, I spent hours making new
outfits. It had no end, for each season I
craved something new. What broke this
cycle? Coming to know Jesus in a real
way, being around people whose needs are
so basic. And Jim's laughing at my
crinoline skirts and picture hats freed me
to distinguish needs from wants. His
preferring me to be "natural" helps, too.

Father God of contentment and satisfaction
in life, today I yield my desires to You for
simplifying . . . in the name of Jesus, who
has overcome the world!

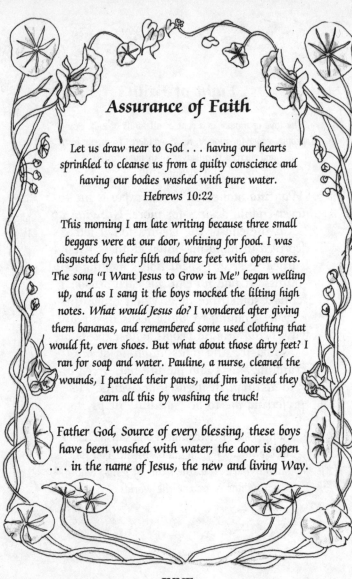

Assurance of Faith

Let us draw near to God . . . having our hearts
sprinkled to cleanse us from a guilty conscience and
having our bodies washed with pure water.
Hebrews 10:22

This morning I am late writing because three small
beggars were at our door, whining for food. I was
disgusted by their filth and bare feet with open sores.
The song "I Want Jesus to Grow in Me" began welling
up, and as I sang it the boys mocked the lilting high
notes. *What would Jesus do?* I wondered after giving
them bananas, and remembered some used clothing that
would fit, even shoes. But what about those dirty feet? I
ran for soap and water. Pauline, a nurse, cleaned the
wounds, I patched their pants, and Jim insisted they
earn all this by washing the truck!

Father God, Source of every blessing, these boys
have been washed with water; the door is open
. . . in the name of Jesus, the new and living Way.

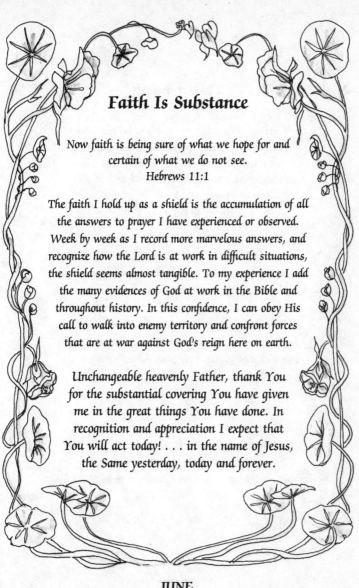

Faith Is Substance

Now faith is being sure of what we hope for and certain of what we do not see.
Hebrews 11:1

The faith I hold up as a shield is the accumulation of all the answers to prayer I have experienced or observed. Week by week as I record more marvelous answers, and recognize how the Lord is at work in difficult situations, the shield seems almost tangible. To my experience I add the many evidences of God at work in the Bible and throughout history. In this confidence, I can obey His call to walk into enemy territory and confront forces that are at war against God's reign here on earth.

Unchangeable heavenly Father, thank You for the substantial covering You have given me in the great things You have done. In recognition and appreciation I expect that You will act today! . . . in the name of Jesus, the Same yesterday, today and forever.

Tested Faith

Consider it pure joy, my brothers, whenever you
face trials of many kinds, because you know that
the testing of your faith develops perseverance.
Perseverance must finish its work so that you
may be mature and complete, not lacking
anything.
James 1:2–4

Here I am, in the midst of spiritual battles with
temptations coming at me, banging against my shield of
faith again. At the moment it seems a terrible hardship,
no fun at all, but James advises me to recognize the
situation as "pure joy"! Perseverance and maturity in
the Lord are two positive results. Just as the butterfly
cannot emerge strong to fly from the cocoon if someone
opens it for him, so I need the practice of resisting the
pressures of the world and the fierce, subtle attacks
of Satan.

Father God, my Rock, show me the joy in
the trials . . . in the name of Jesus,
Tempted in every way yet pure.

Ask in Faith

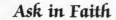

If any of you lacks wisdom, he should ask God
. . . and it will be given to him. But when he
asks, he must believe and not doubt.
James 1:5–6

For years I doubted that one Man's death could mean so
much, that resurrection is possible, that God answers
prayer. Even after Jesus' presence filled me with
certainty, I did not know the dynamic empowering of
His Holy Spirit. I doubted the existence of Satan, had no
idea of my authority as a believer and was wary of
spiritual healing. My need drove me to seek more of
God. Since that initial releasing of God's Spirit, I find I
still have doubts. Recently when Jim was shaking
uncontrollably with dangerously high fever from malaria,
I ran to find Doña Julia and Pastor Sanchez, two prayer
warriors. My faith was not enough, but together there
was victory!

Thank You, Father God, in whom
nothing is impossible, for brothers and
sisters who help me to ask, believing . .
in the name of Jesus, the Answer.

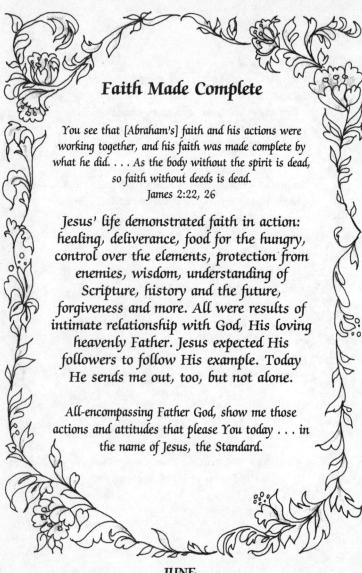

Faith Made Complete

You see that [Abraham's] faith and his actions were working together, and his faith was made complete by what he did. . . . As the body without the spirit is dead, so faith without deeds is dead.
James 2:22, 26

Jesus' life demonstrated faith in action: healing, deliverance, food for the hungry, control over the elements, protection from enemies, wisdom, understanding of Scripture, history and the future, forgiveness and more. All were results of intimate relationship with God, His loving heavenly Father. Jesus expected His followers to follow His example. Today He sends me out, too, but not alone.

All-encompassing Father God, show me those actions and attitudes that please You today . . . in the name of Jesus, the Standard.

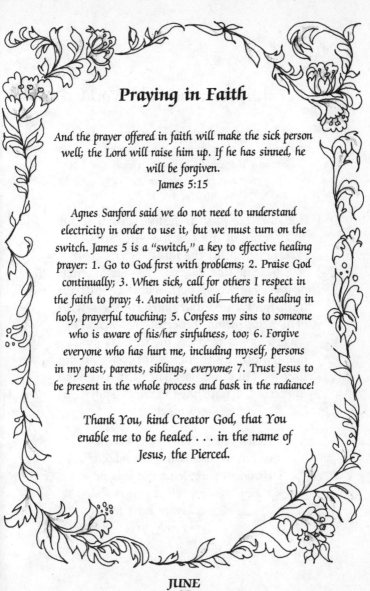

Praying in Faith

And the prayer offered in faith will make the sick person
well; the Lord will raise him up. If he has sinned, he
will be forgiven.
James 5:15

Agnes Sanford said we do not need to understand
electricity in order to use it, but we must turn on the
switch. James 5 is a "switch," a key to effective healing
prayer: 1. Go to God first with problems; 2. Praise God
continually; 3. When sick, call for others I respect in
the faith to pray; 4. Anoint with oil—there is healing in
holy, prayerful touching; 5. Confess my sins to someone
who is aware of his/her sinfulness, too; 6. Forgive
everyone who has hurt me, including myself, persons
in my past, parents, siblings, *everyone*; 7. Trust Jesus to
be present in the whole process and bask in the radiance!

Thank You, kind Creator God, that You
enable me to be healed . . . in the name of
Jesus, the Pierced.

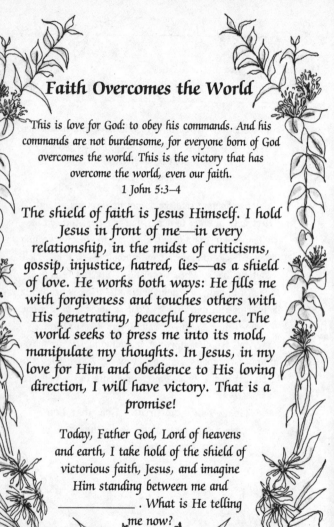

Faith Overcomes the World

This is love for God: to obey his commands. And his commands are not burdensome, for everyone born of God overcomes the world. This is the victory that has overcome the world, even our faith.

1 John 5:3–4

The shield of faith is Jesus Himself. I hold Jesus in front of me—in every relationship, in the midst of criticisms, gossip, injustice, hatred, lies—as a shield of love. He works both ways: He fills me with forgiveness and touches others with His penetrating, peaceful presence. The world seeks to press me into its mold, manipulate my thoughts. In Jesus, in my love for Him and obedience to His loving direction, I will have victory. That is a promise!

Today, Father God, Lord of heavens and earth, I take hold of the shield of victorious faith, Jesus, and imagine Him standing between me and _____ . What is He telling me now?

My Salvation and Song

"The Lord, the Lord, is my strength and my song; he
has become my salvation." With joy you will draw
water from the wells of salvation.
Isaiah 12:2–3

Israeli folk dances based on Hebrew Scriptures are a
great way to exercise and praise God at the same time.
One simple, flowing dance is based on Isaiah 12:2–3,
using Y'shua, the name of Jesus, which is "Salvation" in
Hebrew. Imagine a roomful of Jewish people singing and
dancing for joy because they will draw living water from
the wells of salvation—Jesus! If only they knew Him,
the very Jewish Jesus, who came first for them, lived and
died among them, was resurrected and appeared to His
Jewish disciples and His Jewish mother!

Father God of Abraham, Isaac and
Jacob, today as I take up the helmet of
salvation, with what Jewish friends
can I share Your love and Good News?
Prepare the way . . . in the name of
Jesus, Y'shua.

Joy in Salvation

I will wait patiently for the day of calamity to come on
the nation invading us. Though the fig tree does not bud
and there are no grapes on the vines . . . yet I will
rejoice in the Lord, I will be joyful in God my Savior.
Habakkuk 3:16–18

Reading the book of Habakkuk this morning I saw his
plight as never before. Why are greed and luxury allowed
to build on the blood and labor of the poor? How can
one nation use other nations for its own gain? It has
happened time and again in history and still goes on.
Habakkuk's faith in God's salvation was from the
perspective of the oppressed. The poor believer knows
God will intervene in his behalf. If my country is the
offender, if my people are profiting from the resources
and labor of other nations, I must stand with the
oppressed.

Lord of the nations, Father God, help me stand
with those whose only defense is Your salvation
. . . in the name of Jesus, Savior.

Salvation from Enemies

"Praise be to the Lord, the God of Israel, because he has
come and has redeemed his people. He has raised up a
horn of salvation for us in the house of his servant
David . . . salvation from our enemies and from the hand
of all who hate us."
Luke 1:68–69, 71

Reading Zechariah's prophecy, I am struck again by the
political implications of the salvation he proclaimed. It
was not just a spiritual salvation, but freedom from
imperial Rome's military might. Salvation was freedom
to worship as they pleased. It was the fulfillment of
God's promise of land and the ability to live peacefully
in that land, doing justice. God clearly cares what
happens to His people in exploited countries. He takes
sides and expects me to be on His side!

Holy, holy, holy Father God, remove all
political arrogance from me, and show me
how to stand forgiving and
forgiven in Your salvation
plan . . . in the name of
Jesus, the Sent One.

Light of Salvation

"My eyes have seen your salvation, which you have prepared in the sight of all people, a light for revelation to the Gentiles and for glory to your people Israel."
Luke 2:30–32

Jesus Himself is my salvation. Today I need to see my salvation as a relationship, intimate and loving as a bride with her bridegroom. Unlike old Simeon, who took the baby Jesus in his arms and blessed Him as the salvation of the Jews, I see the rejected, resurrected, forgiving Jesus. He takes me in His arms, heals me inside and out, blessing me! He calls me to represent Him among the Jews as their shining glory, and among unbelievers of every race as revelation of God's available love.

Thank You, Father God, Giver of the Law of Moses, for the Person Jesus, who is my salvation, my inheritance . . . in His name, the Firstborn.

Seeing Salvation

"Prepare the way for the Lord. . . . The crooked roads shall become straight, the rough ways smooth. And all mankind will see God's salvation."

Luke 3:4–6

God cares enough to call me to repentance. Without repentance, and certainty that my sins are forgiven, I cannot put on the helmet of salvation. Aware of my own guilt and pardon, I can be an effective part of the process to make crooked roads straight, correct injustices, bring salvation to others. So many thoughts from the world, flesh and devil bombard my mind, cloud my thinking, muddy my spirit. Distortions of the truth twist, confuse me unless I am firmly centered down, open only to His voice.

Father God, Your Presence, Your Salvation, Jesus alone, is the Truth, the One who saves . . . in His name.

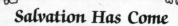

Salvation Has Come

Zacchaeus stood up and said to the Lord, "Look, Lord!
Here and now I give half of my possessions to the poor,
and if I have cheated anybody out of anything, I will
pay back four times the amount."
Luke 19:8

Jesus invited Himself to Zacchaeus' house.
He must have seen something in the little
miser that others had not, or perhaps the
timing was right. Repentance from the
heart healed Zacchaeus of greed. The proof
of that healing was his willingness to
make things right with the very people he
had treated so badly. This is salvation,
Jesus said. As I put on Jesus, my helmet
of salvation, today, I review my life and
must make right whatever is out of order.

Father God, whose heart yearns that all enter into
the joy of salvation, I invite Jesus into my house,
to take control, to enter and clean those rooms
hidden even from myself . . . in the name of Jesus,
incomparable Treasure.

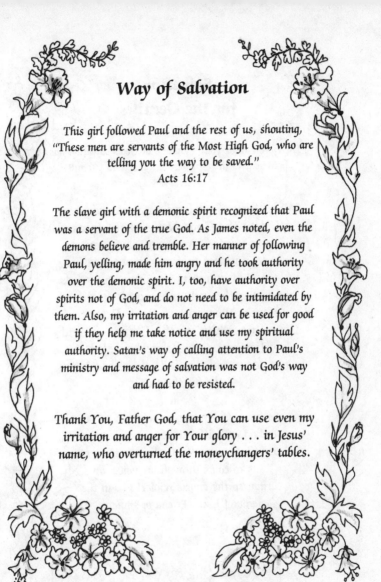

Way of Salvation

This girl followed Paul and the rest of us, shouting, "These men are servants of the Most High God, who are telling you the way to be saved."
Acts 16:17

The slave girl with a demonic spirit recognized that Paul was a servant of the true God. As James noted, even the demons believe and tremble. Her manner of following Paul, yelling, made him angry and he took authority over the demonic spirit. I, too, have authority over spirits not of God, and do not need to be intimidated by them. Also, my irritation and anger can be used for good if they help me take notice and use my spiritual authority. Satan's way of calling attention to Paul's ministry and message of salvation was not God's way and had to be resisted.

Thank You, Father God, that You can use even my irritation and anger for Your glory . . . in Jesus' name, who overturned the moneychangers' tables.

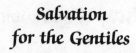

Salvation
for the Gentiles

"Therefore I want you to know that God's salvation has
been sent to the Gentiles, and they will listen!"
Acts 28:28

When hearts are hard, ears closed, eyes
blind to the Good News about Jesus,
healing is needed. As much as I want to, I
can do nothing to bring about healing
unless God appoints, anoints and sends
me out; then my message is heard.
Ananias was sent to Paul, Peter to
Cornelius, Philip to the Ethiopian, and
they listened. The helmet of salvation
is not for me alone; it is the Good News
to be shared.

Father God, Creator, to whom are You
sending me with this joyous message of
new life? I want the healing presence of
Jesus to come through my voice, my
caring, so the angels rejoice! . . . in the
name of Jesus, Friend of sinners.

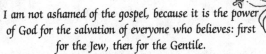

Power of God for Salvation

I am not ashamed of the gospel, because it is the power
of God for the salvation of everyone who believes: first
for the Jew, then for the Gentile.
Romans 1:16

Although putting on the armor of God is a
spiritual action, done in the prayer closet,
what is done in secret is often obvious to
folks around me. The Good News will
radiate from me, unless I block it. The
Liberated Wailing Wall, a singing group
of Jewish believers, has a haunting song
about the power of God for salvation. It
costs them something to declare boldly, "I
am not ashamed of the Gospel."

Father God, Worthy to be praised, what
has it cost me to witness? Today I pray
with Peter for more boldness to witness
even though it be costly . . . in the name
of Jesus, who paid the ultimate price.

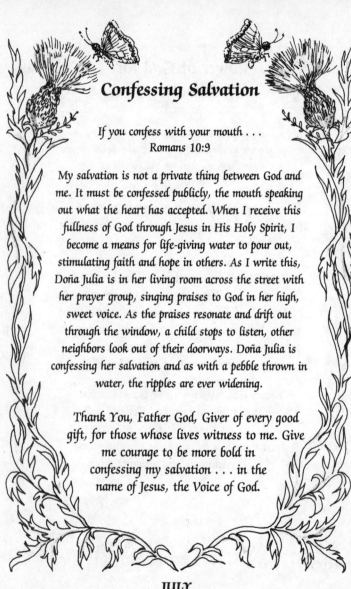

Confessing Salvation

If you confess with your mouth . . .
Romans 10:9

My salvation is not a private thing between God and
me. It must be confessed publicly, the mouth speaking
out what the heart has accepted. When I receive this
fullness of God through Jesus in His Holy Spirit, I
become a means for life-giving water to pour out,
stimulating faith and hope in others. As I write this,
Doña Julia is in her living room across the street with
her prayer group, singing praises to God in her high,
sweet voice. As the praises resonate and drift out
through the window, a child stops to listen, other
neighbors look out of their doorways. Doña Julia is
confessing her salvation and as with a pebble thrown in
water, the ripples are ever widening.

Thank You, Father God, Giver of every good
gift, for those whose lives witness to me. Give
me courage to be more bold in
confessing my salvation . . . in the
name of Jesus, the Voice of God.

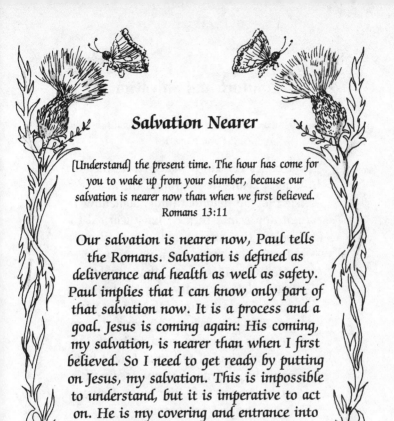

Salvation Nearer

[Understand] the present time. The hour has come for
you to wake up from your slumber, because our
salvation is nearer now than when we first believed.
Romans 13:11

Our salvation is nearer now, Paul tells
the Romans. Salvation is defined as
deliverance and health as well as safety.
Paul implies that I can know only part of
that salvation now. It is a process and a
goal. Jesus is coming again: His coming,
my salvation, is nearer than when I first
believed. So I need to get ready by putting
on Jesus, my salvation. This is impossible
to understand, but it is imperative to act
on. He is my covering and entrance into
perfect health, deliverance, safety.

Thank You, Father God, Provider of
every good and perfect gift, for Your
Son, Jesus . . . in His name who has
come, is come and is coming.

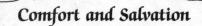

Comfort and Salvation

If we are distressed, it is for your comfort and salvation.
2 Corinthians 1:6

Sometimes certain people irritate me; I just don't want to be around them. Even when they do helpful things, somehow I cannot appreciate them. I have learned to look below the surface and almost always find rejection. This morning, again, I reflected that Daniel has that problem. His mother left six years ago; his father is alcoholic. He is living with us this year and going to high school. Every day I try to reach out to him in order to break the cycle. Many times I fail, and I need him to forgive me. I pray that my needing his forgiveness can help him know Jesus' perfect acceptance.

Thank You, Father God, who yearns for us to come home, that the Gospel is not comfortable, yet You comfort me today as I go about Your business . . . in the name of Jesus, the Rejected One.

Day of Salvation

As God's fellow workers we urge you not to receive God's grace in vain. For he says, "In the time of my favor I heard you, and in the day of salvation I helped you." I tell you, now is the time of God's favor, now is the day of salvation.

2 Corinthians 6:1–2

Paul says this is the day of salvation; do not miss it! He was quoting from Isaiah 49 in which the prophet describes that day as a time when land is restored, captives are freed, the hungry are fed, the thirsty refreshed and the afflicted comforted. In Jesus, my salvation, is God's rule on earth, which makes right the wrongs, heals wounds both physical and emotional, provides enough for everyone—land, houses, food—so that all can live in dignity.

How can I participate in this restorative process today? Show me, Father God, owner of the cattle on a thousand hills . . . in the name of Jesus, the Beginning and the End.

Repentance Unto Salvation

Godly sorrow brings repentance that leads to salvation
and leaves no regret, but worldly sorrow brings death.
See what this godly sorrow has produced in you: what
earnestness, what eagerness to clear yourselves . . .
what longing, what concern.
2 Corinthians 7:10–11

In order to put on the helmet of salvation, I need a
repentant, contrite heart. Godly sorrow sees the wrong
done against the Lord, makes the about-face of sincere
confession, and tries to make things right. This brings
the certainty of being forgiven, of being securely in God's
plan. Sometimes I deceive myself into thinking I don't
need to change; other times I have a false guilt that says
I cannot be forgiven. Both are errors and keep me from
being cleansed and free. Jesus understands every
temptation and trial; He knows the way.

Perfect Father God, I open myself
today to Your forgiveness, which
protects, covers, heals and sets me
free . . . in the name of Jesus, the
only sinless human.

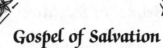

Gospel of Salvation

And you also were included in Christ when you heard
the word of truth, the gospel of your salvation. Having
believed, you were marked in him with a seal, the
promised Holy Spirit, who is a deposit guaranteeing our
inheritance.

Ephesians 1:13–14

It is not enough to hear the word of salvation. I need to
let it permeate my being with the certainty that I am
connected inseparably to God in Jesus. The sign of that
is the Holy Spirit, God's seal of approval. Paul prayed
that we be open to all the treasures available in God's
Spirit: wisdom, discernment, healing, miracles and more!
When I am hungry for more of God, growth follows and
His gifts and fruits become active.

Heavenly Father God, thank You for helping me
see my need. I want to be fervent in my love for
You, not cold and calloused. Set me aglow with
Your salvation today . . . in the name of Jesus,
Lover of my soul.

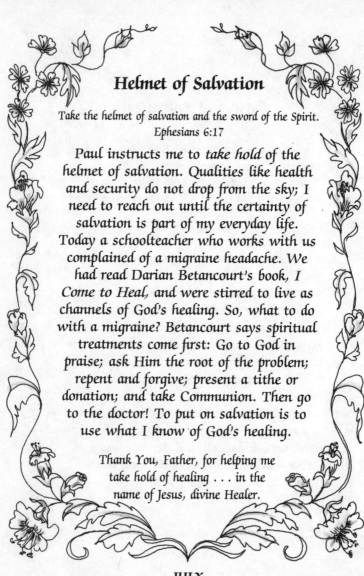

Helmet of Salvation

Take the helmet of salvation and the sword of the Spirit.
Ephesians 6:17

Paul instructs me to *take hold* of the helmet of salvation. Qualities like health and security do not drop from the sky; I need to reach out until the certainty of salvation is part of my everyday life. Today a schoolteacher who works with us complained of a migraine headache. We had read Darian Betancourt's book, *I Come to Heal,* and were stirred to live as channels of God's healing. So, what to do with a migraine? Betancourt says spiritual treatments come first: Go to God in praise; ask Him the root of the problem; repent and forgive; present a tithe or donation; and take Communion. Then go to the doctor! To put on salvation is to use what I know of God's healing.

Thank You, Father, for helping me
take hold of healing . . . in the
name of Jesus, divine Healer.

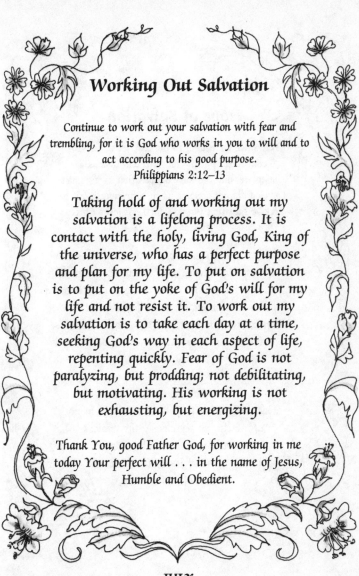

Working Out Salvation

Continue to work out your salvation with fear and trembling, for it is God who works in you to will and to act according to his good purpose.
Philippians 2:12–13

Taking hold of and working out my salvation is a lifelong process. It is contact with the holy, living God, King of the universe, who has a perfect purpose and plan for my life. To put on salvation is to put on the yoke of God's will for my life and not resist it. To work out my salvation is to take each day at a time, seeking God's way in each aspect of life, repenting quickly. Fear of God is not paralyzing, but prodding; not debilitating, but motivating. His working is not exhausting, but energizing.

Thank You, good Father God, for working in me today Your perfect will . . . in the name of Jesus, Humble and Obedient.

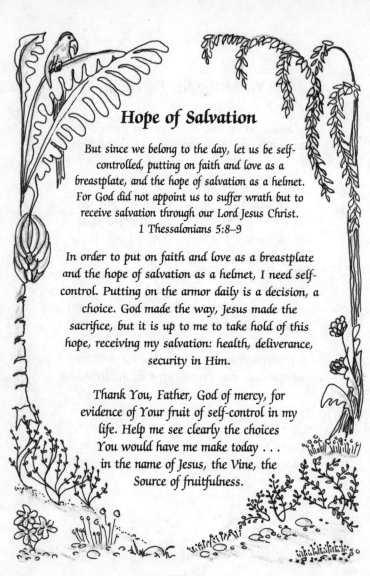

Hope of Salvation

But since we belong to the day, let us be self-controlled, putting on faith and love as a breastplate, and the hope of salvation as a helmet. For God did not appoint us to suffer wrath but to receive salvation through our Lord Jesus Christ.
1 Thessalonians 5:8–9

In order to put on faith and love as a breastplate and the hope of salvation as a helmet, I need self-control. Putting on the armor daily is a decision, a choice. God made the way, Jesus made the sacrifice, but it is up to me to take hold of this hope, receiving my salvation: health, deliverance, security in Him.

Thank You, Father, God of mercy, for evidence of Your fruit of self-control in my life. Help me see clearly the choices You would have me make today . . . in the name of Jesus, the Vine, the Source of fruitfulness.

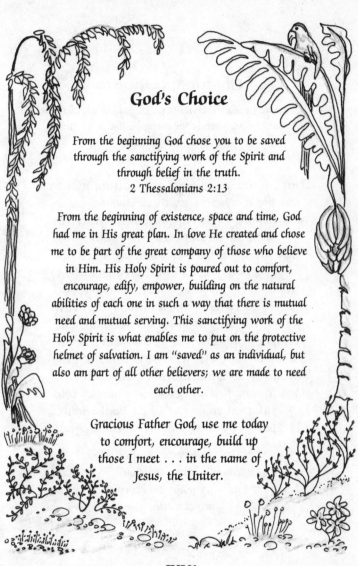

God's Choice

From the beginning God chose you to be saved
through the sanctifying work of the Spirit and
through belief in the truth.
2 Thessalonians 2:13

From the beginning of existence, space and time, God
had me in His great plan. In love He created and chose
me to be part of the great company of those who believe
in Him. His Holy Spirit is poured out to comfort,
encourage, edify, empower, building on the natural
abilities of each one in such a way that there is mutual
need and mutual serving. This sanctifying work of the
Holy Spirit is what enables me to put on the protective
helmet of salvation. I am "saved" as an individual, but
also am part of all other believers; we are made to need
each other.

Gracious Father God, use me today
to comfort, encourage, build up
those I meet . . . in the name of
Jesus, the Uniter.

Obtain Salvation

Therefore I endure everything for the sake of the elect, that they too may obtain the salvation that is in Christ Jesus, with eternal glory.
2 Timothy 2:10

This morning I have been swatting flies in our patio where I wash clothes by hand and prepare food. We keep a flyswatter by the open-air dining area, too, since they buzz around wherever there are smells of food. "I hate flies!" I muttered countless times this morning, but remind myself that this is one of those things "up with which I must put" in order to share the Gospel in Nicaragua. I remember Corrie ten Boom's experiences with lice and fleas in the Nazi concentration camp. "Thank God for the fleas," her sister, Betsie, told her, and good came out of it. Paul endured the chains of prison and I will endure flies.

Father God, in control of all creation, I give You all I cannot change . . . in the name of Jesus, far above all principalities!

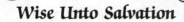

Wise Unto Salvation

From infancy you have known the holy Scriptures,
which are able to make you wise for salvation through
faith in Christ Jesus. All Scripture is God-breathed and
is useful for . . . training in righteousness, so that the
man of God may be thoroughly equipped for every good
work.

2 Timothy 3:15–17

Fully equipped for every good work is another way of
describing the armor of God. The Scriptures stimulate
hunger for God's ways, which lead to wisdom and
salvation. The Bible had been an integral part of
Timothy's life since childhood. It had shaped his
thinking, his understanding of God and human nature,
and had prepared him for a life filled with God's Spirit
growing in Jesus' love and service.

Thank You, heavenly Father, Giver of the Law of
Moses, for the Spirit-breathed words of Scripture.
May they be my daily guide, companion and
covering as I walk with You in the
garden of my circumstances . . . in the
name of Jesus, the living Word.

Grace Brings Salvation

The grace of God that brings salvation . . . teaches us to
say "No" to ungodliness and worldly passions, and to
live self-controlled, upright and godly lives.
Titus 2:11–12

Salvation is freely available to every person, but not
without cost. It costs to say no to pride. It costs to
grow in self-control. I can say no to Jesus' love and
quench His generous Spirit, or I can be open to the
variety of new experiences His salvation means.
The last few days I have been angry at the constant
stream of kids at our door, barging into our bedroom,
making noise, staying for meals, tracking dirt all over.
Praying through tears, I faced my motives and saw I
was resisting God's plan. Yes, I can get someone to help
me clean, put more potatoes in the pot and see Jesus in
those who knock. I can know when it is time to close
doors, too.

Help me, Father God, to put myself today in
Your grace, which offers soup and salvation
to others . . . in the name of
Jesus, who stands at
the door.

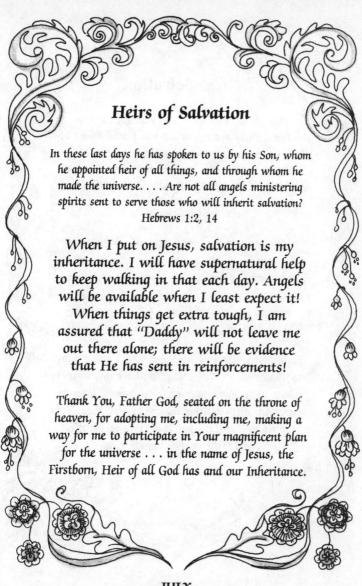

Heirs of Salvation

In these last days he has spoken to us by his Son, whom
he appointed heir of all things, and through whom he
made the universe. . . . Are not all angels ministering
spirits sent to serve those who will inherit salvation?
Hebrews 1:2, 14

When I put on Jesus, salvation is my
inheritance. I will have supernatural help
to keep walking in that each day. Angels
will be available when I least expect it!
When things get extra tough, I am
assured that "Daddy" will not leave me
out there alone; there will be evidence
that He has sent in reinforcements!

Thank You, Father God, seated on the throne of
heaven, for adopting me, including me, making a
way for me to participate in Your magnificent plan
for the universe . . . in the name of Jesus, the
Firstborn, Heir of all God has and our Inheritance.

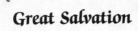

Great Salvation

How shall we escape if we ignore such a great
salvation? This salvation, which was first announced by
the Lord, was confirmed to us by those who heard him.
God also testified to it by signs, wonders and various
miracles, and gifts of the Holy Spirit distributed
according to his will.

Hebrews 2:3–4

"We must pay more careful attention,"
the writer of Hebrews says, "to what we
have heard, so that we do not drift away."
What a great salvation we have been
given, a way of living filled with the
health and security that are in Jesus!

Father God, absolute, unchangeable Love, I want
to appreciate the salvation You have given me. I
want to discover more each day what I have to
share, earnestly desiring all the gifts of Your Holy
Spirit . . . in the name of Jesus, the Miracle-
Worker, the compassionate Healer.

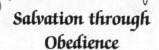

Salvation through Obedience

Although he was a son, he learned obedience from what he suffered and, once made perfect, he became the source of eternal salvation for all who obey him.

Hebrews 5:8–9

My example is Jesus and He was obedient to all God asked Him to do. It is fitting that I put the helmet of salvation on my head, for it is in the imagination and thoughts, conscious and subconscious, that choices are made to go my own way or God's. It always helps to know someone else has gone through all the agony of my circumstances; Jesus has done just that, and will be with me through it all if I exchange my will for His.

Father God, thank You for the example of Jesus. Though Your will for Him meant pain and suffering, Jesus was willing for my sake to give up His life. I want to be willing also . . . in the name of Jesus, sweet, fragrant Offering.

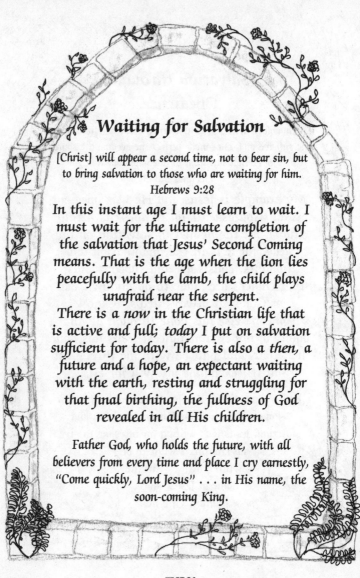

Waiting for Salvation

[Christ] will appear a second time, not to bear sin, but to bring salvation to those who are waiting for him.

Hebrews 9:28

In this instant age I must learn to wait. I must wait for the ultimate completion of the salvation that Jesus' Second Coming means. That is the age when the lion lies peacefully with the lamb, the child plays unafraid near the serpent.

There is a *now* in the Christian life that is active and full; *today* I put on salvation sufficient for today. There is also a *then*, a future and a hope, an expectant waiting with the earth, resting and struggling for that final birthing, the fullness of God revealed in all His children.

Father God, who holds the future, with all believers from every time and place I cry earnestly, "Come quickly, Lord Jesus" . . . in His name, the soon-coming King.

Joy of Salvation

Though you have not seen him, you love him; and even though you do not see him now, you believe in him and are filled with an inexpressible and glorious joy, for you are receiving the goal of your faith, the salvation of your souls.
1 Peter 1:8–9

A single wall separates our Nicaraguan neighbors from us. Once again the husband is drunk and foul-mouthed. The wife, at the end of her rope, is screaming at him to leave. It is difficult to focus on the Scripture about the joy of our salvation when conflict rages all around, but that is reality. It is also reality that there is a hope, peace and joy in Jesus that covers us and can reach out and touch our neighbors.

Show me, Father God, glorious One who lifts up my head, how to share Your "inexpressible and glorious joy" . . . in the name of Jesus, the Son, the Anointed One.

Patience of Jesus in Salvation

[At] the day of the Lord . . . the heavens will disappear
with a roar; the elements will be destroyed by fire, and
the earth and everything in it will be laid bare. . . .
Make every effort to be found spotless, blameless and at
peace with him. Bear in mind that our Lord's patience
means salvation.
2 Peter 3:10, 14–15

Jesus wants all who will come to Him to
have time to make that decision freely. It
is this salvation, the best choice, that
keeps me, even though the earth and
elements disintegrate in flames.

Father God of great mercy, I want to make the
best use possible of my time today, and be alert to
opportunities to share the Good News with
someone You have prepared to hear . . . in the
name of Jesus, who is tenderly calling.

Overcoming Salvation

Then I heard a loud voice in heaven say: "Now have come the salvation and the power and the kingdom of our God, and the authority of his Christ. For the accuser of our brothers, who accuses them before our God day and night, has been hurled down. They overcame him by the blood of the Lamb and by the word of their testimony."
Revelation 12:10–11

When I hear an inner voice accusing my brother or sister Christian, I can recognize it is not of God, but rather a voice to be rejected. As I learn to put on the helmet of salvation—health, wholeness and security in Him—I learn the same is available to my brothers and sisters, through the poured-out blood of Jesus and the word of witnesses to His power.

Father God who reigns forever, cleanse with the blood of Jesus the voices that tear down. Give me, instead, Your thoughts toward others . . . in the name of Jesus, our Passover.

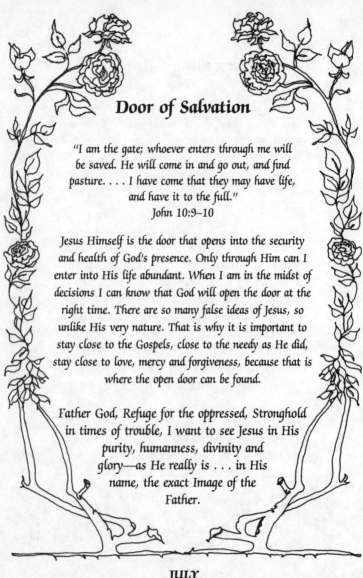

Door of Salvation

"I am the gate; whoever enters through me will
be saved. He will come in and go out, and find
pasture. . . . I have come that they may have life,
and have it to the full."
John 10:9–10

Jesus Himself is the door that opens into the security
and health of God's presence. Only through Him can I
enter into His life abundant. When I am in the midst of
decisions I can know that God will open the door at the
right time. There are so many false ideas of Jesus, so
unlike His very nature. That is why it is important to
stay close to the Gospels, close to the needy as He did,
stay close to love, mercy and forgiveness, because that is
where the open door can be found.

Father God, Refuge for the oppressed, Stronghold
in times of trouble, I want to see Jesus in His
purity, humanness, divinity and
glory—as He really is . . . in His
name, the exact Image of the
Father.

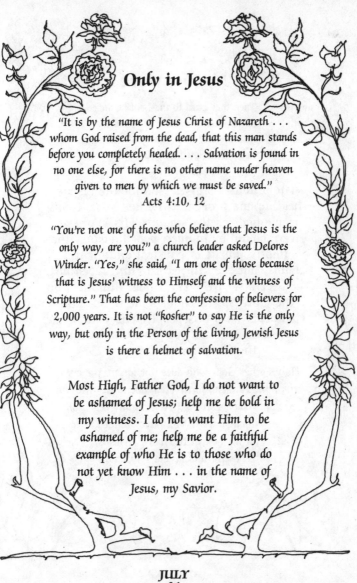

Only in Jesus

"It is by the name of Jesus Christ of Nazareth . . .
whom God raised from the dead, that this man stands
before you completely healed. . . . Salvation is found in
no one else, for there is no other name under heaven
given to men by which we must be saved."
Acts 4:10, 12

"You're not one of those who believe that Jesus is the
only way, are you?" a church leader asked Delores
Winder. "Yes," she said, "I am one of those because
that is Jesus' witness to Himself and the witness of
Scripture." That has been the confession of believers for
2,000 years. It is not "kosher" to say He is the only
way, but only in the Person of the living, Jewish Jesus
is there a helmet of salvation.

Most High, Father God, I do not want to
be ashamed of Jesus; help me be bold in
my witness. I do not want Him to be
ashamed of me; help me be a faithful
example of who He is to those who do
not yet know Him . . . in the name of
Jesus, my Savior.

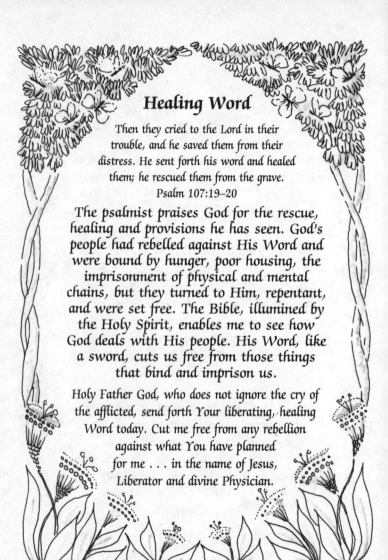

Healing Word

Then they cried to the Lord in their
trouble, and he saved them from their
distress. He sent forth his word and healed
them; he rescued them from the grave.

Psalm 107:19–20

The psalmist praises God for the rescue,
healing and provisions he has seen. God's
people had rebelled against His Word and
were bound by hunger, poor housing, the
imprisonment of physical and mental
chains, but they turned to Him, repentant,
and were set free. The Bible, illumined by
the Holy Spirit, enables me to see how
God deals with His people. His Word, like
a sword, cuts us free from those things
that bind and imprison us.

Holy Father God, who does not ignore the cry of
the afflicted, send forth Your liberating, healing
Word today. Cut me free from any rebellion
against what You have planned
for me . . . in the name of Jesus,
Liberator and divine Physician.

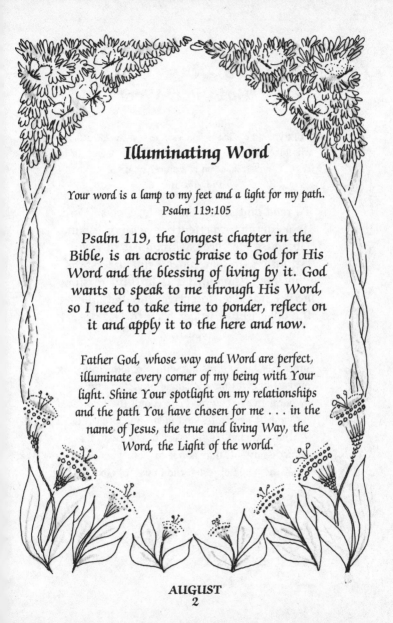

Illuminating Word

Your word is a lamp to my feet and a light for my path.
Psalm 119:105

Psalm 119, the longest chapter in the Bible, is an acrostic praise to God for His Word and the blessing of living by it. God wants to speak to me through His Word, so I need to take time to ponder, reflect on it and apply it to the here and now.

Father God, whose way and Word are perfect, illuminate every corner of my being with Your light. Shine Your spotlight on my relationships and the path You have chosen for me . . . in the name of Jesus, the true and living Way, the Word, the Light of the world.

God's Pure Word

"Every word of God is flawless; he is a shield to those
who take refuge in him. Do not add to his words, or he
will rebuke you and prove you a liar."
Proverbs 30:5–6

To read and study the Bible, God's Word,
is a lifetime experience, a way of living,
because He speaks through it in every
situation. If sometimes I misunderstand
what He is saying, He is faithful to show
me the mistake, to correct me and give me
the opportunity to get back to His perfect
path.

Father God, who arms me with strength, trains me
for battle, gives me the shield of victory, prepares
my path, thank You for Your Word, the two-edged
sword. It penetrates and judges me as well as
those around me, in order to cut away the
unnecessary, all that is not in Your plan . . . in
the name of Jesus, the Power of God.

Word of Deliverance

He drove out the spirits with a word and healed all the sick. This was to fulfill what was spoken through the prophet Isaiah: "He took up our infirmities and carried our diseases."
Matthew 8:16–17

God spoke and out of chaos came creation; His Spirit hovered over the darkness and brought forth light. Jesus, the living Word of God in human form, stepped into the specifics of Jewish culture and drove out spirits with a word. What was that word? It must have been a command, spoken with authority, because He knew God's will in the situation.

Father God of unfailing kindness to Your people, I want to know Your will and be ready to speak the Word that sets people free—because Jesus is living within me . . . in the name of Jesus, the Scepter of God's authority.

Sowing the Word

"The farmer sows the word. . . . Others, like seed sown
on good soil, hear the word, accept it, and produce
a crop—thirty, sixty or even a hundred times
what was sown."
Mark 4:14, 20

The Word of God is like good seed planted
by God's Spirit. God wants to plow up the
hardened places in me, remove the rocks
and pull up weeds by the roots. Then God
spreads on some manure and soaks me
thoroughly with water and sun. This
prepares the soil of my life to produce the
good fruit and vegetables God planned.

Father God, great King and Gardener of all the
earth, thank You for the seasons of life and for the
good seed You plant in me. Prepare me to receive
Your Word today, and to give away
good fruit to the hungry . . . in the
name of Jesus, the Seed, the living
Word.

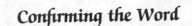

Confirming the Word

"Go into all the world and preach the good news to all creation. . . . These signs will accompany those who believe: In my name they will drive out demons . . . speak in new tongues . . . pick up snakes . . . [not be hurt by] poison . . . place their hands on sick people . . . [who] will get well." . . . And the Lord . . . confirmed his word by the signs that accompanied it.
Mark 16:15, 17–18, 20

This confirming of the Word by supernatural acts that I cannot perform humanly takes the Christian life out of my control. It must be under God's direction, in God's dimension. This is scary, because here I am on the invisible ground of faith, but it is here I must begin.

Father God, worthy to be praised, in obedience I want to step out, bringing Your Good News to those who do not know Your love. Confirm my going and speak through me, letting them know it is really You . . . in the name of Jesus, the Mediator.

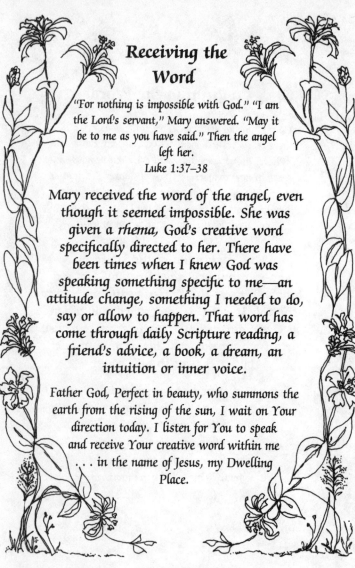

Receiving the Word

"For nothing is impossible with God." "I am the Lord's servant," Mary answered. "May it be to me as you have said." Then the angel left her.
Luke 1:37–38

Mary received the word of the angel, even though it seemed impossible. She was given a *rhema*, God's creative word specifically directed to her. There have been times when I knew God was speaking something specific to me—an attitude change, something I needed to do, say or allow to happen. That word has come through daily Scripture reading, a friend's advice, a book, a dream, an intuition or inner voice.

Father God, Perfect in beauty, who summons the earth from the rising of the sun, I wait on Your direction today. I listen for You to speak and receive Your creative word within me . . . in the name of Jesus, my Dwelling Place.

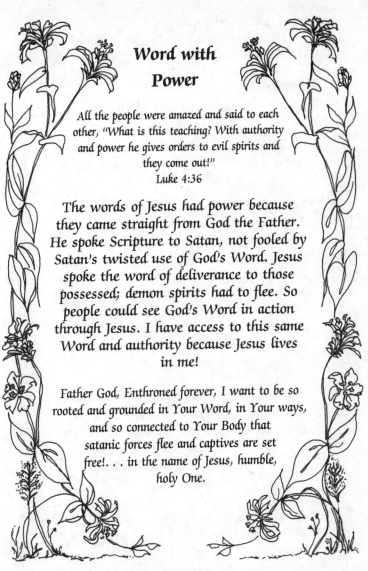

Word with Power

All the people were amazed and said to each other, "What is this teaching? With authority and power he gives orders to evil spirits and they come out!"
Luke 4:36

The words of Jesus had power because they came straight from God the Father. He spoke Scripture to Satan, not fooled by Satan's twisted use of God's Word. Jesus spoke the word of deliverance to those possessed; demon spirits had to flee. So people could see God's Word in action through Jesus. I have access to this same Word and authority because Jesus lives in me!

Father God, Enthroned forever, I want to be so rooted and grounded in Your Word, in Your ways, and so connected to Your Body that satanic forces flee and captives are set free!. . . in the name of Jesus, humble, holy One.

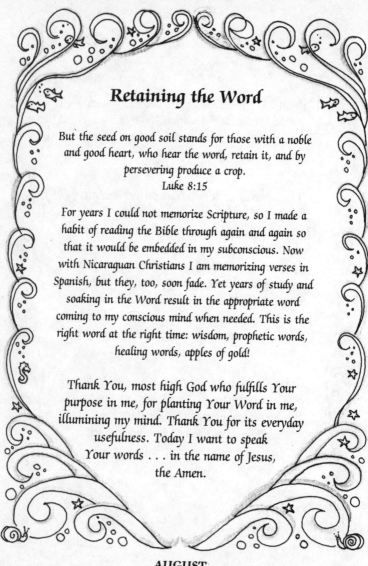

Retaining the Word

But the seed on good soil stands for those with a noble
and good heart, who hear the word, retain it, and by
persevering produce a crop.
Luke 8:15

For years I could not memorize Scripture, so I made a
habit of reading the Bible through again and again so
that it would be embedded in my subconscious. Now
with Nicaraguan Christians I am memorizing verses in
Spanish, but they, too, soon fade. Yet years of study and
soaking in the Word result in the appropriate word
coming to my conscious mind when needed. This is the
right word at the right time: wisdom, prophetic words,
healing words, apples of gold!

Thank You, most high God who fulfills Your
purpose in me, for planting Your Word in me,
illumining my mind. Thank You for its everyday
usefulness. Today I want to speak
Your words . . . in the name of Jesus,
the Amen.

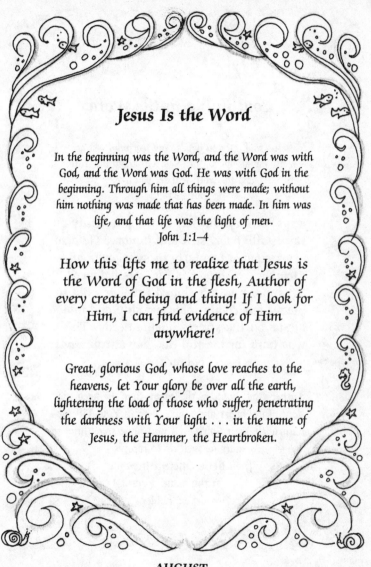

Jesus Is the Word

In the beginning was the Word, and the Word was with
God, and the Word was God. He was with God in the
beginning. Through him all things were made; without
him nothing was made that has been made. In him was
life, and that life was the light of men.

John 1:1–4

How this lifts me to realize that Jesus is
the Word of God in the flesh, Author of
every created being and thing! If I look for
Him, I can find evidence of Him
anywhere!

Great, glorious God, whose love reaches to the
heavens, let Your glory be over all the earth,
lightening the load of those who suffer, penetrating
the darkness with Your light . . . in the name of
Jesus, the Hammer, the Heartbroken.

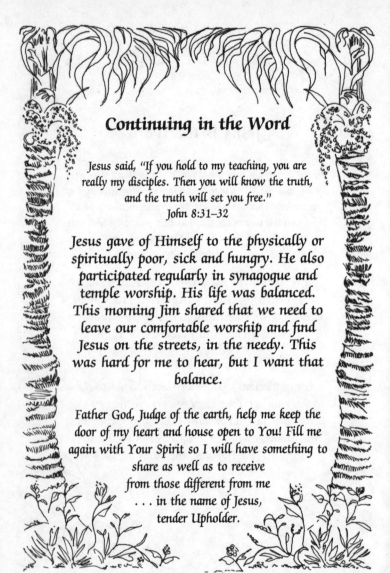

Continuing in the Word

Jesus said, "If you hold to my teaching, you are really my disciples. Then you will know the truth, and the truth will set you free."
John 8:31–32

Jesus gave of Himself to the physically or spiritually poor, sick and hungry. He also participated regularly in synagogue and temple worship. His life was balanced. This morning Jim shared that we need to leave our comfortable worship and find Jesus on the streets, in the needy. This was hard for me to hear, but I want that balance.

Father God, Judge of the earth, help me keep the door of my heart and house open to You! Fill me again with Your Spirit so I will have something to share as well as to receive from those different from me . . . in the name of Jesus, tender Upholder.

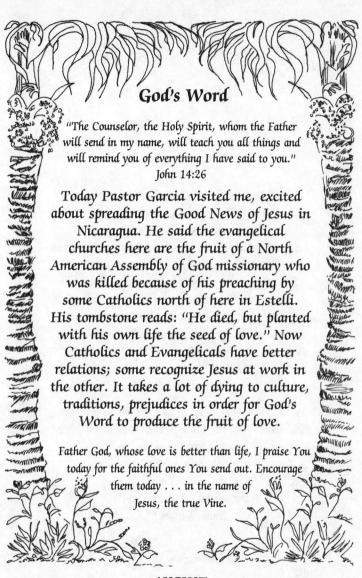

God's Word

"The Counselor, the Holy Spirit, whom the Father will send in my name, will teach you all things and will remind you of everything I have said to you."
John 14:26

Today Pastor Garcia visited me, excited about spreading the Good News of Jesus in Nicaragua. He said the evangelical churches here are the fruit of a North American Assembly of God missionary who was killed because of his preaching by some Catholics north of here in Estelli. His tombstone reads: "He died, but planted with his own life the seed of love." Now Catholics and Evangelicals have better relations; some recognize Jesus at work in the other. It takes a lot of dying to culture, traditions, prejudices in order for God's Word to produce the fruit of love.

Father God, whose love is better than life, I praise You today for the faithful ones You send out. Encourage them today . . . in the name of Jesus, the true Vine.

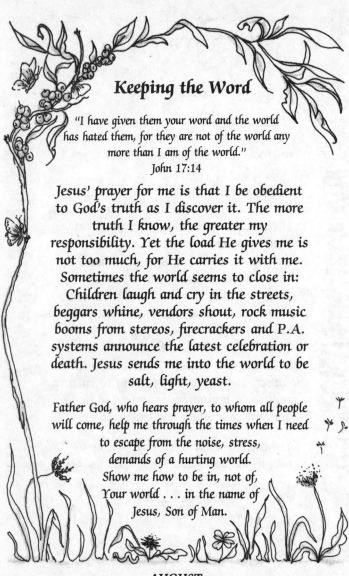

Keeping the Word

"I have given them your word and the world
has hated them, for they are not of the world any
more than I am of the world."
John 17:14

Jesus' prayer for me is that I be obedient
to God's truth as I discover it. The more
truth I know, the greater my
responsibility. Yet the load He gives me is
not too much, for He carries it with me.
Sometimes the world seems to close in:
Children laugh and cry in the streets,
beggars whine, vendors shout, rock music
booms from stereos, firecrackers and P.A.
systems announce the latest celebration or
death. Jesus sends me into the world to be
salt, light, yeast.

Father God, who hears prayer, to whom all people
will come, help me through the times when I need
to escape from the noise, stress,
demands of a hurting world.
Show me how to be in, not of,
Your world . . . in the name of
Jesus, Son of Man.

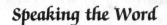

Speaking the Word

"Now, Lord, consider their threats and enable your
servants to speak your word with great boldness. Stretch
out your hand to heal and perform miraculous signs and
wonders through the name of your holy servant Jesus."
. . . They were all filled with the Holy Spirit and spoke
the word of God boldly.

Acts 4:29–31

Jesus does the same healing, miraculous
signs and wonders today as when He
walked in Galilee if I, with other
believers, boldly speak His Word. If I
never use the Word, never speak out that
inner conviction, the Spirit is quenched
and the gifts are not given to those who
need them.

Father God, who tests and refines me, whose deeds
are awesome, I want to be available and bold in
using Your healing words . . . in the
name of Jesus, the Cornerstone.

Ministry of the Word

"Brothers, choose seven men from among you
who are known to be full of the Spirit and
wisdom. We will turn this responsibility over to
them and will give our attention to prayer and
the ministry of the word."

Acts 6:3–4

I have a function as a believer in Christ, a
ministry to be fulfilled. In order to be fully
equipped for my part, I need to soak in
and study God's Word daily. Some may be
called to devote all their time to this
function. If I do my part, they are freed to
communicate more effectively, planting the
seeds far and wide for a bountiful harvest.

Father God, who hears prayer, who calls forth
songs of joy, today I pray for those who minister
Your Word, that they be faithful, effective,
encouraged. Show me my part . . . in
the name of Jesus, Prophet, Priest,
King.

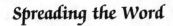

Spreading the Word

When Paul placed his hands on them, the Holy
Spirit came on them. . . . Handkerchiefs and
aprons that had touched him were taken to the
sick, and their illnesses were cured and the evil
spirits left them. . . . In this way the word of the
Lord spread widely and grew in power.
Acts 19:6, 12, 20

Miracles and expulsion of evil spirits were
visible evidence of the reality of Paul's
message. When I become open to the
"something more" that God's Holy Spirit
offers, Paul's message comes alive. Evil
supernatural activity does exist, but God
is more powerful.

Father God, who ransoms me unharmed from the
battle waged against me, God enthroned forever, I
reject all occult activity and am
willing for You to use me today . . . in
the name of Jesus, Creator and Ruler
over all thrones, powers and
authorities, visible or invisible.

Confessing the Word

"The word is near you; it is in your mouth and in your heart," that is, the word of faith we are proclaiming: That if you confess with your mouth, "Jesus is Lord," and believe in your heart that God raised him from the dead, you will be saved.

Romans 10:8–9

"Jesus is my Lord." This is the rhema word, the personal word of faith God has given with my name on it. When this word is a living Person reigning in me, then I will hear through God's Word a personal word that daily cuts through the world's confusion. "Jesus loves me, this I know," because He has spoken to me through the Bible in a personal way.

Father God, exalted above the nations yet very near, use me to share Your saving Word with those around me who have not yet heard in a way they can receive . . . in the name of Jesus, faithful Witness.

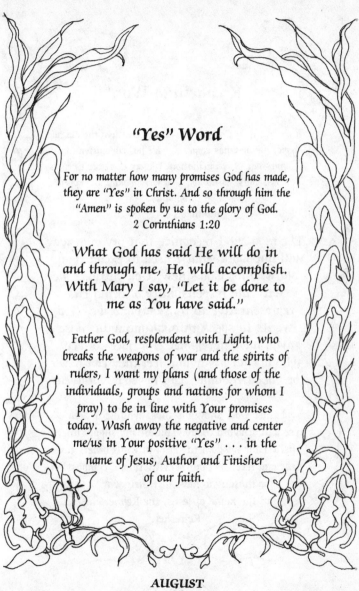

"Yes" Word

For no matter how many promises God has made,
they are "Yes" in Christ. And so through him the
"Amen" is spoken by us to the glory of God.
2 Corinthians 1:20

What God has said He will do in
and through me, He will accomplish.
With Mary I say, "Let it be done to
me as You have said."

Father God, resplendent with Light, who
breaks the weapons of war and the spirits of
rulers, I want my plans (and those of the
individuals, groups and nations for whom I
pray) to be in line with Your promises
today. Wash away the negative and center
me/us in Your positive "Yes" . . . in the
name of Jesus, Author and Finisher
of our faith.

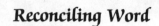

Reconciling Word

If anyone is in Christ, he is a new creation; the old has
gone, the new has come! . . . He has committed to us
the message of reconciliation. We are therefore Christ's
ambassadors, as though God were making his appeal
through us.
2 Corinthians 5:17, 19–20

The moment I recognize that my own way
will not work, that I need to exchange my
old way for God's new, God entrusts me
with the responsibility of being His
representative to those around me. God
wants to speak through me with those
who have never met Him face to face,
who are far away and feel they can never
be "good enough," can never be forgiven.

Father God, show me those who need Your
reconciling Word today. You are my supply line. I
need Your wisdom to speak in ways others can
hear and receive, Your sensitivity and compassion
for those who have lost their way . . .
in the name of Jesus, the Refiner and
Refresher.

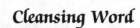

Cleansing Word

*Be filled with the Spirit. Speak to one another with
psalms, hymns and spiritual songs. Sing and make music
in your heart to the Lord, always giving thanks to God
the Father for everything, in the name of our Lord Jesus
Christ.*
Ephesians 5:18–20

Jesus spoke of pruning the vine to make it
more fruitful when He told the disciples,
"You are already clean because of the
word I have spoken to you" (John 15:3).
His rhema, specific word of forgiveness to
me from the cross, is what washes and
makes me holy, not my own striving. This
morning in the shower the song came
forth from deep within, "Clean before the
Lord I stand, and not one blemish does He
see."

Thank You, Father God, who restores and revives
Your people, for Your liberation of men and
women! . . . in the name of Jesus, the New
Wine.

Sword of the Spirit

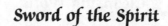

Take the helmet of salvation and the sword of the Spirit,
which is the word of God.
Ephesians 6:17

This resurrected Jesus, God's living Word,
is my offensive weapon against evil
supernatural forces. It is my responsibility
to take hold, grasp and use God's Word,
however, only as the Holy Spirit directs.
Jesus had harsh words for the self-
righteous religious, but merciful words for
repentant sinners, healing and liberating
words for the sick, poor and imprisoned.

Father God, Abounding in love to all who call upon
You, I want the living Word to speak through me
today. Train my tongue to speak Your Word with
authority. Cut away my preconceptions and get to
the heart of the matter—that Jesus is Lord of
heaven and earth . . . in His name.

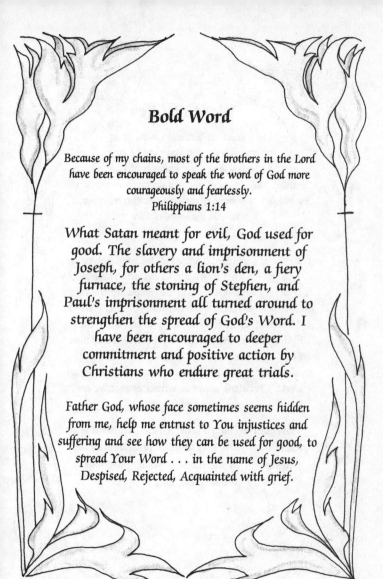

Bold Word

Because of my chains, most of the brothers in the Lord
have been encouraged to speak the word of God more
courageously and fearlessly.
Philippians 1:14

What Satan meant for evil, God used for
good. The slavery and imprisonment of
Joseph, for others a lion's den, a fiery
furnace, the stoning of Stephen, and
Paul's imprisonment all turned around to
strengthen the spread of God's Word. I
have been encouraged to deeper
commitment and positive action by
Christians who endure great trials.

Father God, whose face sometimes seems hidden
from me, help me entrust to You injustices and
suffering and see how they can be used for good, to
spread Your Word . . . in the name of Jesus,
Despised, Rejected, Acquainted with grief.

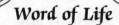

Word of Life

Do everything without complaining
or arguing, so that you may become
blameless and pure, children of God
without fault in a crooked and depraved generation,
in which you shine like stars in the universe as you
hold out the word of life.
Philippians 2:14–16

Yesterday we watched "Witness," the movie about an
Amish boy who witnessed a drug murder. The way of
life of the Amish stood out in clear simplicity and purity
against the "rat race" of the twentieth century. Here in
Nicaragua, as in other third world countries, the
simplicity comes more often from poverty rather than
choice, and many who could move in the fast track
would gladly do so. In this confusing, chaotic, corrupt
world, Christians are to be witnesses that we are
sinners saved by grace.

Covenant-keeping Father God, I want those
around me to see You in my words and actions
today . . . in the name of Jesus, pure and
blameless One.

Dividing
the Word

Do your best to present yourself to God as
one approved, a workman who does not
need to be ashamed and who correctly
handles the word of truth.
2 Timothy 2:15

To make a straight cut and not waste
material is something seamstresses and
carpenters learn early. The Greek verb for
dividing the Word has that same thought,
in the context of Paul's advice to Timothy
to be a good workman. Focused on the
foundation of the Word, the good
workman does not get diverted into
pointless, picky discussions about the
Bible that only confuse, nor does he gossip
idly about things that do not lead back to
the foundation—Jesus.

Everlasting Father God who returns me to the
dust, show me Your balance in my use of
words, and cleanse them of
everything not of You . . .
in the name of Jesus,
Word made flesh.

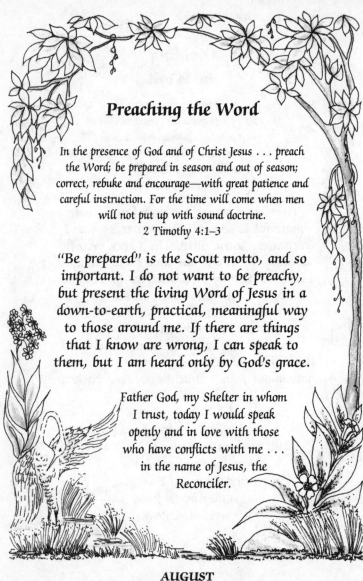

Preaching the Word

In the presence of God and of Christ Jesus . . . preach the Word; be prepared in season and out of season; correct, rebuke and encourage—with great patience and careful instruction. For the time will come when men will not put up with sound doctrine.

2 Timothy 4:1–3

"Be prepared" is the Scout motto, and so important. I do not want to be preachy, but present the living Word of Jesus in a down-to-earth, practical, meaningful way to those around me. If there are things that I know are wrong, I can speak to them, but I am heard only by God's grace.

Father God, my Shelter in whom I trust, today I would speak openly and in love with those who have conflicts with me . . . in the name of Jesus, the Reconciler.

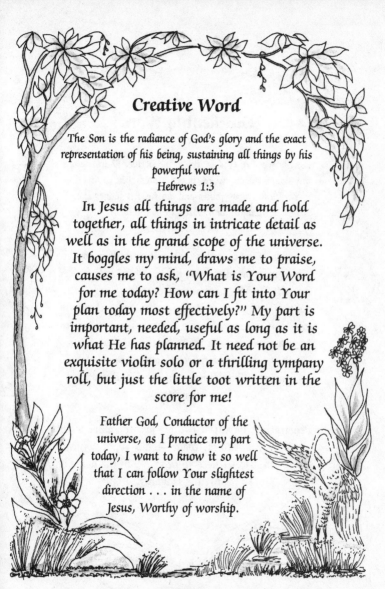

Creative Word

The Son is the radiance of God's glory and the exact
representation of his being, sustaining all things by his
powerful word.
Hebrews 1:3

In Jesus all things are made and hold
together, all things in intricate detail as
well as in the grand scope of the universe.
It boggles my mind, draws me to praise,
causes me to ask, "What is Your Word
for me today? How can I fit into Your
plan today most effectively?" My part is
important, needed, useful as long as it is
what He has planned. It need not be an
exquisite violin solo or a thrilling tympany
roll, but just the little toot written in the
score for me!

Father God, Conductor of the
universe, as I practice my part
today, I want to know it so well
that I can follow Your slightest
direction . . . in the name of
Jesus, Worthy of worship.

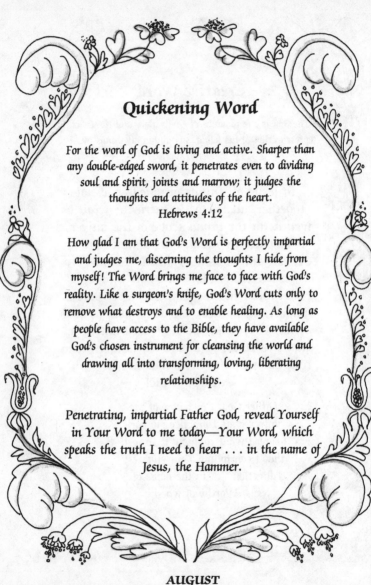

Quickening Word

For the word of God is living and active. Sharper than any double-edged sword, it penetrates even to dividing soul and spirit, joints and marrow; it judges the thoughts and attitudes of the heart.
Hebrews 4:12

How glad I am that God's Word is perfectly impartial and judges me, discerning the thoughts I hide from myself! The Word brings me face to face with God's reality. Like a surgeon's knife, God's Word cuts only to remove what destroys and to enable healing. As long as people have access to the Bible, they have available God's chosen instrument for cleansing the world and drawing all into transforming, loving, liberating relationships.

Penetrating, impartial Father God, reveal Yourself in Your Word to me today—Your Word, which speaks the truth I need to hear . . . in the name of Jesus, the Hammer.

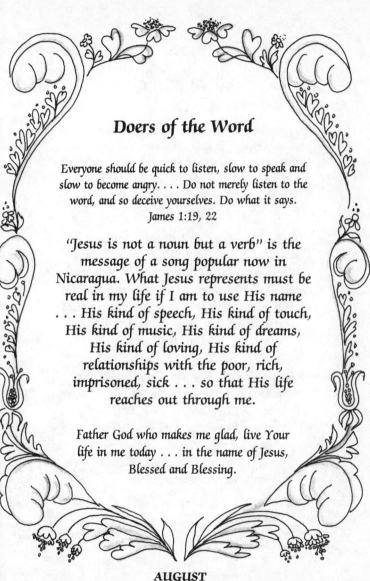

Doers of the Word

Everyone should be quick to listen, slow to speak and
slow to become angry. . . . Do not merely listen to the
word, and so deceive yourselves. Do what it says.
James 1:19, 22

"Jesus is not a noun but a verb" is the
message of a song popular now in
Nicaragua. What Jesus represents must be
real in my life if I am to use His name
. . . His kind of speech, His kind of touch,
His kind of music, His kind of dreams,
His kind of loving, His kind of
relationships with the poor, rich,
imprisoned, sick . . . so that His life
reaches out through me.

Father God who makes me glad, live Your
life in me today . . . in the name of Jesus,
Blessed and Blessing.

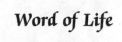

Word of Life

Do everything without complaining or arguing, so that
you may become blameless and pure, children of God
without fault . . . as you hold out the word of life—in
order that I may boast on the day of Christ that I did
not run or labor for nothing.

Philippians 2:14–16

"Get that whine out of your voice!" Jim
has said to me more than once. "Don't
allow yourself a 'pity party,' " a friend,
Dee Goodwin, used to say. How easy it is
to slip into whining or self-pity, yet how
those attitudes drag down the whole
family!

Father God, my Resting Place, Jesus did not
complain even on the cross. He cried out in agony
to You, but accepted Your decision.
I want to accept with joy all You
have for me today . . . in the name
of Jesus, the Answer who did not
answer His accusers.

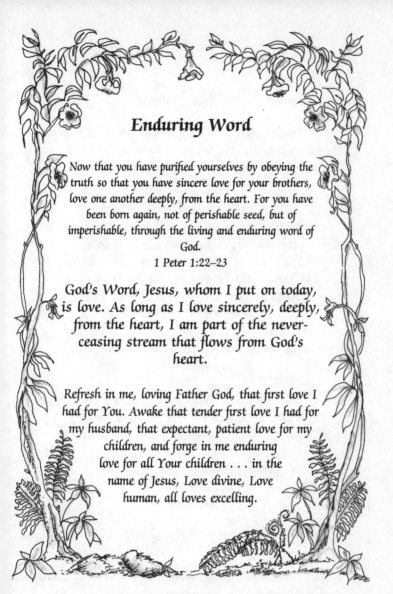

Enduring Word

Now that you have purified yourselves by obeying the
truth so that you have sincere love for your brothers,
love one another deeply, from the heart. For you have
been born again, not of perishable seed, but of
imperishable, through the living and enduring word of
God.

1 Peter 1:22–23

God's Word, Jesus, whom I put on today,
is love. As long as I love sincerely, deeply,
from the heart, I am part of the never-
ceasing stream that flows from God's
heart.

Refresh in me, loving Father God, that first love I
had for You. Awake that tender first love I had for
my husband, that expectant, patient love for my
children, and forge in me enduring
love for all Your children . . . in the
name of Jesus, Love divine, Love
human, all loves excelling.

Abiding Word

If anyone obeys his word, God's love is truly made
complete in him. This is how we know we are in him:
Whoever claims to live in him must walk as Jesus did.
1 John 2:5–6

Each day as I look back over the
interactions within the family and
community, I hold up the standard
"What would Jesus do?" Immersed in the
Word, picturing vividly the Jesus of the
Gospels, His way of relating to those
around Him, His obedience to God's
direction, I can see more clearly what He
would do in the particular situation where
He has me.

Father God, my Rock in whom there is no
wickedness, thank You that I can keep short
accounts, that You cover all that I give to You.
You are with me every step, to
plunge through the day with Your
joy . . . in the name of Jesus, my
All in all.

Praise Continually

I will extol the Lord at all times; his praise will always
be on my lips. My soul will boast in the Lord; let the
afflicted hear and rejoice. . . . I sought the Lord, and he
answered me; he delivered me from all my fears.

Psalm 34:1–2, 4

Sometimes I come into God's presence
with noisy joy, other times with moans of
grief or pain or confession, sometimes in
quiet, other times crying out. It is a
comfort to know God is always present,
always the same. God is love. God is for
me. I can look up, lift up everything I am
to God, and as I praise, all that God is
fills and heals.

You are worthy, sovereign Father
God, to be praised with every
breath, with all my being. You
alone are worthy! . . . in the name
of Jesus, the Same yesterday, today
and forever.

Lips Praise

O God, you are my God, earnestly I seek you; my
soul thirsts for you, my body longs for you, in a dry
and weary land where there is no water. . . . Because
your love is better than life, my lips will glorify you.
I will praise you as long as I live, and in your name
I will lift up my hands. . . . With singing lips my
mouth will praise you.

Psalm 63:1, 3–5

How important are my words! Words of
faith come from the heart. David from the
desert of trying circumstances praised God
using the Hebrew word that means a
command, a shout of triumph. Sometimes
praise is quiet, but sometimes it wells up
from a grateful soul united to God's Spirit
in a great shout, a certainty that God has
overcome in the situation.

When I see You, almighty loving Father, I can
see circumstances from Your
perspective. Nothing is impossible
to You! . . . in the name of Jesus,
my Praise.

Willing to Praise

Praise the Lord, O my soul. I will praise the Lord all
my life; I will sing praise to my God as long as I live.
Do not put your trust in princes, in mortal men, who
cannot save. . . . The Maker of heaven and earth . . .
remains faithful forever.
Psalm 146:1–3, 6

Sometimes the psalmist had to instruct his inner self to
praise the Lord. Praise is not always spontaneous, but is
as much a part of life as breathing or hearts beating,
and is part of forever. This Hebrew word for praise
means to be clear, to shine forth, celebrating, even being
clamorously foolish in exulting God, for God is worthy.
As I focus on who God is, what God has done, hardness
cracks, coldness melts, depression lifts,
and I can see.

Father God of the immense universe, I extol You
with high praises that well up when I see Your
greatness, yet know intimately and
securely Your closeness and care
. . . in the name of Jesus, God's
visible Image.

Praise for Details

For you created my inmost being; you knit me
together in my mother's womb. I praise you
because I am fearfully and wonderfully made; your
works are wonderful, . . . your eyes saw my
unformed body.
Psalm 139:13–14, 16

How marvelous to see a baby born, every
part intricately fit together to function
perfectly! Humans, with all their scientific
knowledge, cannot approach that beauty,
nor breathe living spirit into what has
been created. With the same care with
which I was formed in my mother's
womb, I am surrounded, encircled by
God, my loving Parent.

Father God, Maker of the universe and of me, how
I worship You, for Your works are beyond
compare! You did not make me and leave me alone,
but are with me always to complete Your creation,
to perfect our love within the body of Believers . . .
in the name of Jesus, in whom all things fit
together.

Garment of Praise

. . . To bestow on them . . . a garment of praise instead
of a spirit of despair. They will be called oaks of
righteousness, a planting of the Lord for the display of
his splendor.
Isaiah 61:3

The mission of Jesus, which He gives to
us—to heal, liberate, preach Good News,
comfort—includes replacing the spirit of
despair with the garment of praise when
God's people grieve. The crown of beauty,
the oil of gladness and the garment (a
song) of praise are all gifts I can give
others to encourage and protect them as
part of their spiritual armor.

Father God, who lifts me, when I see brothers or
sisters uncovered, lacking in some way,
disheartened, grieving, enable me to be a channel
of Holy Spirit resources so they radiate Your praise
once again . . . in the name of Jesus, who
completes His mission.

Thoughts of Praise

Whatever is true, whatever is noble, whatever is right, whatever is pure, whatever is lovely, whatever is admirable—if anything is excellent or praiseworthy—think about such things.

Philippians 4:8

To renew my mind, being transformed, not conformed, to the pressures of the world, is to focus on what is true, right, lovely, pure, worthy of praise. This is part of the armor I put on. As I turn my thoughts to Him in praise, I gradually become more like Him. As lovers who grow old together take on each other's characteristics, so I, made in His image, grow to be like my Lover, Jesus.

Father God, Worthy of all praises, I want these lofty meditations to be lived out on the solid ground where I walk and get my feet dirty every day. Thank You for Jesus, my Companion, who walked this earth before and walks it still with me . . . in His name.

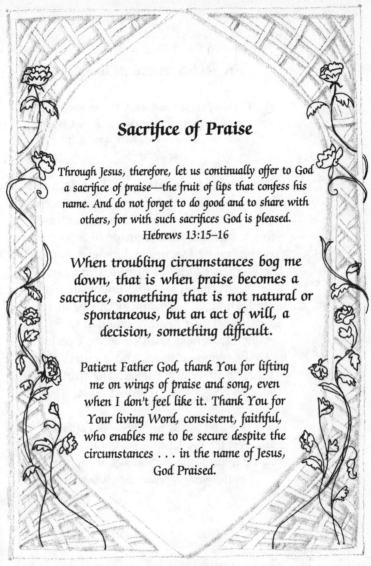

Sacrifice of Praise

Through Jesus, therefore, let us continually offer to God
a sacrifice of praise—the fruit of lips that confess his
name. And do not forget to do good and to share with
others, for with such sacrifices God is pleased.
Hebrews 13:15–16

When troubling circumstances bog me
down, that is when praise becomes a
sacrifice, something that is not natural or
spontaneous, but an act of will, a
decision, something difficult.

Patient Father God, thank You for lifting
me on wings of praise and song, even
when I don't feel like it. Thank You for
Your living Word, consistent, faithful,
who enables me to be secure despite the
circumstances . . . in the name of Jesus,
God Praised.

In Repentance and Rest

. . .The Holy One of Israel, says: "In repentance and rest is your salvation, in quietness and trust is your strength, but you would have none of it."
Isaiah 30:15

"A broken and contrite heart God does not despise," a pastor reminded me as I wept at the altar. Other times I have confessed to my husband, children, or to a prayer partner while jogging or having a cup of tea. Roman Catholics have a strong sense of the freeing, cleansing importance of confession. . . . Though it can be mere ritual, it is a healthy practice to be completely honest with someone I respect as God's representative. Those quiet, alone times with God are where the things I need to confess are revealed most often.

Father God who listens with undivided attention, I praise You, for You hear the cries of my heart and bring me to the place of repentance and rest in You . . . in the name of Jesus, the Hiding Place.

Godly Sorrow

Godly sorrow brings repentance that leads to salvation
and leaves no regret, but worldly sorrow brings death.
See what this godly sorrow has produced in you: what
earnestness, what eagerness to clear yourselves.
2 Corinthians 7:10–11

As far as the East is from the West, as
deep as the unplumbable depths of the sea
are my sins cleansed, erased, forgotten!
This is the joy of salvation, but first I
must recognize the ways my thought
patterns, actions, words are against God.
Only then can the cleansing take place.
My responsibility is to have a godly
sorrow that leads to complete release, not
a worldly sorrow that berates, nags and
condemns.

Totally forgiving Father God, thank You for the
ways You show me what is wrong and false in
myself, yet always make a way to become new,
free, whole . . . in the name of Jesus, the sacrificial
Lamb.

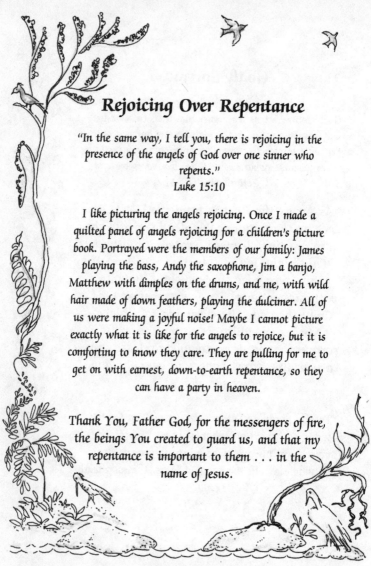

Rejoicing Over Repentance

"In the same way, I tell you, there is rejoicing in the presence of the angels of God over one sinner who repents."
Luke 15:10

I like picturing the angels rejoicing. Once I made a quilted panel of angels rejoicing for a children's picture book. Portrayed were the members of our family: James playing the bass, Andy the saxophone, Jim a banjo, Matthew with dimples on the drums, and me, with wild hair made of down feathers, playing the dulcimer. All of us were making a joyful noise! Maybe I cannot picture exactly what it is like for the angels to rejoice, but it is comforting to know they care. They are pulling for me to get on with earnest, down-to-earth repentance, so they can have a party in heaven.

Thank You, Father God, for the messengers of fire, the beings You created to guard us, and that my repentance is important to them . . . in the name of Jesus.

Confess and Renounce

He who conceals his sins does not prosper, but whoever
confesses and renounces them finds mercy.
Proverbs 28:13

It is not enough to see my sin and be
sorry. I must decide that it is no longer
acceptable and do the things necessary to
turn away from it completely. That
probably means a change in habits, doing
things differently so the temptation cannot
overpower, focusing on the Lord rather
than on my own wretched weakness. The
promise is that in His direction there is
mercy if I but turn to Him.

Thank You, caring Father God, for calling me to
come away from that sin that seems to bind so
close. You sent Jesus, the Deliverer, who took
every sin, grief and sickness on His wounded body
. . . in His name I am free!

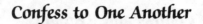

Confess to One Another

Is any one of you sick? He should call the elders of the
church to pray over him and anoint him with oil in the
name of the Lord. . . . Therefore confess your sins to
each other and pray for each other so that you may be
healed.
James 5:14, 16

To let a few others whom I respect in the faith know
me as I really am is a risky, but powerfully liberating,
process. In this relationship the resurrected Jesus reveals
Himself again; in anointing with oil, the Holy Spirit
touches and heals body, soul and spirit. This is
especially precious in the marriage relationship: Jim and
I have a commitment to share openly with each other,
seeing the other as wonderfully made. So our love has
grown.

Thank You, gentle God, for enabling me to have
honest relationships in which I can know the love,
forgiveness and freedom You have prepared for
me/us . . . in the name of Jesus, divine Healer.

Be Baptized

"After me will come one who is more powerful than I, whose sandals I am not fit to carry. He will baptize you with the Holy Spirit and with fire."
Matthew 3:11

The result of my sin is death. Baptism represents the resurrection life of Jesus in place of death brought on by sins. Though I have not been a drug addict or alcoholic, like Nicky Cruz and Cookie Rodriguez, whose tremendous testimonies I am reading now, I am responsible to turn around if I am walking away from God. That means submitting to a baptism, which includes a public sign, water, and God's supernatural seal, the Holy Spirit, and the fire of testing and tempering.

Ever-listening Father God, who sees the hidden motives of my heart, I give all I am into Your creative hands . . . in the name of Jesus, Tempted in every way yet without sin.

Confess Sin

If we confess our sins, he is faithful and just
and will forgive us our sins and purify us from
all unrighteousness.
1 John 1:9

Last night, next door, Concesa's baby died.
One day while she was pregnant, in terrible pain, Concesa cried out to the virgin
Mary. I went over and suggested healing
prayer with Doña Julia and some other
believing neighbors. Together we knelt,
confessing our sinfulness, and prayed for
Concesa. She was healed of several infirmities. Doña Julia, in a knowledge that
came from the Lord, told Concesa that the
child was conceived in adultery; if she did
not stop the relationship, the child would
die. It has been agony to know that, despite
our prayers, Concesa refused to repent.

Jealous Father God, You forgave David of
adultery and murder. You are faithful,
calling Concesa, me and everyone into total
openness, cleansing and freedom . . . in the
name of Jesus, our Sanctuary.

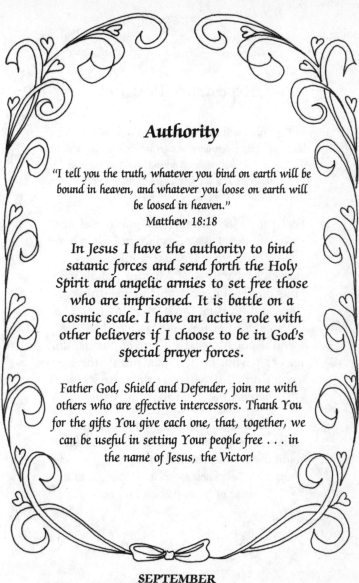

Authority

"I tell you the truth, whatever you bind on earth will be bound in heaven, and whatever you loose on earth will be loosed in heaven."
Matthew 18:18

In Jesus I have the authority to bind satanic forces and send forth the Holy Spirit and angelic armies to set free those who are imprisoned. It is battle on a cosmic scale. I have an active role with other believers if I choose to be in God's special prayer forces.

Father God, Shield and Defender, join me with others who are effective intercessors. Thank You for the gifts You give each one, that, together, we can be useful in setting Your people free . . . in the name of Jesus, the Victor!

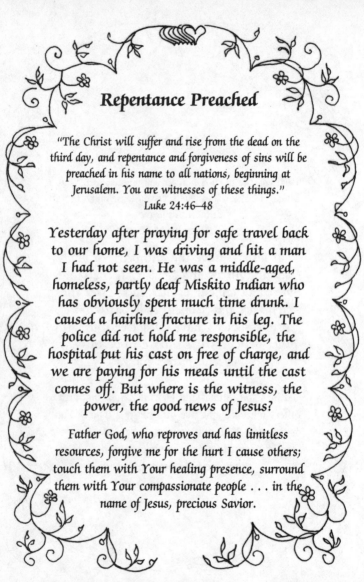

Repentance Preached

"The Christ will suffer and rise from the dead on the third day, and repentance and forgiveness of sins will be preached in his name to all nations, beginning at Jerusalem. You are witnesses of these things."
Luke 24:46–48

Yesterday after praying for safe travel back to our home, I was driving and hit a man I had not seen. He was a middle-aged, homeless, partly deaf Miskito Indian who has obviously spent much time drunk. I caused a hairline fracture in his leg. The police did not hold me responsible, the hospital put his cast on free of charge, and we are paying for his meals until the cast comes off. But where is the witness, the power, the good news of Jesus?

Father God, who reproves and has limitless resources, forgive me for the hurt I cause others; touch them with Your healing presence, surround them with Your compassionate people . . . in the name of Jesus, precious Savior.

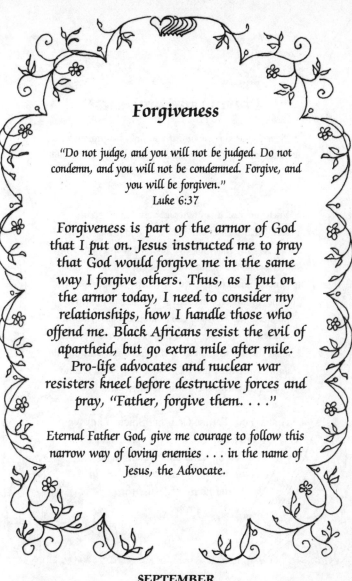

Forgiveness

"Do not judge, and you will not be judged. Do not condemn, and you will not be condemned. Forgive, and you will be forgiven."
Luke 6:37

Forgiveness is part of the armor of God that I put on. Jesus instructed me to pray that God would forgive me in the same way I forgive others. Thus, as I put on the armor today, I need to consider my relationships, how I handle those who offend me. Black Africans resist the evil of apartheid, but go extra mile after mile. Pro-life advocates and nuclear war resisters kneel before destructive forces and pray, "Father, forgive them. . . ."

Eternal Father God, give me courage to follow this narrow way of loving enemies . . . in the name of Jesus, the Advocate.

Praying in Forgiveness

"When you stand praying, if you hold anything against anyone, forgive him, so that your Father in heaven may forgive you your sins."
Mark 11:25

When Jim was away with a work group recently, a robber tried to enter the house. The first night I heard him over my room for two hours; I had a four-hour prayer session, singing praises at the top of my lungs, not forgetting to forgive the intruder—in Spanish! After all, our things are the Lord's. The second night Doña Julia and her husband came running when I heard someone try to enter from the roof. After we prayed through the house, anointing the doorways with oil and sprinkling with water, a symbol that Satan has no authority here, there was no more disturbance.

Thank You, Father God, my Shield, that we do have authority in the name and blood of Jesus against any who would rob or try to hurt us . . . in the name of Jesus, the Protector.

Forgive Like the Lord

Bear with each other and forgive whatever grievances
you may have against one another. Forgive as the
Lord forgave you.
Colossians 3:13

What brings out the strength and good in another? For
weeks I struggled with negative feelings toward Daniel,
the teenager living with us. He only occasionally joined
in the youth program, was not making much effort in
school, but enjoyed the privileges of being part of our
family. When Martina, the teacher who helps us, and I
were taking turns staying up at night to watch and pray
while Jim was gone, Daniel volunteered to help for
several hours. When I expressed my gratitude for the job
well done, his face lit up and he shared with me things
on his heart.

Thank You, Father God, who
knows our hidden needs. I want to
see with Your eyes . . . in the name
of Jesus, the Defender.

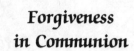

Forgiveness in Communion

"This is my blood of the covenant, which is poured out for many for the forgiveness of sins."
Matthew 26:28

Writing in my journal of a frustrating day I conclude, "Lord, it seems daily forgiveness is as essential as air!" Those churches that emphasize Communion, the Lord's Supper, have available a very specific, regular way of focusing on the giving and receiving of forgiveness. Agnes Sanford taught that there is healing power in Communion, in the blood of Jesus, which fills the universe with His Spirit of forgiveness. Francis MacNutt urges those who need healing to picture the blood from the wounds of Jesus applied to their needs.

Father God, who sanctifies, I praise You for Jesus who showed the way of forgiveness, making new beginnings possible . . . in the name of Jesus, the Reconciler.

Repent and Receive

Peter replied, "Repent and be baptized, every one of
you, in the name of Jesus Christ so that your sins
may be forgiven."
Acts 2:38

In Nicky Cruz' *Run Baby Run,* a
psychiatrist told him he was hopeless,
would die in the electric chair and go to
hell. To read of the cruel violence in
Nicky's life is horrifying, but I, too, had
to repent of the ways in which I tried to
run my own life apart from God. No
matter which path we are on, each must
make that eternal choice. To turn, be
cleansed, be filled with the Holy Spirit is
the only answer that makes sense.

Father God, whose thoughts toward me cannot be
numbered, You know me so intimately. Use me, O
God, in Your great plan to bring all who will come
into Your great love . . . in the name of Jesus,
Friend of sinners.

Enter with Thanksgiving

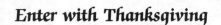

Shout for joy to the Lord, all the earth. . . . Enter his
gates with thanksgiving and his courts with praise; give
thanks to him and praise his name. For the Lord is good
and his love endures forever.
Psalm 100:1, 4–5

Catherine Marshall wrote in *Something
More* that praise is a miraculous key, an
act of will. "We stop fighting the evil or
less-than-good circumstances. With that,
resentment goes; self-pity goes. Perspective
comes. We . . . are looking steadily at
God. We are acting out our belief in the
character of God—His goodness, His
love."

Most excellent Father God, with all the saints in
glory, all the angels and stars and moon, with all
the trees, birds and beasts of the field, I join in
praise and thanksgiving for everything . . . in
the name of Jesus, the Upholder.

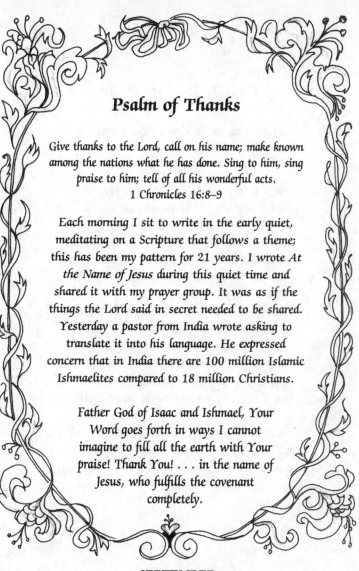

Psalm of Thanks

Give thanks to the Lord, call on his name; make known among the nations what he has done. Sing to him, sing praise to him; tell of all his wonderful acts.
1 Chronicles 16:8–9

Each morning I sit to write in the early quiet, meditating on a Scripture that follows a theme; this has been my pattern for 21 years. I wrote *At the Name of Jesus* during this quiet time and shared it with my prayer group. It was as if the things the Lord said in secret needed to be shared. Yesterday a pastor from India wrote asking to translate it into his language. He expressed concern that in India there are 100 million Islamic Ishmaelites compared to 18 million Christians.

Father God of Isaac and Ishmael, Your Word goes forth in ways I cannot imagine to fill all the earth with Your praise! Thank You! . . . in the name of Jesus, who fulfills the covenant completely.

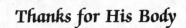

Thanks for His Body

The Lord Jesus, on the night he was betrayed, took
bread, and when he had given thanks. . . .
1 Corinthians 11:23–24

Jesus knew that the bread represented
His body, that it would be cruelly
broken within hours; still He gave
thanks. He knew His blood would be
poured out; He still gave thanks and
offered the cup to His disciples. It
was as if He were saying, "You will
suffer death in many ways, but that
is not what is important. Recognize
in believers all over the world the
sacrifices they are making, and give
thanks. In this appreciation and
thanksgiving are strength and health."

Exalted Father God, thank You for all who call on
Your name through Jesus, Your Son. Thank You
that each sacrifice I make is only a servant's duty
. . . in the name of Jesus, the perfect Sacrifice.

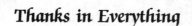

Thanks in Everything

Be joyful always; pray continually; give thanks in all circumstances, for this is God's will for you in Christ Jesus.
1 Thessalonians 5:16–18

I resist when someone urges me to be joyful or thankful, even though that is wisdom. Watchman Nee, before he died in a Chinese solitary confinement cell, wrote that he had learned the secret of continual joy. Jon Trott, editor of *Cornerstone* magazine, speaks of feeling rage when he sees hunger, homelessness, injustice. I think both are right; I must learn to live a balance between continual thanksgiving and continual impatience for justice to triumph.

Father God, just Judge, today I put on thanksgiving, wrapping around me those myriad ways You have encouraged me, shown me Your love. I want my life to be a praise to You that others utter . . . in the name of Jesus, the Succorer.

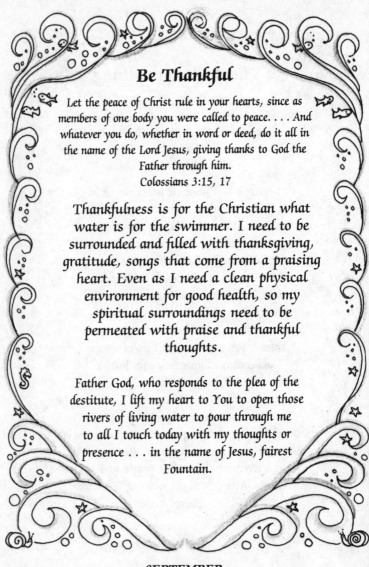

Be Thankful

Let the peace of Christ rule in your hearts, since as members of one body you were called to peace. . . . And whatever you do, whether in word or deed, do it all in the name of the Lord Jesus, giving thanks to God the Father through him.

Colossians 3:15, 17

Thankfulness is for the Christian what water is for the swimmer. I need to be surrounded and filled with thanksgiving, gratitude, songs that come from a praising heart. Even as I need a clean physical environment for good health, so my spiritual surroundings need to be permeated with praise and thankful thoughts.

Father God, who responds to the plea of the destitute, I lift my heart to You to open those rivers of living water to pour through me to all I touch today with my thoughts or presence . . . in the name of Jesus, fairest Fountain.

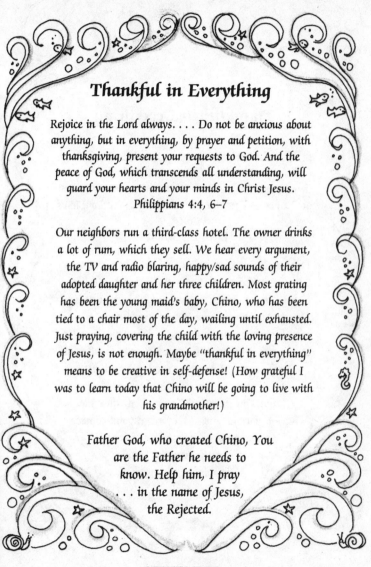

Thankful in Everything

Rejoice in the Lord always. . . . Do not be anxious about anything, but in everything, by prayer and petition, with thanksgiving, present your requests to God. And the peace of God, which transcends all understanding, will guard your hearts and your minds in Christ Jesus.
Philippians 4:4, 6–7

Our neighbors run a third-class hotel. The owner drinks a lot of rum, which they sell. We hear every argument, the TV and radio blaring, happy/sad sounds of their adopted daughter and her three children. Most grating has been the young maid's baby, Chino, who has been tied to a chair most of the day, wailing until exhausted. Just praying, covering the child with the loving presence of Jesus, is not enough. Maybe "thankful in everything" means to be creative in self-defense! (How grateful I was to learn today that Chino will be going to live with his grandmother!)

Father God, who created Chino, You
are the Father he needs to
know. Help him, I pray
. . . in the name of Jesus,
the Rejected.

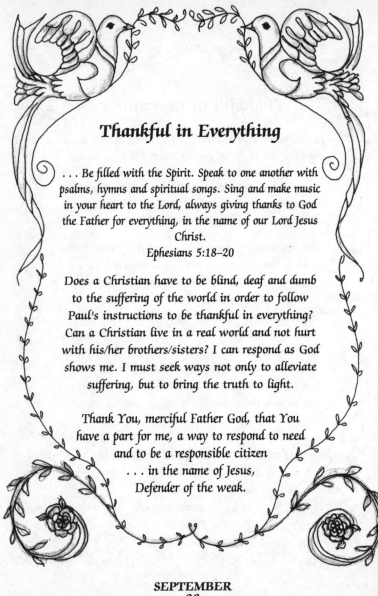

Thankful in Everything

. . . Be filled with the Spirit. Speak to one another with psalms, hymns and spiritual songs. Sing and make music in your heart to the Lord, always giving thanks to God the Father for everything, in the name of our Lord Jesus Christ.
Ephesians 5:18–20

Does a Christian have to be blind, deaf and dumb to the suffering of the world in order to follow Paul's instructions to be thankful in everything? Can a Christian live in a real world and not hurt with his/her brothers/sisters? I can respond as God shows me. I must seek ways not only to alleviate suffering, but to bring the truth to light.

Thank You, merciful Father God, that You have a part for me, a way to respond to need and to be a responsible citizen
. . . in the name of Jesus,
Defender of the weak.

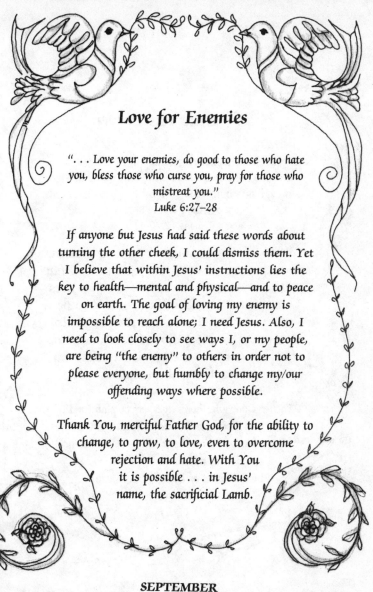

Love for Enemies

"... Love your enemies, do good to those who hate
you, bless those who curse you, pray for those who
mistreat you."
Luke 6:27–28

If anyone but Jesus had said these words about
turning the other cheek, I could dismiss them. Yet
I believe that within Jesus' instructions lies the
key to health—mental and physical—and to peace
on earth. The goal of loving my enemy is
impossible to reach alone; I need Jesus. Also, I
need to look closely to see ways I, or my people,
are being "the enemy" to others in order not to
please everyone, but humbly to change my/our
offending ways where possible.

Thank You, merciful Father God, for the ability to
change, to grow, to love, even to overcome
rejection and hate. With You
it is possible ... in Jesus'
name, the sacrificial Lamb.

The Generous Prayer

"If your enemy is hungry, feed him; if he is thirsty, give
him something to drink. In doing this, you will heap
burning coals on his head." Do not be overcome by evil,
but overcome evil with good.
Romans 12:20–21

Father Darian Betancourt teaches that the
most generous prayer asks God to do what
will give Him the most glory. What does
God want? What will cause God to be
more known, blessed and praised? This
means that what I think I want may not
happen; it opens the possibility that my
own life is dispensable.

Father God, who holds the perfect plan for the
universe in Your hand, today I release my desires
and my life into Your keeping. I want Your good
to reign in me no matter what . . .
in the name of Jesus, Preserver and
Rewarder.

Mary's Listening Prayer

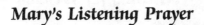

Mary . . . sat at the Lord's feet listening to what he
said.
Luke 10:39

Someone has said God gave us two ears and one
mouth because we need to listen more than to
speak. Each of my meditation books has been an
experiment in listening. When I began writing I
did not know if God would speak to me each day,
illuminating the attributes of Jesus. Though I used
dictionaries and other resources, it was the quiet
listening and writing the thoughts that came that
spoke most to me. Many, many times others have
told me the Lord speaks the wise word just right
for their situations in the same way.

Thank You, only wise Father God,
that You speak in countless ways and
enable me to hear Your voice . . . in
the name of Jesus, the great Shepherd
whose sheep know His voice.

Listening for Wisdom

Listen to [wisdom's] instruction and be wise; do not
ignore it. For whoever finds [it] finds life.
Proverbs 8:33, 35

The Holy Spirit's gifts of wisdom, understanding,
knowledge, prophecy depend on an attitude of
alert listening. I enjoy bringing prayer concerns to
my neighbor, Doña Julia, because she unerringly
"hears" the hidden roots and is guided in prayer
to the remedy just right for the situation. Doña
Julia hears with spiritual ears. She is tuned in to
God's station, which means other channels do not
get turned on. When she speaks the very word
needed in a situation about which she could know
nothing, I know God is at work!

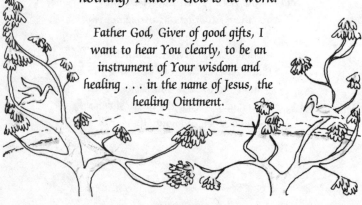

Father God, Giver of good gifts, I
want to hear You clearly, to be an
instrument of Your wisdom and
healing . . . in the name of Jesus, the
healing Ointment.

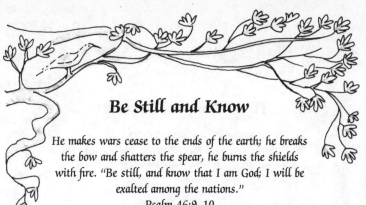

Be Still and Know

He makes wars cease to the ends of the earth; he breaks
the bow and shatters the spear, he burns the shields
with fire. "Be still, and know that I am God; I will be
exalted among the nations."
Psalm 46:9–10

God spoke to Elijah in a still, small voice,
a gentle whisper at a time when Elijah
was discouraged over the triumph of evil in
his land. He felt all alone; but that was not true.
There were 7,000 others who had not worshiped
false gods. After that he found Elisha, the one
who would work faithfully with him and carry
on his ministry.

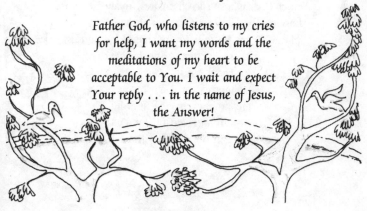

Father God, who listens to my cries
for help, I want my words and the
meditations of my heart to be
acceptable to You. I wait and expect
Your reply . . . in the name of Jesus,
the Answer!

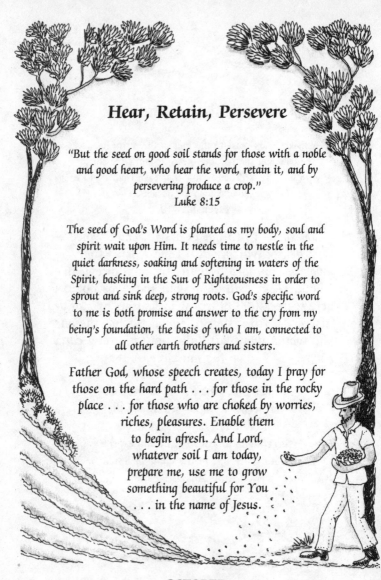

Hear, Retain, Persevere

"But the seed on good soil stands for those with a noble
and good heart, who hear the word, retain it, and by
persevering produce a crop."
Luke 8:15

The seed of God's Word is planted as my body, soul and
spirit wait upon Him. It needs time to nestle in the
quiet darkness, soaking and softening in waters of the
Spirit, basking in the Sun of Righteousness in order to
sprout and sink deep, strong roots. God's specific word
to me is both promise and answer to the cry from my
being's foundation, the basis of who I am, connected to
all other earth brothers and sisters.

Father God, whose speech creates, today I pray for
those on the hard path . . . for those in the rocky
place . . . for those who are choked by worries,
riches, pleasures. Enable them
to begin afresh. And Lord,
whatever soil I am today,
prepare me, use me to grow
something beautiful for You
. . . in the name of Jesus.

OCTOBER
4

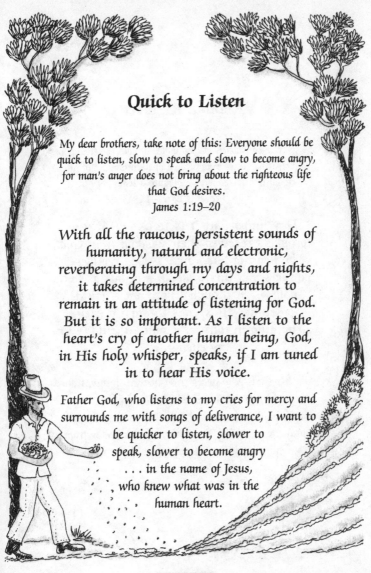

Quick to Listen

My dear brothers, take note of this: Everyone should be
quick to listen, slow to speak and slow to become angry,
for man's anger does not bring about the righteous life
that God desires.

James 1:19–20

With all the raucous, persistent sounds of
humanity, natural and electronic,
reverberating through my days and nights,
it takes determined concentration to
remain in an attitude of listening for God.
But it is so important. As I listen to the
heart's cry of another human being, God,
in His holy whisper, speaks, if I am tuned
in to hear His voice.

Father God, who listens to my cries for mercy and
surrounds me with songs of deliverance, I want to
be quicker to listen, slower to
speak, slower to become angry
. . . in the name of Jesus,
who knew what was in the
human heart.

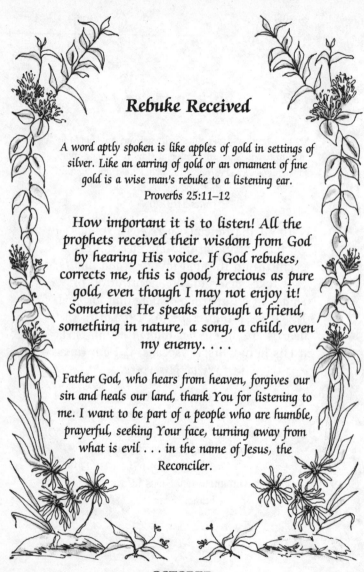

Rebuke Received

A word aptly spoken is like apples of gold in settings of
silver. Like an earring of gold or an ornament of fine
gold is a wise man's rebuke to a listening ear.
Proverbs 25:11–12

How important it is to listen! All the
prophets received their wisdom from God
by hearing His voice. If God rebukes,
corrects me, this is good, precious as pure
gold, even though I may not enjoy it!
Sometimes He speaks through a friend,
something in nature, a song, a child, even
my enemy. . . .

Father God, who hears from heaven, forgives our
sin and heals our land, thank You for listening to
me. I want to be part of a people who are humble,
prayerful, seeking Your face, turning away from
what is evil . . . in the name of Jesus, the
Reconciler.

Hear and Understand

"But blessed are your eyes because they see, and your
ears because they hear. . . . But what was sown on good
soil is the man who hears the word and understands it.
He produces a crop, yielding a hundred, sixty or thirty
times what was sown."
Matthew 13:16, 23

The evidence of my hearing and understanding God's
Word can be seen and tested as good fruit by others.
God measures my fruitfulness by how much His Word
multiplies (thirty, sixty, one hundred times) through me
to others. This is a reproduction of the living, Spirit-
infused Jesus, which happens as I get out of the way
thirty, sixty or one hundred percent!

Father to the fatherless, Defender of widows, who
sets the lonely in families and leads forth the
prisoners with singing, I want to be available to
You today to hear and understand . . . in the
name of Jesus, the Firstfruits.

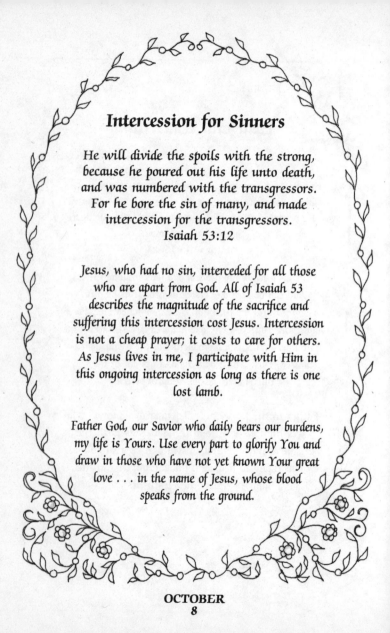

Intercession for Sinners

He will divide the spoils with the strong,
because he poured out his life unto death,
and was numbered with the transgressors.
For he bore the sin of many, and made
intercession for the transgressors.
Isaiah 53:12

Jesus, who had no sin, interceded for all those
who are apart from God. All of Isaiah 53
describes the magnitude of the sacrifice and
suffering this intercession cost Jesus. Intercession
is not a cheap prayer; it costs to care for others.
As Jesus lives in me, I participate with Him in
this ongoing intercession as long as there is one
lost lamb.

Father God, our Savior who daily bears our burdens,
my life is Yours. Use every part to glorify You and
draw in those who have not yet known Your great
love . . . in the name of Jesus, whose blood
speaks from the ground.

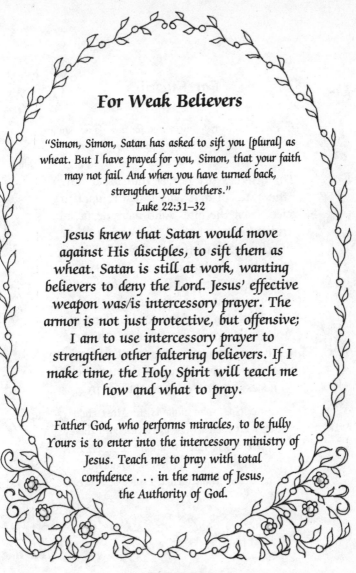

For Weak Believers

"Simon, Simon, Satan has asked to sift you [plural] as wheat. But I have prayed for you, Simon, that your faith may not fail. And when you have turned back, strengthen your brothers."
Luke 22:31–32

Jesus knew that Satan would move against His disciples, to sift them as wheat. Satan is still at work, wanting believers to deny the Lord. Jesus' effective weapon was/is intercessory prayer. The armor is not just protective, but offensive; I am to use intercessory prayer to strengthen other faltering believers. If I make time, the Holy Spirit will teach me how and what to pray.

Father God, who performs miracles, to be fully Yours is to enter into the intercessory ministry of Jesus. Teach me to pray with total confidence . . . in the name of Jesus, the Authority of God.

For Enemies

Jesus said, "Father, forgive them, for they do not know
what they are doing."
Luke 23:34

The intercessory prayer that broke down
the gates of hell was Jesus' refusal to
reject even the ones who were despising,
ridiculing, torturing, murdering Him.
"Father, forgive them, they don't know
what they are doing" was His cry from
the cross. What did they not know? The
plan of God was to conquer the world He
had created through love instead of
through force. As I enter into the
intercession of Jesus, this must become my
heart cry as well, and go through hell if
necessary to set the captives free.

Father God, who alone is the Most High
over all the earth, I intercede with the
forgiveness of Jesus today for _____
. . . in the name of Jesus, Wonderful
Counselor, Mighty God, Prince of Peace.

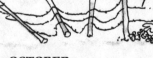

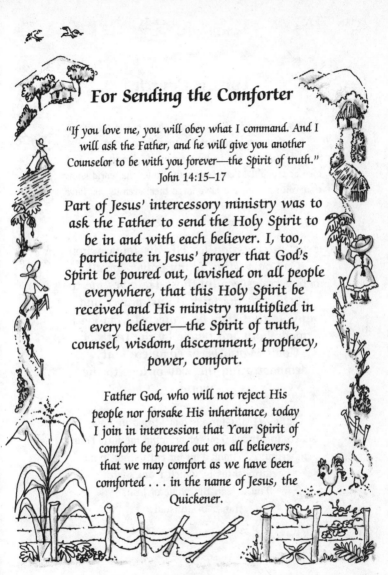

For Sending the Comforter

"If you love me, you will obey what I command. And I will ask the Father, and he will give you another Counselor to be with you forever—the Spirit of truth."
John 14:15–17

Part of Jesus' intercessory ministry was to ask the Father to send the Holy Spirit to be in and with each believer. I, too, participate in Jesus' prayer that God's Spirit be poured out, lavished on all people everywhere, that this Holy Spirit be received and His ministry multiplied in every believer—the Spirit of truth, counsel, wisdom, discernment, prophecy, power, comfort.

Father God, who will not reject His people nor forsake His inheritance, today I join in intercession that Your Spirit of comfort be poured out on all believers, that we may comfort as we have been comforted . . . in the name of Jesus, the Quickener.

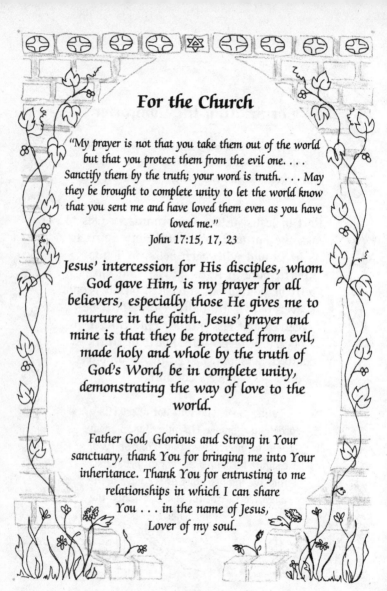

For the Church

"My prayer is not that you take them out of the world but that you protect them from the evil one. . . . Sanctify them by the truth; your word is truth. . . . May they be brought to complete unity to let the world know that you sent me and have loved them even as you have loved me."

John 17:15, 17, 23

Jesus' intercession for His disciples, whom God gave Him, is my prayer for all believers, especially those He gives me to nurture in the faith. Jesus' prayer and mine is that they be protected from evil, made holy and whole by the truth of God's Word, be in complete unity, demonstrating the way of love to the world.

Father God, Glorious and Strong in Your sanctuary, thank You for bringing me into Your inheritance. Thank You for entrusting to me relationships in which I can share You . . . in the name of Jesus, Lover of my soul.

Intercede in God's Will

. . . The Spirit helps us in our weakness. We do not know what we ought to pray, but the Spirit himself intercedes for us with groans that words cannot express.
Romans 8:26

What is God's will? There is One who always knows God's will in every situation. The Holy Spirit intercedes for me and helps me pray for others in a way that bonds with God's own highest and best. Sometimes I have experienced a wordless groaning prayer that, like a dentist's drill, bores into the decay to remove it. Then God works to fill the weak place with His strength.

Father God, as I confront a disturbing situation that I am unable to change, I lift it to You in a prayer beyond my capacity, that the Spirit's intercession will get the job done . . . in the name of Jesus, our measureless Immortality.

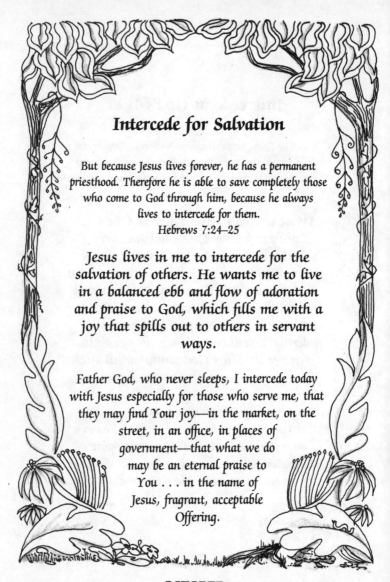

Intercede for Salvation

But because Jesus lives forever, he has a permanent
priesthood. Therefore he is able to save completely those
who come to God through him, because he always
lives to intercede for them.
Hebrews 7:24–25

Jesus lives in me to intercede for the
salvation of others. He wants me to live
in a balanced ebb and flow of adoration
and praise to God, which fills me with a
joy that spills out to others in servant
ways.

Father God, who never sleeps, I intercede today
with Jesus especially for those who serve me, that
they may find Your joy—in the market, on the
street, in an office, in places of
government—that what we do
may be an eternal praise to
You . . . in the name of
Jesus, fragrant, acceptable
Offering.

Heal Our Land

"If my people, who are called by my name, will humble
themselves and pray and seek my face and turn from
their wicked ways, then will I hear from heaven and
will forgive their sin and will heal their land.
2 Chronicles 7:14

God wants to restore paradise to His
people, but requires His people to
participate actively. As I write, ragged
Nicaraguan children of our neighborhood
play, laughing in the street outside my
door. What will it take for there to be
healing of their war-torn land? I have
walked dusty roads with Christians here,
and knelt on burning pavement, praying.
God's Word is true. He will heal their
land, but my people must recognize and
repent of ways we have hurt others.

Father God, our lands need healing.
Come quickly, Lord Jesus. Lead
Your people in the way of
humility. Enable us to see
and turn from all
wickedness.

Heal Waywardness

"Come, let us return to the Lord. He has torn us to
pieces but he will heal us; he has injured us but he will
bind up our wounds." "I will heal their waywardness
and love them freely, for my anger has turned away from
them."

Hosea 6:1, 14:4

Little Israel trusted in military might, in alliances with
superpowers of her day, and worshiped gods made with
her own hands.

This rebellion, waywardness led her away from God and
His protection. God took sides politically as well as
spiritually. He wanted leaders who again and again
would bring His people back to deeds of love and justice.

Father God, who comes to judge the world in
righteousness, the peoples with equity, today I
intercede for my people who call You God, that we
trust only You, worship only You . . . in the name
of Jesus, God's King, the Key.

Jehovah - JESUS: our HEALER

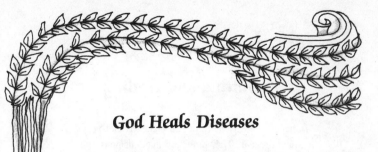

God Heals Diseases

Praise the Lord, O my soul, and forget not all his
benefits. He forgives all my sins and heals all my
diseases; he redeems my life from the pit and crowns me
with
love and compassion.
Psalm 103:2–4

This entire psalm is a witness, a praise to the writer's
experience of who God is. I pray today clothed in my
provision from the generous God of the universe, the
armor of light, which is salvation, truth, justice, love,
peace, faith and the Word of God inspired by the Holy
Spirit. This Word says God heals all my diseases,
forgives all my sins and much more. The resurrected
Jesus, who lives in me, touches me with healing and
reaches out through me to touch another.

Father God, Compassionate and Gracious, today I
yield my will, my imagination, my body and
spirit into Your healing hands . . . in the name
of Jesus, the Potter.

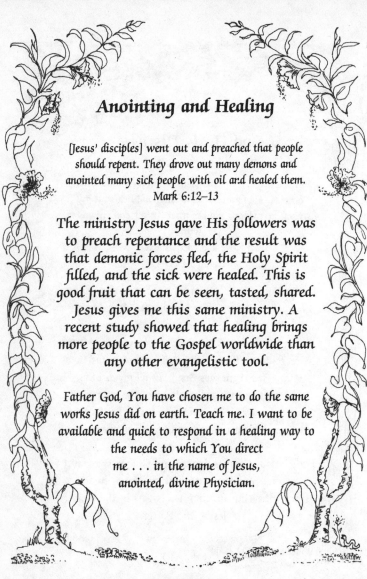

Anointing and Healing

[Jesus' disciples] went out and preached that people
should repent. They drove out many demons and
anointed many sick people with oil and healed them.
Mark 6:12–13

The ministry Jesus gave His followers was
to preach repentance and the result was
that demonic forces fled, the Holy Spirit
filled, and the sick were healed. This is
good fruit that can be seen, tasted, shared.
Jesus gives me this same ministry. A
recent study showed that healing brings
more people to the Gospel worldwide than
any other evangelistic tool.

Father God, You have chosen me to do the same
works Jesus did on earth. Teach me. I want to be
available and quick to respond in a healing way to
the needs to which You direct
me . . . in the name of Jesus,
anointed, divine Physician.

Healing from Satan's Power

"This is the message God sent to the people of Israel, . . . how God anointed Jesus of Nazareth with the Holy Spirit and power, and how he went around doing good and healing all who were under the power of the devil, because God was with him."

Acts 10:36, 38

Jesus has won the victory over all the principalities—the chiefs in the ranks of evil—and powers—the superhuman forces of privilege and control. Jesus shares His authority, His dynamic, miraculous power, with all believers. As I desire intensely to be clothed in His gifts and stay in tune with His creative song, the instruments of despair, depression and death are defeated.

Father God, who sends forth
Your Word to heal, I consecrate
myself to be Your humble
instrument of peace and of
liberating power today . . . in
the name of Jesus, Name above
all names.

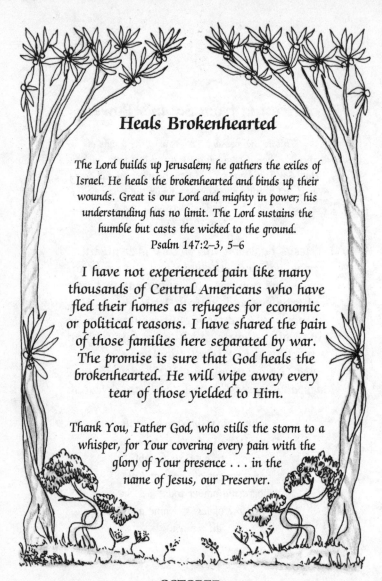

Heals Brokenhearted

The Lord builds up Jerusalem; he gathers the exiles of
Israel. He heals the brokenhearted and binds up their
wounds. Great is our Lord and mighty in power; his
understanding has no limit. The Lord sustains the
humble but casts the wicked to the ground.
Psalm 147:2–3, 5–6

I have not experienced pain like many
thousands of Central Americans who have
fled their homes as refugees for economic
or political reasons. I have shared the pain
of those families here separated by war.
The promise is sure that God heals the
brokenhearted. He will wipe away every
tear of those yielded to Him.

Thank You, Father God, who stills the storm to a
whisper, for Your covering every pain with the
glory of Your presence . . . in the
name of Jesus, our Preserver.

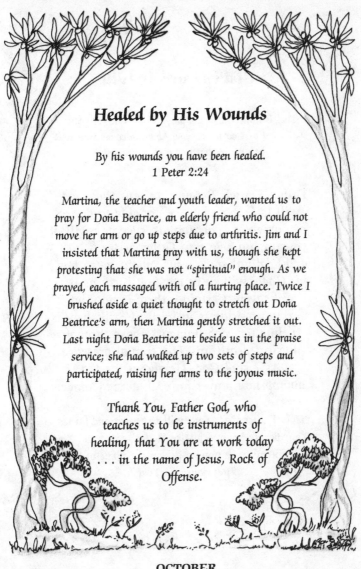

Healed by His Wounds

By his wounds you have been healed.
1 Peter 2:24

Martina, the teacher and youth leader, wanted us to
pray for Doña Beatrice, an elderly friend who could not
move her arm or go up steps due to arthritis. Jim and I
insisted that Martina pray with us, though she kept
protesting that she was not "spiritual" enough. As we
prayed, each massaged with oil a hurting place. Twice I
brushed aside a quiet thought to stretch out Doña
Beatrice's arm, then Martina gently stretched it out.
Last night Doña Beatrice sat beside us in the praise
service; she had walked up two sets of steps and
participated, raising her arms to the joyous music.

Thank You, Father God, who
teaches us to be instruments of
healing, that You are at work today
. . . in the name of Jesus, Rock of
Offense.

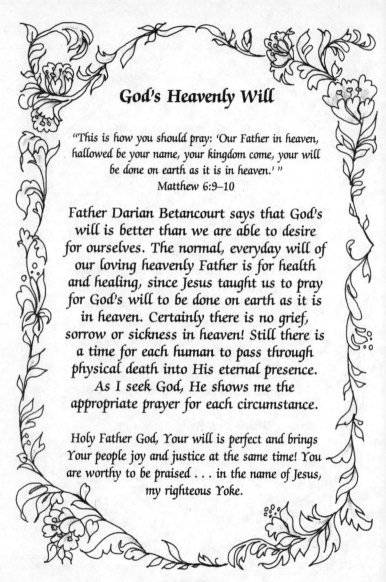

God's Heavenly Will

"This is how you should pray: 'Our Father in heaven,
hallowed be your name, your kingdom come, your will
be done on earth as it is in heaven.' "
Matthew 6:9–10

Father Darian Betancourt says that God's
will is better than we are able to desire
for ourselves. The normal, everyday will of
our loving heavenly Father is for health
and healing, since Jesus taught us to pray
for God's will to be done on earth as it is
in heaven. Certainly there is no grief,
sorrow or sickness in heaven! Still there is
a time for each human to pass through
physical death into His eternal presence.
As I seek God, He shows me the
appropriate prayer for each circumstance.

Holy Father God, Your will is perfect and brings
Your people joy and justice at the same time! You
are worthy to be praised . . . in the name of Jesus,
my righteous Yoke.

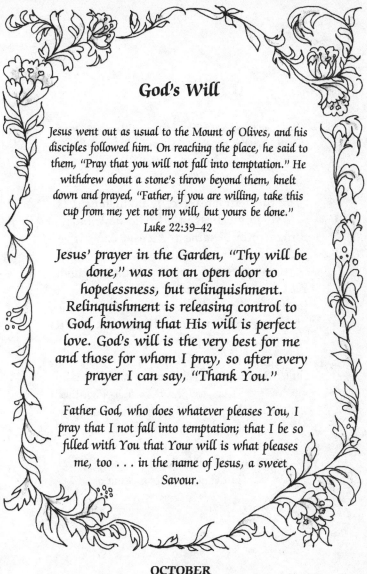

God's Will

Jesus went out as usual to the Mount of Olives, and his disciples followed him. On reaching the place, he said to them, "Pray that you will not fall into temptation." He withdrew about a stone's throw beyond them, knelt down and prayed, "Father, if you are willing, take this cup from me; yet not my will, but yours be done."
Luke 22:39–42

Jesus' prayer in the Garden, "Thy will be done," was not an open door to hopelessness, but relinquishment. Relinquishment is releasing control to God, knowing that His will is perfect love. God's will is the very best for me and those for whom I pray, so after every prayer I can say, "Thank You."

Father God, who does whatever pleases You, I pray that I not fall into temptation; that I be so filled with You that Your will is what pleases me, too . . . in the name of Jesus, a sweet Savour.

Yielding

Jesus called out with a loud voice, "Father, into your hands I commit my spirit." When he had said this, he breathed his last.

Luke 23:46

The ultimate prayer of relinquishment is, first, forgiveness of all who have hurt, then total yielding to God of one's life. God does the resurrection work, totally destroying Satan's power. This was done on the cross, and my part is to participate in the forgiveness, the yielding and the joy of resurrection triumph. Death has lost its sting! Hallelujah!

Father God, who has delivered my soul from death, my eyes from tears, my feet from stumbling, that I may walk before the Lord in the land of the living (Psalm 116), reveal to me ways I have not yielded to You, so that Your will will reign in me today . . . in the name of Jesus, King of the Jews.

Good from Evil

And we know that in all things God works for the
good of those who love him, who have been called
according to his purpose.
Romans 8:28

This does not mean that my life is sitting
on a silk cushion with no conflict. I am in
but not of the world, so I will experience
every worldly temptation, even as Jesus
did. The martyrs of the faith in the Bible
(Hebrews 11) and now were/are not
comfortable in their hunger, tortures,
imprisonment, death, but good does come.
Not one tear or drop of blood is wasted in
the bringing about of God's happy reign on
earth.

Father God, today I pray for all who are suffering
for their faith in any way. Strengthen, encourage
them, demonstrate Your supreme
power to the principalities and
powers, and bring good out of the
evil . . . in the name of Jesus, the
Forerunner.

Submit Desires to God

When you ask, you do not receive, because you ask with wrong motives, that you may spend what you get on your pleasures. Submit yourselves . . . to God. Resist the devil, and he will flee from you.

James 4:3, 7

In the context of answered prayers, God sees the motives for my asking. God knows my doublemindedness, the ways I am drawn to the comforts and things of the world rather than to that which builds up love and peace in the world. God knows I need grace, mercy in order to learn the lessons that strip me of pride and greed. God teaches me to recognize and resist the devil, and so rejoice in answered prayer.

Father God, who answers me in my anguish, who helps me triumph over Satan, purify my heart today and show me the prayer of Your heart . . . in the name of Jesus, Heir to the Kingdom of heaven.

In God's Will

This is the assurance we have in approaching God: that
if we ask anything according to his will, he hears us.
And if we know that he hears us—whatever we
ask—we know that we have what we asked of him.
1 John 5:14–15

God wants me to pray because He has
designed my prayers to be part of the
liberating force that sets people free from
sin, death and Satan's traps. I don't
understand this, but part of the benefit
and obligation of union with God in Jesus'
name is that I participate in God's will
being done *now*, here in concrete physical
ways and in invisible spiritual ways.

Father God, my Strength, Song and Salvation,
today I participate with You in specific prayer for
_____ , cutting off the enemy . . . in
the name of Jesus, the Avenger.

The Lord's Prayer

In the awareness that the great God of the
universe is my loving Parent and I am
joined in a great family of believers, I
acknowledge God's perfect holiness, God's
perfect authority to govern all the earth in
the same way He governs the glorious
realm of heaven, where there is no sorrow,
sickness or death. I ask, confident that it
is God's will, that today all God's family
and mine have enough to eat, that all
God's family and mine be forgiven for
every sin in the same way we forgive
every sin against us. I ask, confident that
it is God's will, that today we walk in
paths of peace, not of temptation. Today
we resist and triumph over all the evil
forces of Satan . . . in the name of Jesus,
who prays with me.
Matthew 6:9–13,
paraphrased

Delight in the Lord

Delight yourself in the Lord and he will give you the
desires of your heart. Commit your way to the Lord;
trust in him and he will do this: He will make your
righteousness shine like the dawn, the justice of your
cause like the noonday sun.

Psalm 37:4–6

As I delight in the Lord, the desires of my
heart conform to the things that please
Him. As I trust in the Lord, that God's
justice will be done in all the earth, that
those who look to God will have their
needs met, I release anger and striving,
and become a person of peace, making
peace in a peaceful way. This is a good
message for my birthday!

Father God, You have made this day, so I
rejoice and am glad in it! Today I commit
my desires and my direction totally to You
. . . in the name of Jesus, Desired of all
nations.

Perfect in Love

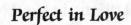

> "Be perfect, therefore, as your heavenly Father is
> perfect."
> Matthew 5:48

In Jesus' teaching on the Mount, He describes every
facet of human life: money and possessions, sex and
marriage, prayer, fasting, judging, murder and anger, the
poor, the enemy, the persecuted. He states I must be
perfect, whole, complete in every area; but surely this is
impossible! Why would Jesus teach such ideals? Perhaps
He wants me to see how penetrating God's standard is
to the core of my daily life and the motives of my heart.
That removes any possibility of pride and sets me on the
same footing as any other human being—in need of
God's mercy.

Father God, who has made Your light shine on
me, I praise You that in Your love and mercy all
believers are joined to You, made whole, complete
. . . in the name of Jesus, our Consolation.

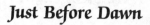

Just Before Dawn

On my bed I remember you; I think of you
through the watches of the night. Because you
are my help, I sing in the shadow of your wings.
Psalm 63:6–7

Doña Julia's favorite time for prayer, and
advice for those who would receive more
from God, is to pray "just before dawn."
The stillness of human activity encourages
listening. Penetrating insights come that
can be acted on later in the day. It is a
time of communion, of being bathed in
God's light through the darkness, of seeing
things as they really are. Some are called
to watch before dawn, others late at
night, but each needs to find that space
and time of quiet listening.

Father God, Father of lights, I want my quality
time to be all Yours, so that I do not miss what
You want to communicate . . . in
the name of Jesus, my Treasure.

Armor of Light

Let us put aside the deeds of darkness and put on the armor of light. . . . Clothe yourselves with the Lord Jesus Christ.
Romans 13:12, 14

Agnes Sanford's *The Healing Light* first caused me to wonder if there wasn't more to the Christian life than my shabby efforts. She urged her readers to picture Jesus as filled with light. When there are conflicts or disease or any prayer concern, I can imagine Jesus in the center of the situation, His light touching, consuming, cleansing, making brilliantly new both me and the person/situation for whom I pray. The Greek word for *light* means "to shine, make manifest by rays, luminousness, fire." This is the armor I put on today.

Father God, today I use sanctified imagination to touch all I see with Your glorious light . . . in the name of Jesus, the Brightness of God's glory.

Yoke

"Take my yoke upon you and learn from me, for I am gentle and humble in heart, and you will find rest for your souls. For my yoke is easy and my burden is light."
Matthew 11:29–30

Jesus calls me to come to Him in my weariness and give Him my burdens in exchange for His yoke, which is easy and light. Here in Nicaragua, farmers still use oxen, which pull together by carved wooden yokes. So many times I take on burdens too heavy for me, or go in directions not good for me. His yoke is lightweight, custom-made, designed to give me refreshment. It recreates my body, soul and spirit, as I am joined harmoniously with other believers, my husband, children, neighbors. . . .

Father God, who watches over my coming in and going out now and forever, today I put on the yoke of Jesus, and rest in Your will with those You give me . . . in the name of Jesus, my Shelter, Shade.

Wedding Garment

"Friend," he asked, "how did you get in here without
wedding clothes?" The man was speechless.
Matthew 22:12

It was our custom to bring groups of campers from the
top of the mountain at Pioneer Plunge to worship in a
small Baptist church in the valley. We carried peanut
butter sandwiches and dried fruit to eat afterward. One
sunny day was the church's homecoming celebration.
They spread out tables, filling every space with steaming
casseroles of vegetables, huge hams, fried chicken, fruit
pies. Our laughing campers joined in, heaping borrowed
plates with the feast, while I chose to sit, dejected, on
the grass with my dry peanut butter sandwich
embarrassed by their "gluttony." God's quiet voice spoke,
You are the only one here without a wedding garment.

Father God, who invites me, prepare me to
receive as well as to give . . . in the name of
Jesus, who wants
our joy full.

Put on Trust

"Therefore I tell you, do not worry about your life,
what you will eat; or about your body, what you
will wear. Life is more than food and the body more
than clothes."
Luke 12:22–23

It is terrible to see someone clothed in
worry: anxious lines on the face, darting
eyes, bowed back, as if all the world's
burdens are there. It is awesome to see
trust, like a light shining forth in the
midst of dark circumstances. To worry or
trust is a choice, a decision. I have seen
both in rich and in poor. I have
experienced the crushing weight of worry
and the expectant glow of trust. I choose
this day and each day whom to serve.

Father God, Covenant-Keeper, eminently
Trustworthy, guide me in the trust-filled way . . .
in the name of Jesus, Kinsman-Redeemer.

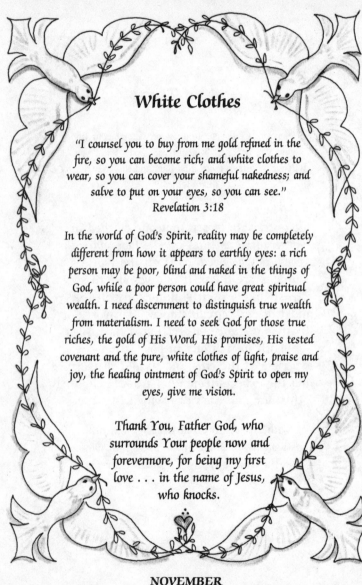

White Clothes

"I counsel you to buy from me gold refined in the
fire, so you can become rich; and white clothes to
wear, so you can cover your shameful nakedness; and
salve to put on your eyes, so you can see."
Revelation 3:18

In the world of God's Spirit, reality may be completely
different from how it appears to earthly eyes: a rich
person may be poor, blind and naked in the things of
God, while a poor person could have great spiritual
wealth. I need discernment to distinguish true wealth
from materialism. I need to seek God for those true
riches, the gold of His Word, His promises, His tested
covenant and the pure, white clothes of light, praise and
joy, the healing ointment of God's Spirit to open my
eyes, give me vision.

Thank You, Father God, who
surrounds Your people now and
forevermore, for being my first
love . . . in the name of Jesus,
who knocks.

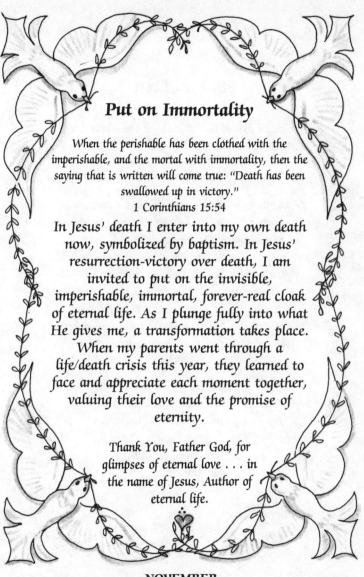

Put on Immortality

When the perishable has been clothed with the imperishable, and the mortal with immortality, then the saying that is written will come true: "Death has been swallowed up in victory."
1 Corinthians 15:54

In Jesus' death I enter into my own death now, symbolized by baptism. In Jesus' resurrection-victory over death, I am invited to put on the invisible, imperishable, immortal, forever-real cloak of eternal life. As I plunge fully into what He gives me, a transformation takes place. When my parents went through a life/death crisis this year, they learned to face and appreciate each moment together, valuing their love and the promise of eternity.

Thank You, Father God, for glimpses of eternal love . . . in the name of Jesus, Author of eternal life.

Put on Christ

You are all sons of God through faith in Christ Jesus,
for all of you who were baptized into Christ have
clothed yourselves with Christ.
Galatians 3:26–27

To describe being clothed with Christ, the apostle Paul
says we are inheritors of God's promise and God chooses
not to distinguish between Jew and Greek, slave and
free, male and female. Jim would include young and old,
black and white, rich and poor. All believers have the
advantages and responsibilities of being heirs. Jesus' way
of love, of service, His treatment of conflicts and
enemies is what influences and motivates me, rather
than my class, race, culture, sex, age or religious
orientation.

Father God, forgive me for ways I emphasize
divisive things You have covered with the blood of
Jesus—in me and in others. Cleanse me of
anything that does not build up Your Body
. . . in the name of Jesus,
our Advocate.

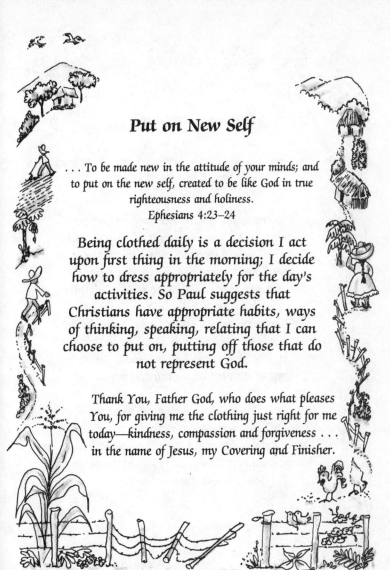

Put on New Self

... To be made new in the attitude of your minds; and to put on the new self, created to be like God in true righteousness and holiness.

Ephesians 4:23–24

Being clothed daily is a decision I act upon first thing in the morning; I decide how to dress appropriately for the day's activities. So Paul suggests that Christians have appropriate habits, ways of thinking, speaking, relating that I can choose to put on, putting off those that do not represent God.

Thank You, Father God, who does what pleases You, for giving me the clothing just right for me today—kindness, compassion and forgiveness ... in the name of Jesus, my Covering and Finisher.

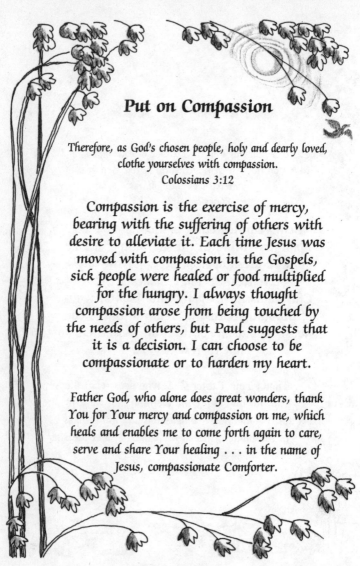

Put on Compassion

Therefore, as God's chosen people, holy and dearly loved,
clothe yourselves with compassion.
Colossians 3:12

Compassion is the exercise of mercy,
bearing with the suffering of others with
desire to alleviate it. Each time Jesus was
moved with compassion in the Gospels,
sick people were healed or food multiplied
for the hungry. I always thought
compassion arose from being touched by
the needs of others, but Paul suggests that
it is a decision. I can choose to be
compassionate or to harden my heart.

Father God, who alone does great wonders, thank
You for Your mercy and compassion on me, which
heals and enables me to come forth again to care,
serve and share Your healing . . . in the name of
Jesus, compassionate Comforter.

Put on Kindness

Therefore, as God's chosen people, holy and dearly loved,
clothe yourselves with . . . kindness.
Colossians 3:12

Today I put on kindness: usefulness,
moral excellence in character, gentleness,
goodness. What can I do as special acts of
kindness, maybe as anonymous surprises,
that would bless someone?

Father God, who is kind to the ungrateful, lead me
in Your ways of kindness to others today, whether
or not they deserve it, whether or not I feel like it
. . . in the name of Jesus, Longsuffering and Kind.

Put on Humility

Therefore, as God's chosen people, holy and dearly
loved, clothe yourselves with . . . humility.
Colossians 3:12

Today I put on humility, recognizing the
lowliness of my understanding, the
earthiness of my feelings, the limits of my
wisdom, as I look at the incomparable
greatness of Jesus. The Nicaraguan folk
mass describes Jesus as God of the poor,
picturing Him sunburned, sweaty in the
street; God the laborer, Christ the worker.
This picture offends some who want an
ethereal God to worship from afar, but
Jesus promised we would be serving Him
as we serve the poor. Today I want to
serve in such a way that those I serve see
Jesus in themselves and so rejoice!

Father God, whose greatness no one
can fathom, show me today the
path of true humility and gratitude
. . . in the name of Jesus, Servant
of all.

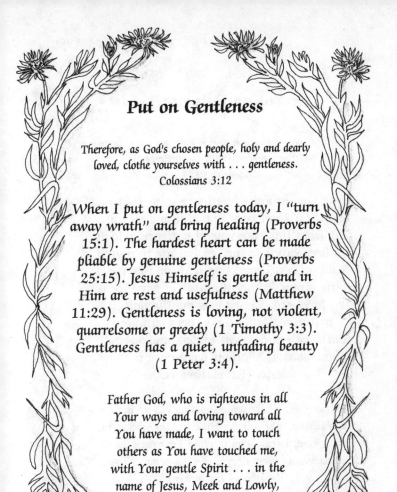

Put on Gentleness

Therefore, as God's chosen people, holy and dearly
loved, clothe yourselves with . . . gentleness.
Colossians 3:12

When I put on gentleness today, I "turn
away wrath" and bring healing (Proverbs
15:1). The hardest heart can be made
pliable by genuine gentleness (Proverbs
25:15). Jesus Himself is gentle and in
Him are rest and usefulness (Matthew
11:29). Gentleness is loving, not violent,
quarrelsome or greedy (1 Timothy 3:3).
Gentleness has a quiet, unfading beauty
(1 Peter 3:4).

Father God, who is righteous in all
Your ways and loving toward all
You have made, I want to touch
others as You have touched me,
with Your gentle Spirit . . . in the
name of Jesus, Meek and Lowly,
Gracious in every way.

Put on Patience

Therefore, as God's chosen people, holy and dearly loved,
clothe yourselves with . . . patience.
Colossians 3:12

Jesus has unlimited patience with sinners. For that I am very thankful and so can take from this reservoir of patience, which has been given to me, as I relate to myself and others. Love is patient, and as the Spirit grows in me, the fruit of patience is produced. That takes me through irritations, afflictions, persecutions. Patience brings great understanding and calms quarrels. Patient endurance is mine in Jesus (Revelation 1:9).

Father God, whose understanding has no limit, who sustains the humble but casts the wicked to the ground, I trust You to grow Your patience in me today, and every day . . . in the name of Jesus, Repairer of the broken.

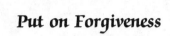

Put on Forgiveness

Bear with each other and forgive whatever grievances
you may have against one another. Forgive as the
Lord forgave you.
Colossians 3:13

Frankly, freely forgive, pardon or rescue in
kindness, as a favor granted. God has
placed me in a family, a neighborhood, a
church, a nation. As I learn more of Jesus,
I must learn how to forgive, for there will
be daily testings. When I turn the
spotlight away from the other person's
wrongs onto my own failures and
shortcomings, it will be easier to forgive,
for I will recognize my own need.

Father God, who sets prisoners free and gives sight
to the blind, open my eyes to see the good in those
who need my forgiveness today . . . in the name of
Jesus, the Sanctifier.

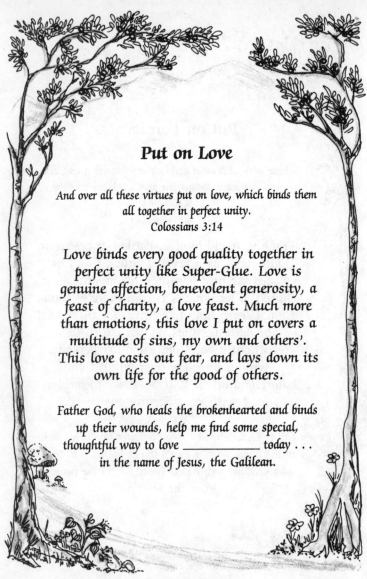

Put on Love

And over all these virtues put on love, which binds them
all together in perfect unity.
Colossians 3:14

Love binds every good quality together in
perfect unity like Super-Glue. Love is
genuine affection, benevolent generosity, a
feast of charity, a love feast. Much more
than emotions, this love I put on covers a
multitude of sins, my own and others'.
This love casts out fear, and lays down its
own life for the good of others.

Father God, who heals the brokenhearted and binds
up their wounds, help me find some special,
thoughtful way to love _____ today . . .
in the name of Jesus, the Galilean.

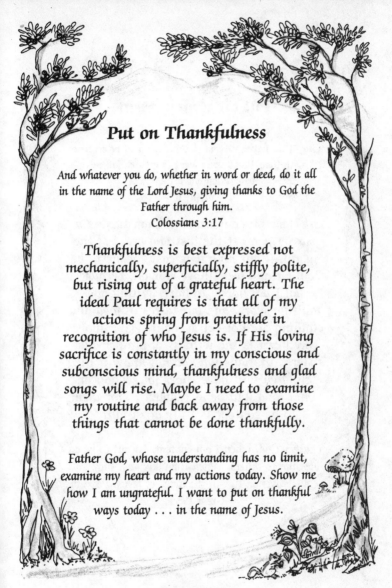

Put on Thankfulness

And whatever you do, whether in word or deed, do it all in the name of the Lord Jesus, giving thanks to God the Father through him.
Colossians 3:17

Thankfulness is best expressed not mechanically, superficially, stiffly polite, but rising out of a grateful heart. The ideal Paul requires is that all of my actions spring from gratitude in recognition of who Jesus is. If His loving sacrifice is constantly in my conscious and subconscious mind, thankfulness and glad songs will rise. Maybe I need to examine my routine and back away from those things that cannot be done thankfully.

Father God, whose understanding has no limit, examine my heart and my actions today. Show me how I am ungrateful. I want to put on thankful ways today . . . in the name of Jesus.

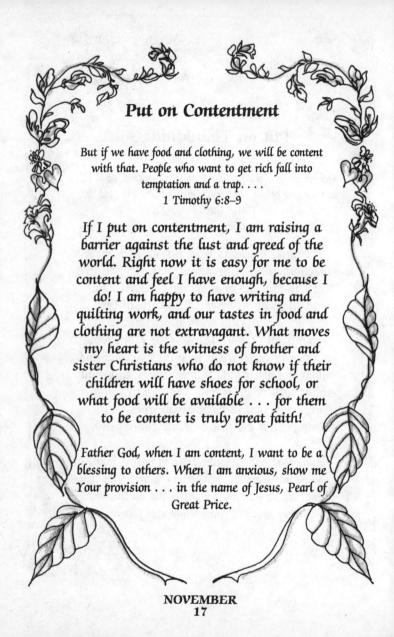

Put on Contentment

But if we have food and clothing, we will be content
with that. People who want to get rich fall into
temptation and a trap. . . .
1 Timothy 6:8–9

If I put on contentment, I am raising a
barrier against the lust and greed of the
world. Right now it is easy for me to be
content and feel I have enough, because I
do! I am happy to have writing and
quilting work, and our tastes in food and
clothing are not extravagant. What moves
my heart is the witness of brother and
sister Christians who do not know if their
children will have shoes for school, or
what food will be available . . . for them
to be content is truly great faith!

Father God, when I am content, I want to be a
blessing to others. When I am anxious, show me
Your provision . . . in the name of Jesus, Pearl of
Great Price.

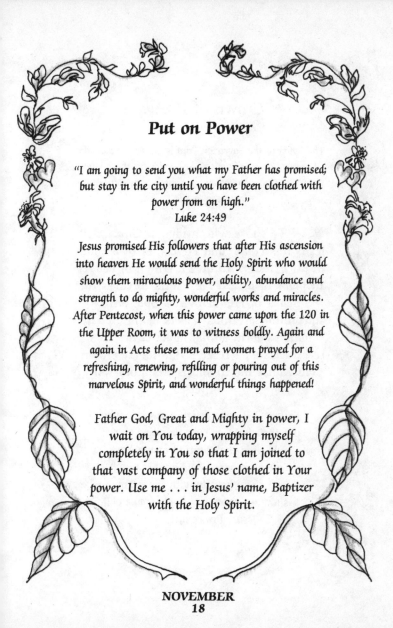

Put on Power

"I am going to send you what my Father has promised;
but stay in the city until you have been clothed with
power from on high."
Luke 24:49

Jesus promised His followers that after His ascension
into heaven He would send the Holy Spirit who would
show them miraculous power, ability, abundance and
strength to do mighty, wonderful works and miracles.
After Pentecost, when this power came upon the 120 in
the Upper Room, it was to witness boldly. Again and
again in Acts these men and women prayed for a
refreshing, renewing, refilling or pouring out of this
marvelous Spirit, and wonderful things happened!

Father God, Great and Mighty in power, I
wait on You today, wrapping myself
completely in You so that I am joined to
that vast company of those clothed in Your
power. Use me . . . in Jesus' name, Baptizer
with the Holy Spirit.

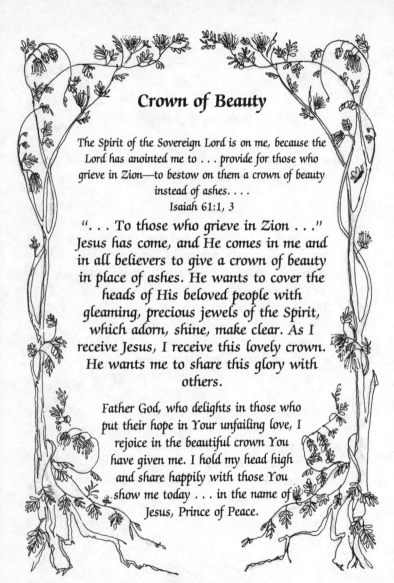

Crown of Beauty

The Spirit of the Sovereign Lord is on me, because the
Lord has anointed me to . . . provide for those who
grieve in Zion—to bestow on them a crown of beauty
instead of ashes. . . .

Isaiah 61:1, 3

". . . To those who grieve in Zion . . ."
Jesus has come, and He comes in me and
in all believers to give a crown of beauty
in place of ashes. He wants to cover the
heads of His beloved people with
gleaming, precious jewels of the Spirit,
which adorn, shine, make clear. As I
receive Jesus, I receive this lovely crown.
He wants me to share this glory with
others.

Father God, who delights in those who
put their hope in Your unfailing love, I
rejoice in the beautiful crown You
have given me. I hold my head high
and share happily with those You
show me today . . . in the name of
Jesus, Prince of Peace.

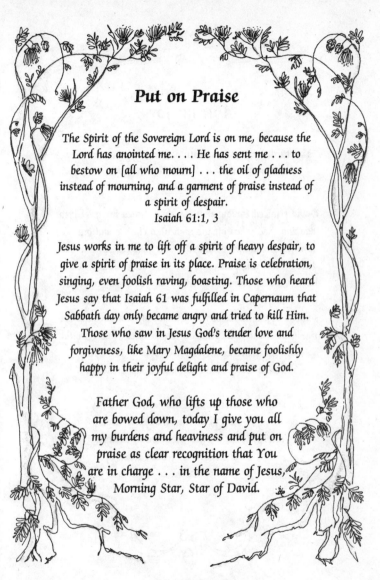

Put on Praise

The Spirit of the Sovereign Lord is on me, because the
Lord has anointed me. . . . He has sent me . . . to
bestow on [all who mourn] . . . the oil of gladness
instead of mourning, and a garment of praise instead of
a spirit of despair.
Isaiah 61:1, 3

Jesus works in me to lift off a spirit of heavy despair, to
give a spirit of praise in its place. Praise is celebration,
singing, even foolish raving, boasting. Those who heard
Jesus say that Isaiah 61 was fulfilled in Capernaum that
Sabbath day only became angry and tried to kill Him.
Those who saw in Jesus God's tender love and
forgiveness, like Mary Magdalene, became foolishly
happy in their joyful delight and praise of God.

Father God, who lifts up those who
are bowed down, today I give you all
my burdens and heaviness and put on
praise as clear recognition that You
are in charge . . . in the name of Jesus,
Morning Star, Star of David.

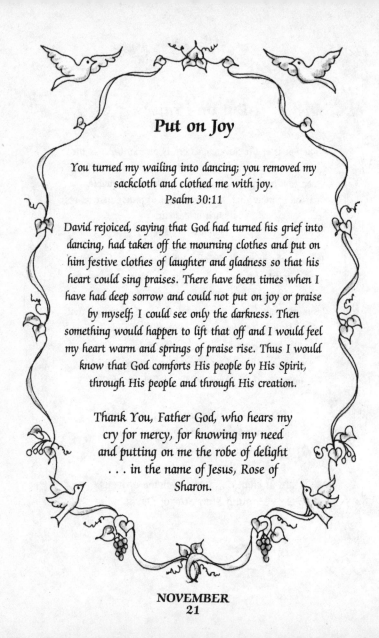

Put on Joy

*You turned my wailing into dancing; you removed my
sackcloth and clothed me with joy.*
Psalm 30:11

David rejoiced, saying that God had turned his grief into
dancing, had taken off the mourning clothes and put on
him festive clothes of laughter and gladness so that his
heart could sing praises. There have been times when I
have had deep sorrow and could not put on joy or praise
by myself; I could see only the darkness. Then
something would happen to lift that off and I would feel
my heart warm and springs of praise rise. Thus I would
know that God comforts His people by His Spirit,
through His people and through His creation.

Thank You, Father God, who hears my
cry for mercy, for knowing my need
and putting on me the robe of delight
. . . in the name of Jesus, Rose of
Sharon.

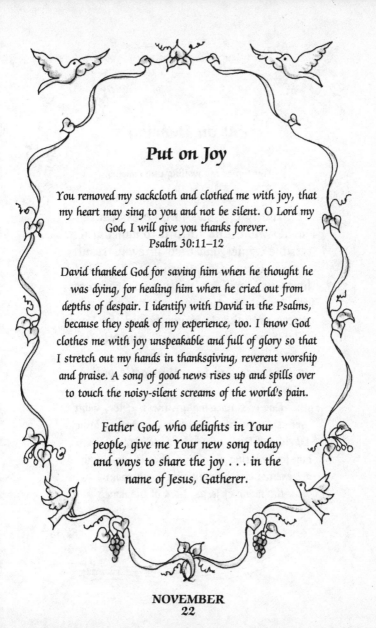

Put on Joy

You removed my sackcloth and clothed me with joy, that
my heart may sing to you and not be silent. O Lord my
God, I will give you thanks forever.
Psalm 30:11–12

David thanked God for saving him when he thought he
was dying, for healing him when he cried out from
depths of despair. I identify with David in the Psalms,
because they speak of my experience, too. I know God
clothes me with joy unspeakable and full of glory so that
I stretch out my hands in thanksgiving, reverent worship
and praise. A song of good news rises up and spills over
to touch the noisy-silent screams of the world's pain.

Father God, who delights in Your
people, give me Your new song today
and ways to share the joy . . . in the
name of Jesus, Gatherer.

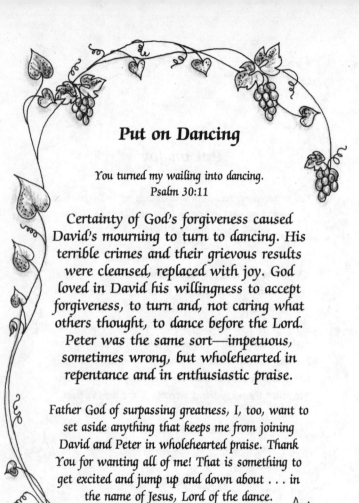

Put on Dancing

You turned my wailing into dancing.
Psalm 30:11

Certainty of God's forgiveness caused David's mourning to turn to dancing. His terrible crimes and their grievous results were cleansed, replaced with joy. God loved in David his willingness to accept forgiveness, to turn and, not caring what others thought, to dance before the Lord. Peter was the same sort—impetuous, sometimes wrong, but wholehearted in repentance and in enthusiastic praise.

Father God of surpassing greatness, I, too, want to set aside anything that keeps me from joining David and Peter in wholehearted praise. Thank You for wanting all of me! That is something to get excited and jump up and down about . . . in the name of Jesus, Lord of the dance.

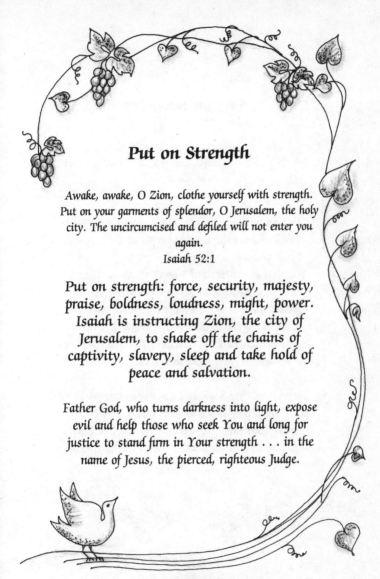

Put on Strength

Awake, awake, O Zion, clothe yourself with strength.
Put on your garments of splendor, O Jerusalem, the holy
city. The uncircumcised and defiled will not enter you
again.
Isaiah 52:1

Put on strength: force, security, majesty,
praise, boldness, loudness, might, power.
Isaiah is instructing Zion, the city of
Jerusalem, to shake off the chains of
captivity, slavery, sleep and take hold of
peace and salvation.

Father God, who turns darkness into light, expose
evil and help those who seek You and long for
justice to stand firm in Your strength . . . in the
name of Jesus, the pierced, righteous Judge.

Put on Splendor

. . . Put on your garments of splendor, O Jerusalem,
the holy city. The uncircumcised and defiled will not
enter you again.
Isaiah 52:1

Put on beauty, bravery, glory, honor, majesty,
Isaiah advises the captive people of God. Is this
"pull yourself up by your bootstraps," positive
thinking or confession? I don't think so. Despite
desperate and discouraging circumstances, God
speaks the word of encouragement through His
prophet. In order to act on this word, I need to be
utterly convinced I am hearing from God, receiving
His clear direction.

Father God, my Rock and my Redeemer, all glory
and honor and majesty are Yours. As You cover me
with Your presence today, may I reflect Your
beauty . . . in the name of Jesus, the Refiner.

Put on Strength

*She is clothed with strength and dignity; she can
laugh at the days to come.*
Proverbs 31:25

A wife of noble character, by her very being, puts on
strength: security, power, praise. She seeks good for her
husband. She is a woman of prayer, a woman
competently involved in ordering her household,
providing for her family's needs and helping the poor.
She is creative, shrewd in business and wise. Her
example instructs me in knowing my source of strength
is God, and in His becoming the glue that holds the
family together.

Father God, who arms me with strength, thank You for
the fulfillment You give me as I seek my husband's and
family's good, as I seek You in how to use the creativity
and wisdom You give me. May You get all the praise
. . . in the name of Jesus, the Almighty, the Arm of the
Lord.

Put on Dignity

She is clothed with strength and dignity. . . .
Proverbs 31:25

The woman of God is clothed in dignity: magnificence,
beauty, excellency, glory, majesty. When I think of
women whose lives are examples of Christ's sacrificial
love, none would assume these titles for herself, but
there is a radiant beauty, an inner nobility that beams
forth. Yesterday I sat with Doña Julia as her son
staggered in drunk and belligerent, after a year of not
drinking. As we prayed under our breath, he quieted,
vomited and finally lay snoring on the couch, his small
son obediently at his side. Doña Julia's closeness to God
is stronger than the circumstances around her, stronger
than evil.

Thank You, Father God, who is
faithful to those who are faithful, for
human examples to follow . . . in the
name of Jesus, the Overcomer.

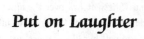

Put on Laughter

*She makes linen garments and sells them, and supplies
the merchants with sashes. She is clothed with strength
and dignity; she can laugh at the days to come.*
Proverbs 31:24–25

I never pictured the godly Proverbs woman laughing
with pleasure, making merry, playing, enjoying sports
and fun times with her family, but this is the sense of
the Hebrew word. She is a hard worker, worthy of honor
and dignity, yet is so in touch with her family that she
enjoys them in the here and now. She is so confident in
God that she does not fear what the future may bring.

Father God, my Shepherd who provides,
leads and guides me, sometimes I am too
serious; I take on burdens I am not meant
to carry. Help me enter into the laughter
and rejoicing You want for our family . . .
in the name of Jesus, the Pleasure of God.

Put on Wisdom

She speaks with wisdom, and faithful instruction is on her tongue. She watches over the affairs of her household and does not eat the bread of idleness. Her children arise and call her blessed; her husband also, and he praises her: "Many women do noble things, but you surpass them all."
Proverbs 31:26–29

God Himself is my shield, the source of all wisdom. Jesus Himself is my wisdom. As I seek out His words of wisdom, they penetrate my heart, becoming a part of me. Then, within everyday circumstances, even though my Spanish is terrible, wisdom will come forth as "faithful instruction."

Thank You, Father God, Guide and Teacher, that You confide in me, heighten my intellect, give spiritual depth to my understanding and through me enable others to say, "Praise God!" . . . in the name of Jesus, Rabbi, Master, Teacher.

Put on the Crown of Life

Blessed is the man who perseveres under trial, because when he has stood the test, he will receive the crown of life that God has promised to those who love him.
James 1:12

Putting on the crown of life is not something I can do myself because it is given after I have persevered or endured trials and tests. How I handle poverty or riches is important and God wants me to ask for wisdom, because He wants to give it to me.

Father God of the heavenly lights who gives good and perfect gifts, I need wisdom to manage what You have given, in Your way, in Your timing, according to Your eternal purpose. How should I handle the tests and trials in my life right now? . . . in the name of Jesus, the Wisdom from God.

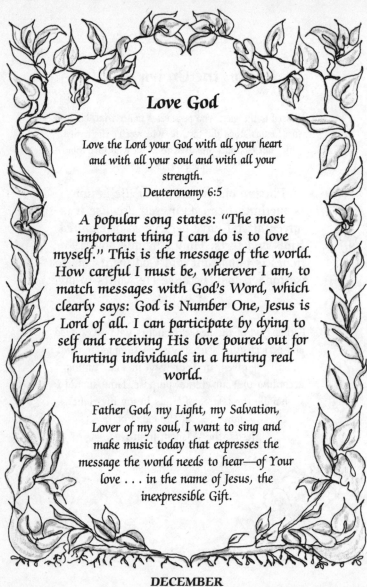

Love God

*Love the Lord your God with all your heart
and with all your soul and with all your
strength.*
Deuteronomy 6:5

A popular song states: "The most
important thing I can do is to love
myself." This is the message of the world.
How careful I must be, wherever I am, to
match messages with God's Word, which
clearly says: God is Number One, Jesus is
Lord of all. I can participate by dying to
self and receiving His love poured out for
hurting individuals in a hurting real
world.

Father God, my Light, my Salvation,
Lover of my soul, I want to sing and
make music today that expresses the
message the world needs to hear—of Your
love . . . in the name of Jesus, the
inexpressible Gift.

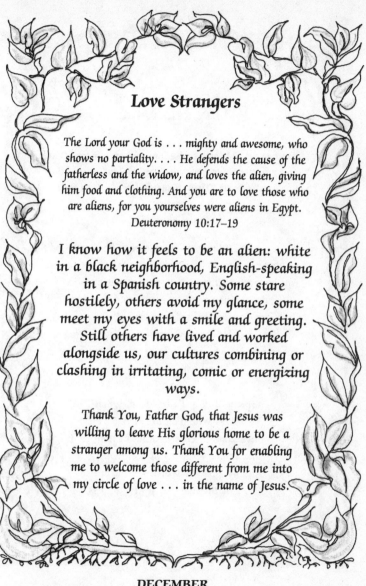

Love Strangers

The Lord your God is . . . mighty and awesome, who shows no partiality. . . . He defends the cause of the fatherless and the widow, and loves the alien, giving him food and clothing. And you are to love those who are aliens, for you yourselves were aliens in Egypt.
Deuteronomy 10:17–19

I know how it feels to be an alien: white in a black neighborhood, English-speaking in a Spanish country. Some stare hostilely, others avoid my glance, some meet my eyes with a smile and greeting. Still others have lived and worked alongside us, our cultures combining or clashing in irritating, comic or energizing ways.

Thank You, Father God, that Jesus was willing to leave His glorious home to be a stranger among us. Thank You for enabling me to welcome those different from me into my circle of love . . . in the name of Jesus.

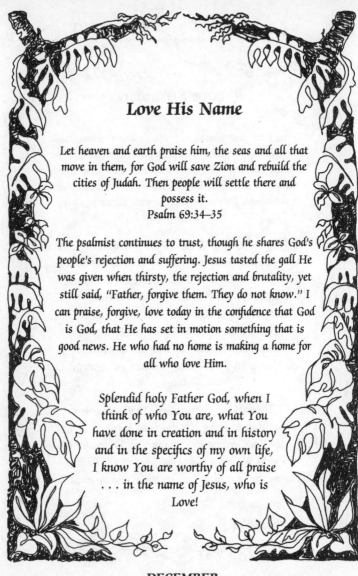

Love His Name

Let heaven and earth praise him, the seas and all that
move in them, for God will save Zion and rebuild the
cities of Judah. Then people will settle there and
possess it.
Psalm 69:34–35

The psalmist continues to trust, though he shares God's
people's rejection and suffering. Jesus tasted the gall He
was given when thirsty, the rejection and brutality, yet
still said, "Father, forgive them. They do not know." I
can praise, forgive, love today in the confidence that God
is God, that He has set in motion something that is
good news. He who had no home is making a home for
all who love Him.

Splendid holy Father God, when I
think of who You are, what You
have done in creation and in history
and in the specifics of my own life,
I know You are worthy of all praise
. . . in the name of Jesus, who is
Love!

DECEMBER
3

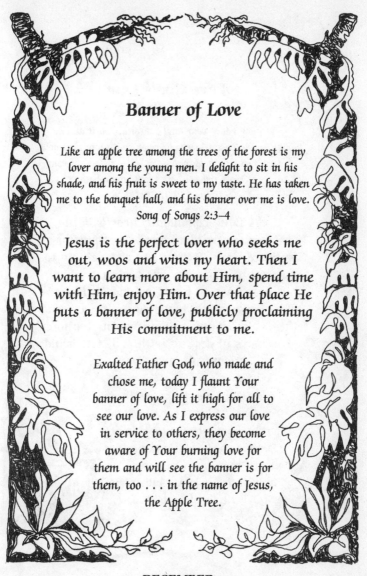

Banner of Love

Like an apple tree among the trees of the forest is my
lover among the young men. I delight to sit in his
shade, and his fruit is sweet to my taste. He has taken
me to the banquet hall, and his banner over me is love.
Song of Songs 2:3–4

Jesus is the perfect lover who seeks me
out, woos and wins my heart. Then I
want to learn more about Him, spend time
with Him, enjoy Him. Over that place He
puts a banner of love, publicly proclaiming
His commitment to me.

Exalted Father God, who made and
chose me, today I flaunt Your
banner of love, lift it high for all to
see our love. As I express our love
in service to others, they become
aware of Your burning love for
them and will see the banner is for
them, too . . . in the name of Jesus,
the Apple Tree.

Love God's Law

Oh, how I love your law! I meditate on it all day long. . . . Because I love your commands more than gold, more than pure gold, and because I consider all your precepts right, I hate every wrong path.
Psalm 119:97, 127–128

God's Law, commands, heart's desire, promises, wisdom can be accepted or rejected. It is up to me to choose how to respond to God. Like the psalmist, today I choose love, to love God and all He is, His ways, even when I do not understand them, His timing, when it seems too long, His ways of dealing with evil, His being in control when I am not.

Father God, who speaks life, thank You for the Bible, Your Word, and for inspiring it by the Holy Spirit. Open my mind and heart to receive all of it in faithful commitment . . . in the name of Jesus, Author and Perfecter of my faith.

Love Jerusalem

Pray for the peace of Jerusalem: "May those who love you be secure. May there be peace within your walls and security within your citadels." For the sake of my brothers and friends, I will say, "Peace be within you."
Psalm 122:6–8

Loving God includes loving those He loves; it is clear God loves Jerusalem, the city of peace. God loves the Jews, the sons and daughters of Israel, wherever they are found on the earth, and wants me to participate in that reaching-out love that includes and draws them in.

Father God, Father of Isaac and Ishmael, I pray for the peace of Jerusalem, that Jesus, the Prince of Peace, reign there. Penetrate the fear with Your love . . . in His name.

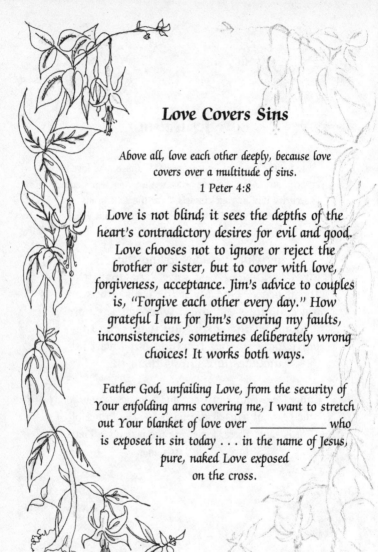

Love Covers Sins

*Above all, love each other deeply, because love
cover over a multitude of sins.*
1 Peter 4:8

Love is not blind; it sees the depths of the
heart's contradictory desires for evil and good.
Love chooses not to ignore or reject the
brother or sister, but to cover with love,
forgiveness, acceptance. Jim's advice to couples
is, "Forgive each other every day." How
grateful I am for Jim's covering my faults,
inconsistencies, sometimes deliberately wrong
choices! It works both ways.

Father God, unfailing Love, from the security of
Your enfolding arms covering me, I want to stretch
out Your blanket of love over _____ who
is exposed in sin today . . . in the name of Jesus,
pure, naked Love exposed
on the cross.

Love Mercy

He has showed you, O man, what is good. And what
does the Lord require of you? To act justly and to love
mercy and to walk humbly with your God.
Micah 6:8

God, portrayed by Micah as a lawyer
presenting his case against Israel, revealed
what kind of people please Him: those
who act justly, love mercy, walk humbly
with God. Love has an object; it is not
some vague, warm-to-hot feeling. God
calls me to love mercy, to value
lovingkindness, to appreciate correction.

O Father God, my ever-present Help, my Sustainer,
I want to be Your kind of person. I want to love
what You love, as You cover me with Your love
. . . in the name of Jesus, our Sanctification.

Love God

"Of all the commandments, which is the most important?" "The most important one," answered Jesus, "is this: 'Hear, O Israel, the Lord our God, the Lord is one. Love the Lord your God with all your heart and with all your soul and with all your mind and with all your strength.' "
Mark 12:28–30

God is love. God defines love and as I learn, experience, recognize God's presence in everything, I am to appreciate, adore, enjoy, give myself unreservedly to Him in love. "Do you really love Me," Jesus asked Peter three times, "with the kind of love that abandons itself in joyful joining, generous giving?"

Father God, infinite Love, show me what it means to love You, through and through, an eternal commitment to see You in everything . . . in the name of Jesus, Love personified.

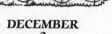

Love Neighbor as Self

"To love [God] with all your heart, with all your
understanding and with all your strength, and to love
your neighbor as yourself is more important than all
burnt offerings and sacrifices."
Mark 12:33

"Who is your neighbor?" Jesus asked and then told the
story of the Good Samaritan. Jesus turned upside-down
the prejudices and stereotypes that excluded some and
built up others. The one in need, who is within my
power to help, is my neighbor. I am to do for him or her
what I would want done if I were in the same situation.

God and Father of all, everything and everyone,
forgive me for times when I have failed to love
You in others, when I have shut out the needs of
my neighbors. I want to be a
good neighbor today, to love
myself and others more . . . in
the name of Jesus, who is in me
and in my neighbor.

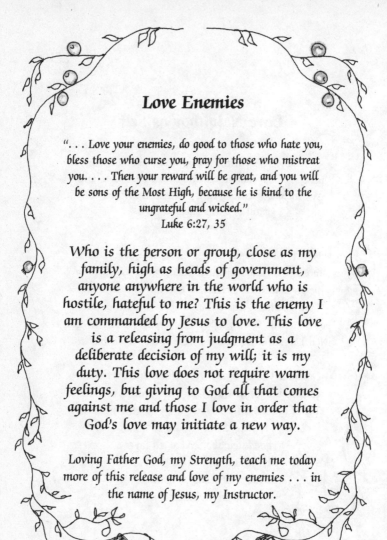

Love Enemies

". . . Love your enemies, do good to those who hate you,
bless those who curse you, pray for those who mistreat
you. . . . Then your reward will be great, and you will
be sons of the Most High, because he is kind to the
ungrateful and wicked."
Luke 6:27, 35

Who is the person or group, close as my
family, high as heads of government,
anyone anywhere in the world who is
hostile, hateful to me? This is the enemy I
am commanded by Jesus to love. This love
is a releasing from judgment as a
deliberate decision of my will; it is my
duty. This love does not require warm
feelings, but giving to God all that comes
against me and those I love in order that
God's love may initiate a new way.

Loving Father God, my Strength, teach me today
more of this release and love of my enemies . . . in
the name of Jesus, my Instructor.

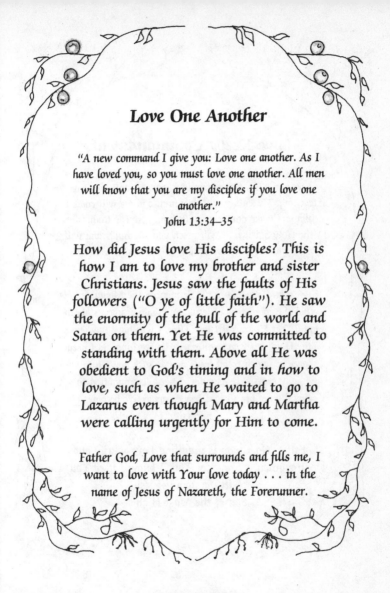

Love One Another

"A new command I give you: Love one another. As I have loved you, so you must love one another. All men will know that you are my disciples if you love one another."
John 13:34–35

How did Jesus love His disciples? This is how I am to love my brother and sister Christians. Jesus saw the faults of His followers ("O ye of little faith"). He saw the enormity of the pull of the world and Satan on them. Yet He was committed to standing with them. Above all He was obedient to God's timing and in *how* to love, such as when He waited to go to Lazarus even though Mary and Martha were calling urgently for Him to come.

Father God, Love that surrounds and fills me, I want to love with Your love today . . . in the name of Jesus of Nazareth, the Forerunner.

Love Keeps Commandments

Jesus replied, "If anyone loves me, he will obey my teaching. My Father will love him, and we will come to him and make our home with him. . . . The Counselor, the Holy Spirit, . . . will teach you all things and will remind you of everything I have said to you."
John 14:23, 26

Even a brief reading of the Sermon on the Mount reveals that the commands of Jesus are humanly impossible to fulfill. Yet He says if I love Him, I will have the help of the Holy Spirit and will obey His teaching. So I need space in which to let Jesus' words soak down into my daily experience as guide. I need determination to simplify my life so that Jesus' perspective becomes my necessity.

Father God, who is unfailing Love, purify and strengthen my love for You. I know I need You . . . in the name of Jesus, Son of the Most High.

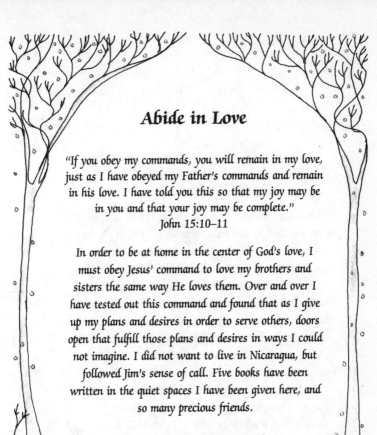

Abide in Love

"If you obey my commands, you will remain in my love, just as I have obeyed my Father's commands and remain in his love. I have told you this so that my joy may be in you and that your joy may be complete."
John 15:10–11

In order to be at home in the center of God's love, I must obey Jesus' command to love my brothers and sisters the same way He loves them. Over and over I have tested out this command and found that as I give up my plans and desires in order to serve others, doors open that fulfill those plans and desires in ways I could not imagine. I did not want to live in Nicaragua, but followed Jim's sense of call. Five books have been written in the quiet spaces I have been given here, and so many precious friends.

Father God, who delivers me from
all my fears, show me Your
balance, Your timing in my plans
. . . in the name of Jesus,
Emmanuel, God with us.

DECEMBER
14

Greatest Love

"Greater love has no one than this, that one lay
down his life for his friends."
John 15:13

When I see someone lay down his/her life for another, it
is an awesome beacon light beckoning: "This is the way,
walk this way." I remember the time a group of young
people hiked on a cold and snowy trail at the wilderness
camp, Pioneer Plunge, that Jim began for Young Life
in North Carolina. One girl's feet were freezing in wet
tennis shoes. On the way back, we found a warm pair of
boots left for her by one of the guys, who walked the
rest of the way barefoot!

Father God, close to the brokenhearted,
giving up my boots and many other
comfortable things seems impossible, but I
pray that today, covered with Your kind of
love, I will be willing . . . in the name of
Jesus, the Life-Giver.

Working Together for Good

And we know that in all things God works for the good of those who love him, who have been called according to his purpose.
Romans 8:28

How could the persecution, torture and horrible deaths of thousands of Christians work together for good? Rome, until Constantine, utterly rejected the Christian Gospel and Paul was speaking to those suffering believers. How can the bombing of poor neighborhoods, torture and rape of Christians work for good? It takes a leap of faith to believe and praise God in everything, but is vital to a life drenched in God's Spirit and responsive to His direction.

Loving Father God, Salvation of the poor and needy, thank You for the myriad ways You have proved Your love for me. I do not want to hide from hard questions . . . in the name of Jesus, the Answer.

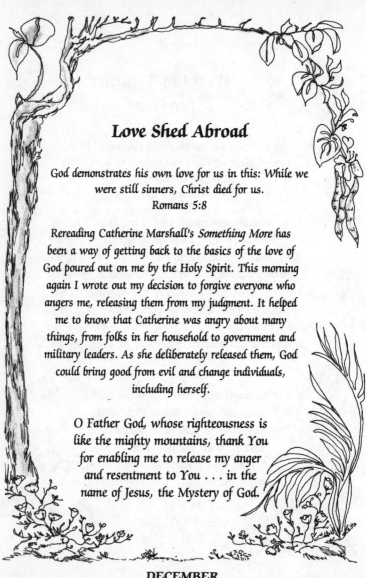

Love Shed Abroad

God demonstrates his own love for us in this: While we
were still sinners, Christ died for us.
Romans 5:8

Rereading Catherine Marshall's *Something More* has
been a way of getting back to the basics of the love of
God poured out on me by the Holy Spirit. This morning
again I wrote out my decision to forgive everyone who
angers me, releasing them from my judgment. It helped
me to know that Catherine was angry about many
things, from folks in her household to government and
military leaders. As she deliberately released them, God
could bring good from evil and change individuals,
including herself.

O Father God, whose righteousness is
like the mighty mountains, thank You
for enabling me to release my anger
and resentment to You . . . in the
name of Jesus, the Mystery of God.

Inseparable in Love

Who shall separate us from the love of Christ? Shall
trouble or hardship or persecution or famine or
nakedness or danger or sword? . . . No, in all these
things we are more than conquerors through him who
loved us.

Romans 8:35, 37

The love shield, which I consciously put
on today, the love of God in Jesus, is
really an inseparable part of me,
penetrating all I am. God's overcoming
love protects me from becoming like the
power of hate, enables me to overcome all
tragedies of life, all evil and horror in
whatever place or time. This love suffers
but comes through victorious!

O great, merciful Father God, I
praise You today for Your
outstretched arms of love in Jesus
on the cross, and His total
acceptance. I want to receive others
today with His love . . . in the
name of Jesus, the slain, resurrected
Lamb.

Love Is Patient

Love is patient, love is kind. It does not envy,
it does not boast, it is not proud. It is not
rude, it is not self-seeking, it is not easily
angered, it keeps no record of wrongs.
1 Corinthians 13:4–5

Love is long on patience, enduring and
suffering through much. Love makes itself
useful, is generous, sharing, quick to
forgive. This is the love I put on today
after washing my body, soul, mind,
thoughts, imagination, memories, spirit
with that cleansing blood of Jesus' love
for me.

Father God, who ransoms me unharmed
from the battle waged against me, when I
look at my past, present and future, may
I see love, Your love for me and through
me . . . in the name of Jesus, the Avenger,
the Atonement.

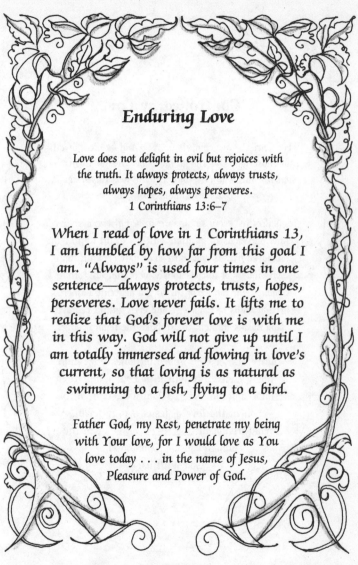

Enduring Love

Love does not delight in evil but rejoices with the truth. It always protects, always trusts, always hopes, always perseveres.
1 Corinthians 13:6–7

When I read of love in 1 Corinthians 13, I am humbled by how far from this goal I am. "Always" is used four times in one sentence—always protects, trusts, hopes, perseveres. Love never fails. It lifts me to realize that God's forever love is with me in this way. God will not give up until I am totally immersed and flowing in love's current, so that loving is as natural as swimming to a fish, flying to a bird.

Father God, my Rest, penetrate my being with Your love, for I would love as You love today . . . in the name of Jesus, Pleasure and Power of God.

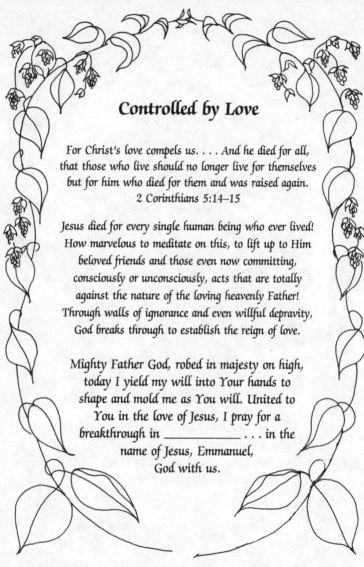

Controlled by Love

For Christ's love compels us. . . . And he died for all,
that those who live should no longer live for themselves
but for him who died for them and was raised again.
2 Corinthians 5:14–15

Jesus died for every single human being who ever lived!
How marvelous to meditate on this, to lift up to Him
beloved friends and those even now committing,
consciously or unconsciously, acts that are totally
against the nature of the loving heavenly Father!
Through walls of ignorance and even willful depravity,
God breaks through to establish the reign of love.

Mighty Father God, robed in majesty on high,
today I yield my will into Your hands to
shape and mold me as You will. United to
You in the love of Jesus, I pray for a
breakthrough in _____ . . . in the
name of Jesus, Emmanuel,
God with us.

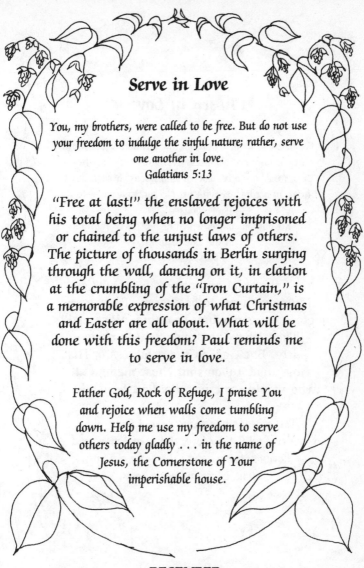

Serve in Love

You, my brothers, were called to be free. But do not use your freedom to indulge the sinful nature; rather, serve one another in love.
Galatians 5:13

"Free at last!" the enslaved rejoices with his total being when no longer imprisoned or chained to the unjust laws of others. The picture of thousands in Berlin surging through the wall, dancing on it, in elation at the crumbling of the "Iron Curtain," is a memorable expression of what Christmas and Easter are all about. What will be done with this freedom? Paul reminds me to serve in love.

Father God, Rock of Refuge, I praise You and rejoice when walls come tumbling down. Help me use my freedom to serve others today gladly . . . in the name of Jesus, the Cornerstone of Your imperishable house.

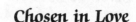

Chosen in Love

For he chose us in him before the creation of the world
to be holy and blameless in his sight. In love he
predestined us to be adopted as his sons through Jesus
Christ, in accordance with his pleasure and will—to the
praise
of his glorious grace, which he has freely given us
in the One he loves.
Ephesians 1:4–6

All the children in my "kids' club" on
Saturdays want to be chosen. They crowd
close, arms waving, shouting, "Pick me!"
Then I have to decide how to choose
fairly. But God, in the greatness of His
love, had a plan that chose me and all
who would come into the love Jesus gives.

Father God, who chooses me, I want to be
covered with Your love, to live and move and
have my being . . . in the name of Jesus,
who is coming again soon.

Grounded in Love

And I pray that you, being rooted and established in love, may have power, together with all the saints, to grasp how wide and long and high and deep is the love of Christ, and to know this love that surpasses knowledge.

Ephesians 3:17–19

Today, amid the glitter and materialism of this season, I focus again on the reason Jesus came and the wonder of His birth among us. His birth is similar to that of millions who are born in poverty, under a cruel government, with religious and political groups in harsh conflict. He came to show the height and depth and fullness of God's love for every single one.

Immeasurable Father God, birth in me this season Your perfect love, which is more than I can ask or imagine. Have Your way with me . . . in the name of Jesus, the Babe, the Child of Mary.

Knit Together

My purpose is that they may be encouraged in heart and united in love, so that they may have the full riches of complete understanding, in order that they may know the mystery of God, namely, Christ, in whom are hidden all the treasures of wisdom and knowledge.

Colossians 2:2–3

Christ in one and in all believers—this is the hope of glory. Christ born in me, growing in wisdom and obedience to God, dying to self, raised in overcoming victory over every force of death, disease, darkness, working His works, loving with His love.

Reigning Father God, let there be peace on earth and let it begin with me . . . in the name of Jesus, the Christ, the best Gift.

DECEMBER
25

Breastplate of Love

But since we belong to the day, let us be self-controlled, putting on faith and love as a breastplate, and the hope of salvation as a helmet. . . . He died for us so that, whether we are awake or asleep, we may live together with him.

1 Thessalonians 5:8, 10

Time keeps moving on, ever closer to the day of Jesus' coming again. Will I be ready? Is there anything I can clear away now that will enable His victory to break through in this earth? Use self-control, Paul urges, in putting on the protection of love and salvation. It is a decision.

Father God, who lifts me from the pit, sets my feet on the rock, and puts a new song of praise in my heart, I release to You _____ so that Your penetrating love can be my armor today . . . in the name of Jesus, Sign of the New Covenant.

Nothing without Love

If I speak in the tongues of men and of angels, but have
not love, I am only a resounding gong or a clanging
cymbal. . . . If I give all I possess to the poor and
surrender my body to the flames, but have not love, I
gain nothing.
1 Corinthians 13:1, 3

Without love I am nothing; I am a hollow
shell. Nothing I do can gain favor with
God. Even the greatest sacrifices and
generosity, the most marvelous insights
and strongest faith are empty, worthless.
Only love ultimately gains. Only love
changes wrong to right. Only love is
perfect.

Fill me today, Father God, my Joy and my Delight,
with Your love. Let me see all my
accomplishments and failures as worth nothing
unless they are bathed in Your love, for Your
praise . . . in the name of Jesus, beloved
Bridegroom.

God Dwells in Love

Dear friends, let us love one another, for love comes from God. Everyone who loves has been born of God and knows God. . . . If we love each other, God lives in us and his love is made complete in us.

1 John 4:7, 12

This morning as I took Communion with a roomful of Young Life urban leaders, I meditated on the love that brought us together through the years: black and white, rich and poor, young and old, from many cities. One black brother stood bashfully and said, with choking voice, "I just want to thank You, Lord, for the pain, because it helps me communicate Your love, that You understand." The others nodded, echoing with resonant, heartfelt voices.

Thank You, Father God, for Your unconquerable, indefatigable, exhilarating, all-consuming love . . . in the name of Jesus, the Sun of Righteousness risen with healing in His wings.

God Is Love

And so we know and rely on the love God has for us.
God is love. Whoever lives in love lives in God, and God
in him.
1 John 4:16

I am in God and God is in me when I
recognize and receive Jesus as God's Son. I
am in God and God is in me when I live
in that kind of self-giving love that God
is. Love is who Jesus is and if I know
Him as in the intimate discovery of lovers,
there will be a touching of others with
love that spills over. Love cannot be
contained; its nature is to be shared.

Father God almighty, who makes wars cease to
the ends of the earth, who will be exalted among
the nations, open me today to the meaning of
being in Your love, and Your love in me . . . in the
name of Jesus, Lover of my soul.

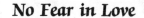

No Fear in Love

Love is made complete among us so that we will have
confidence on the day of judgment, because in this world
we are like him. There is no fear in love. But perfect
love drives out fear, because fear has to do with
punishment.
1 John 4:17–18

As I put on God's love as a shining cloak,
as God's love within flows out through
my imagination, dreams, thoughts, words,
actions, and this fuses with God's love in
my brother and sister believers, there is
ever-increasing ability to accept and reach
out to those trapped in beliefs and
behavior that are against Jesus and all for
which He stands.

Immense, eternally loving Father God, I want to
be like a ray of Your healing, warming, revealing
light today, touching tenderly those to whom You
direct me . . . in the name of Jesus, glorious
Lord, Image of God.

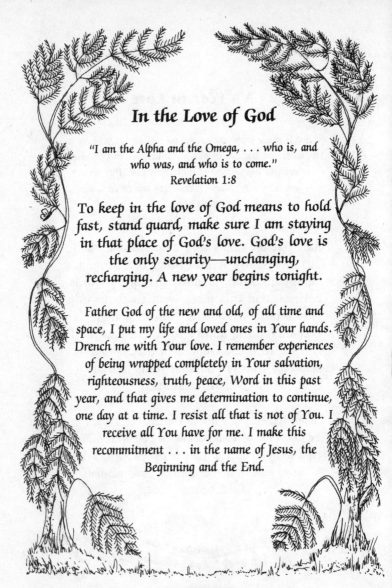

In the Love of God

"I am the Alpha and the Omega, . . . who is, and
who was, and who is to come."
Revelation 1:8

To keep in the love of God means to hold
fast, stand guard, make sure I am staying
in that place of God's love. God's love is
the only security—unchanging,
recharging. A new year begins tonight.

Father God of the new and old, of all time and
space, I put my life and loved ones in Your hands.
Drench me with Your love. I remember experiences
of being wrapped completely in Your salvation,
righteousness, truth, peace, Word in this past
year, and that gives me determination to continue,
one day at a time. I resist all that is not of You. I
receive all You have for me. I make this
recommitment . . . in the name of Jesus, the
Beginning and the End.